MATHEMATICS & ECONOMICS

CONNECTIONS FOR LIFE • GRADES 9–12

This publication was made possible through funding of State Farm Insurance Companies.

NCEE

National Council on Economic Education

Authors:

Rich MacDonald is the assistant director of the Center for Economic Education and a member of the economics faculty at St. Cloud State University. In recent years, Dr. MacDonald has been a frequent contributor to EconEdLink and has authored adult economic education materials for the Business Roundtable. He is currently the president-elect of the National Association of Economic Educators.

Lisa Breidenbach teaches mathematics at Tecumseh Middle School, Lafayette, Indiana. Ms. Breidenbach's varied experience includes teaching sixth through twelfth grade mathematics, writing curriculum materials, organizing and conducting professional development experiences, and speaking at teacher conferences from the local to national levels.

Evelyn L. Doetschman is Mathematics Department Chair at Vestal Senior High School in Vestal, New York where she teaches both mathematics and computer science. In addition to her studies in the United States, Ms. Doetschman studied mathematics at the Australian National University in Canberra, Australia. She has also written Sequential Mathematics 1 Regents questions for 3 years for the State Education Department of New York State.

Project Director:

John E. Clow is the Director of the Leatherstocking Center for Economic Education at the New York State University College at Oneonta and Professor Emeritus of that college. He is a national award-winning college teacher, speaker and author in the fields of personal finance, economics, and business education.

ISBN 1-56183-602-8

5 4 3 2 1

Contents

Acknowledgments

The members of the writing team express their deepest gratitude to the many individuals who were involved with this project.

Economics Reviewers:

Steven L. Cobb, Director
Center for Economic Education
University of North Texas
Denton, TX

Mathematics Reviewers:

Mary Jo Aiken, Secondary Mathematics Teacher (Retired)
Edina, MN

Patricia Lamphere Jordan, Associate Professor
School of Curriculum and Educational Leadership
Oklahoma State University
Stillwater, OK

Tom Lester, Mathematics Consultant
California Department of Education
Sacramento, CA

Deborah K. Lyman, Mathematics Specialist
Virginia Department of Education
Richmond, VA

Barbara Montalto, Director of Mathematics
Division of Curriculum and Professional Development
Texas Education Agency
Austin, TX

Teachers involved in field testing:

Gayle Town
Winchester High School
Winchester, MA

Linda Ray
Liberty High School
Sykesville, MD

Foreword

This excellent book is aptly named. Bringing mathematics and economics together—to connect them in the minds of our students—will give those students very important skills they can use in their lives, all their lives.

For more than 50 years, the National Council on Economic Education (NCEE) has been the nation's leader in getting economics effectively into the curriculum, K–12 , by teaching teachers and equipping them with outstanding materials. This publication, however, is a "first" for NCEE. It is especially written for high school mathematics teachers. It will have significant reach and impact, in terms of core educational experiences for thousands of young people. We are very grateful to The State Farm Insurance Companies for making this splendid resource for teachers possible. NCEE is proud of this outstanding "connection" with State Farm—and of the product.

Because understanding economics is so important for life, NCEE is constantly seeking ways to ensure that economics is incorporated into teaching and learning in various subject areas, especially the social studies, such as government, history, geography, and now mathematics. This new teaching resource will certainly help to advance economic literacy, because of the central place math has in the curriculum in all schools.

Whether the course is basic algebra or AP calculus, there are lessons in this book designed to help reinforce the mathematics concepts and processes taught, by using examples from economics. Using the four basic mathematical manipulations of addition, subtraction, multiplication, and division, students will understand how interest on a credit card debt can cost them large sums of money. Or using factorials, they can determine their odds of winning a lottery. Calculus students can use derivatives to determine the shape of a marginal cost function and understand its importance. This book is especially designed to help math teachers answer the proverbial question asked by students, "Why do I have to learn this? Am I ever going to use it?"

On the other hand, mathematics teachers may ask the question, "Do I need to take a course in economics in order to use this curriculum guide?" The answer is, "No." This book was specifically written for math educators, in consultation with math educators. It provides the needed economics, as well as the answers to problems/questions. However, if you or your students have questions to which you do not know the economics answer, please visit our website www.ncee.net to find the nearest NCEE Council or Center Director—who can certainly help you.

The primary author of this work, an outstanding economic educator, Richard MacDonald, consulted with two math educators, Evy Doetschman and Lisa Breidenbach, and we are most grateful to them.

Special thanks also go to John Clow, Director of the Leatherstocking Center for Economic Education in Oneonta, New York, for his work in getting this project well launched, and to Elizabeth Volard, former Senior Vice President at NCEE, for her vision for developing curriculum materials for mathematics teachers that reinforce mathematics concepts using examples from economics. NCEE is especially appreciative of the powerful partnership with the National Council of Teachers of Mathematics (NCTM), which, with the support of State Farm, truly made this good work possible.

Robert F. Duvall, Ph.D.
President & Chief Executive Officer
The National Council on Economic Education

Introduction

Mathematics and Economics: Connection for Life, 9–12 is a set of 15 lessons showing how mathematical processes and concepts may be applied in the study of economics and personal finance. In this volume, mathematics educators will find lessons connecting mathematics instruction to practical problems and issues that students will encounter through their lifetimes.

In the study of these problems and issues, economics and mathematics are natural intellectual allies. Economics is, after all, the study of peoples' attempts to make good decisions in an uncertain world endowed with limited resources. The tools that economists use—for example, those related to optimization and informed decision-making—gain power, elegance, and visual appeal as they are represented mathematically in models. Indeed, one might think of economics as "first quadrant math" since economic magnitudes only rarely take on a negative sign. Research indicates that students with a strong background in mathematics are more likely than others to succeed in their introductory college-level economics classes.

But the lessons presented here are not designed exclusively for college-bound students. Several of them are intended to serve a general education purpose, providing knowledge and skills that students will use subsequently as savers, investors, consumers, producers, and informed citizens.

Using the Lessons

The minimum level of mathematics students will need for each lesson is noted in the Mathematics Focus section in each lesson. Each lesson begins with a mathematical warm-up activity to introduce the mathematics content of the economics lesson. Activity sheets, answers, visuals for making overhead transparencies, and extension activities are provided in each lesson, ready to be copied for use. Each lesson also includes a detailed lesson procedure section with ample background on the concepts presented. (A more detailed discussion of the basic economic tools of supply and demand can be found under "Economics Background of Lessons 1–4.")

These lessons are NOT intended for use in teaching mathematics processes and concepts per se; rather, they illustrate economic and personal finance applications for the mathematics knowledge and skills students have already acquired in their mathematics classes. The lessons are therefore well suited for use in culminating activities in mathematics courses, or they may be used between units to offer a change of pace and a meaningful application of mathematics in real-world problems.

When students find the mathematics simple, they can focus more easily on the economic ideas that are being illustrated. Thus, lessons requiring a minimum of mathematics can be used very successfully even with advanced mathematics students. With advanced students, teachers can expect more discussion of the economic ideas underlying the lesson materials, especially since more advanced, older students will perhaps have begun to encounter those ideas in their daily lives.

Overview of the Lessons

Lessons 1–4 are foundational lessons on supply and demand, the primary tools of economic analysis. These initial lessons are written at an Algebra I level. They involve a great deal of graphical analysis as well as the use of algebraic solutions. If possible, they should be taught as one unit. Together they provide the background needed for Lessons 5 and 6. Lesson 5 calls for an application of the foundational lessons; the application involves the solution of inequalities and the calculation of triangular and rectangular areas. This lesson is certainly appropriate for use in the Algebra II classroom and may also be useful to some Algebra I teachers. In Lesson 6, written at the Algebra I level, students will find a tool—the concept of elasticity—that explains the strength of the relationship between economic variables. Lessons 7–9 involve some uses of calculus (calculus is optional for Algebra II students). In Lesson 7, students are asked to explore a production possibilities curve. This is a curve with several interesting economic properties; it is modeled as both a circle and an ellipse. In Lesson 8, a cubic function is used to help explain the real-world behavior of firm costs. This is followed in Lesson 9 by a demonstration of the decision-making process that a firm uses in determining the optimal amount it should produce in order to maximize profits. Calculus is used in this lesson to determine a point of extrema as well as to verify that this is indeed a maximum point.

Lessons 10–15 cover familiar economic applications from everyday life, including games of chance, present and future value of money, implicit and explicit costs of owning and operating an automobile, taxes, savings, and credit card use. Lessons 12 and 13 are appropriate for the pre-Algebra level, while lessons 10 and 11 are for more advanced students. Lessons 14 and 15 vary in difficulty level from pre-Algebra through Algebra II. All of these lessons may be taught as independent units, and all are potentially useful in analyses of the life experience of students in grades 9–12. Lesson 10 is most appropriately placed in a data analysis or algebra class. Students calculate and replicate probabilities of winning lottery prizes and determine the expected return on each dollar spent on these unfair games. In Lesson 11, students verify that the cash equivalent of a lottery prize is the actuarial equivalent of the annuity value of the prize. Students also discover the future value of the dollars that are spent on undesirable activities, such as smoking.

Lessons 12 and 13 are both appropriate for use at the pre-Algebra level. Lesson 12 looks at the costs associated with owning and operating an automobile as well as the economic cost of various transportation options. Lesson 13 involves the simple mathematics of taxation and helps uncover some of the mysteries that underlie the numbers that are found in tax tables.

Finally, Lessons 14 and 15 provide personal finance applications. Lesson 14 looks at future value calculations and methods for understanding the accumulations that can arise from a commitment to saving. Lesson 15 demonstrates how the numbers on a credit card statement are obtained as well as how the fixed payment on an auto loan is determined.

Economics Background of Lessons 1–4

Supply and demand is the foundation upon which the study of economics rests. These first four lessons lay the groundwork for further study of the mathematical and economic concepts that are explored in this volume. While the instruction suggested in most lessons of this volume is self-contained, these first four foundational lessons will help mathematics students begin to develop the "economic way of thinking." Both graphical and algebraic models are developed to illustrate the concepts of supply and demand. Graphical models are derived from hypothetical data tables that represent real world economic relationships. Algebraic models are specified as simple linear expressions of supply and demand forces. The properties of slopes and intercepts, among other things, are considered in these economic applications to mathematical processes and concepts. Teachers are strongly urged to introduce students to the use of supply and demand tools by covering (at least elements of) these initial lessons.

Lesson 1 develops an economic understanding of the *law of demand.* Demand is determined by the value that people attach to products in the marketplace. A *demand curve* is a graphical representation that reflects a negative relationship between the amount of a product that people are willing and able to purchase and its price, assuming all things besides price that might affect peoples' desires to purchase the product are held constant. A demand curve is most accurately derived from a *demand schedule*, which relates alternative quantities of the product demanded to various prices. A variation in the *quantity demanded* of a product is caused by a change in the product's price. This is the only thing that can cause a change in quantity demanded. By tradition, economists refer to a downward sloping relationship between price and quantity demanded as a "demand curve" even though this relationship might be linear. A change in quantity demanded is a *movement along* the downward-sloping demand curve. Note that other factors that influence peoples' desires to buy the product (such as changes in *income*, tastes, the prices of *substitutes* or *complements*, etc.) cause a change in *demand.* A change in demand leads to a *shift* (or translation) in the demand curve, the topic of Lesson 4.

Lesson 2 considers the nature of supply. Supply is related to how costly it is for a seller to produce and bring her product to market. A *supply curve* is a graphical representation that maps the positive relationship between the price of a product and sellers' willingness and ability to offer various quantities of the product at alternative prices, assuming all other things besides price are held constant. The supply curve is typically derived from a *supply schedule.* Like the demand curve, the upward sloping "supply curve" is referred to as a curve even though it might represent a linear relationship. A change in *quantity supplied* is caused by a change in the product's price. It is represented by a *movement along* the upward sloping supply curve. Changes in factors other than price that affect sellers' willingness and ability to offer their product (such as productivity, the cost of energy, materials, and labor, etc.) cause a change in *supply*. A change in supply leads to a *shift* (or translation) in the supply curve (which is addressed in Lesson 4).

Lesson 3 develops graphical and algebraic explanations of the forces that influence the prices that people pay and the amounts that they purchase in a modern market economy. In general terms, the two factors that affect prices and quantities are supply and demand. *Equilibrium* is said to occur at the point at which quantity supplied equals quantity demanded. In equilibrium, all conflicting forces are in balance and there is no tendency to change. In most situations that are relevant to understanding economics at this level, the equilibrium that is observed is unique in the sense that there is only one price-quantity combination that will satisfy the condition that quantity supplied equals quantity demanded. The concept of equilibrium also helps us to see that market prices and quantities behave very predictably in response to changes in supply and demand.

At times, prices are set away from their equilibrium level. If prices are too low, then quantity demanded is greater than quantity supplied and a *shortage* is said to exist. When prices are too high, quantity supplied exceeds quantity demanded and a *surplus* arises. As long as market forces are allowed to operate, prices tend to increase in response to a shortage and decrease in response to a surplus. These adjustments occur impersonally, without the direction of any centralized authority. Ultimately, adjustments occur until equilibrium is restored. States of *disequilibrium* would therefore not be expected to persist in an ordinary market setting.

The final lesson in this foundational section considers the factors that cause a change in supply and/or a change in demand. Many factors influence the amount of a product that people are willing and able to purchase at each and every price. Such factors as income, tastes and preferences, the prices of related goods, the number of buyers, and expected future prices influence the *demand* for a product. When we observe a change in any of these factors, we normally expect to experience *a change in demand* for the product. A change in demand causes a *parallel shift* (or translation) of the demand curve. This is distinct from a movement along the demand curve, which (as noted in Lesson 1) is called a change in quantity demanded. A change in quantity demanded can only be caused by a change in the price of the product.

An increase in demand is represented by a *rightward* shift (away from the origin) in the demand curve. This can be caused by an increase in income, an increase in the prices of substitute goods, higher expected future prices, an increase in the number of buyers, or a favorable change in tastes and preferences. Holding everything else constant, an increase in demand leads to higher prices and greater quantities exchange. A decrease in demand is represented by a *leftward* shift (toward the origin) in the demand curve. This might be caused by a decrease in income, a decrease in the prices of substitute goods, lower expected future prices, a decrease in the number of buyers, or an unfavorable change in tastes and preferences. A decrease in demand usually causes a decrease in price and quantity exchanged.

Factors that influence the amount of a product that people are willing and able to sell at each and every price affect the *supply* of a product. Such factors include the prices of productive *inputs* (such as *capital, labor,* energy, and materials), expectations of future prices, technology, or the number of sellers. Changes in any of these factors cause a *parallel shift* (or translation) of the supply curve, also known as a *change in supply.* This is to be distinguished from a change in quantity supplied, which is caused by a change in the price of a product and is represented by a movement along the supply curve.

An increase in supply is represented by a *rightward* shift (moving it closer to the horizontal axis) in the supply curve. This can be caused by a decrease in input prices, a technological advance, an increase in the number of sellers, or producer expectations of lower future product prices. Holding everything else constant, an increase in supply leads to lower prices and greater quantities exchanged. A decrease in supply is represented by a *leftward* shift (moving it further away from the horizontal axis) in the supply curve. This might be caused by rising input prices, technological regress, a decrease in the number of sellers, or producer expectations of higher future product prices. A decrease in supply leads to higher prices and lower quantities exchanged.

Changes in demand and supply are restricted to the first quadrant because price and quantity (which are respectively measured on the vertical and horizontal axes) must both be positive numbers. An increase in demand is therefore represented by an increase in the vertical intercept while a decrease in demand leads to a decrease in the value of the vertical intercept. Likewise, an increase in supply leads to a decrease in the value of the vertical intercept and a decrease in supply increases the vertical intercept.

Correlation of *Mathematics and Economics: Connections for Life* Lessons with the National Standards for Mathematics

Mathematics Standards	Lesson 1	Lesson 2	Lesson 3	Lesson 4	Lesson 5	Lesson 6	Lesson 7	Lesson 8	Lesson 9	Lesson 10	Lesson 11	Lesson 12	Lesson 13	Lesson 14	Lesson 15
1. Number and Operations	X	X	X	X	X	X	X	X	X	X	X	X	X	X	X
2. Algebra	X	X	X	X	X	X	X	X	X	X	X	X	X	X	
3. Geometry		X	X	X	X	X	X	X	X	X					
4. Measurement					X	X			X						
5. Data Analysis & Probability	X	X	X	X	X	X	X	X	X	X	X	X	X	X	X
6. Problem Solving	X	X	X	X	X	X	X	X	X	X	X	X	X	X	X
7. Reasoning and Proof	X	X	X	X	X	X	X	X	X	X	X	X	X	X	X
8. Communication	X	X	X	X	X	X	X	X	X	X	X	X	X	X	X
9. Connections	X	X	X	X	X	X	X	X	X	X	X	X	X	X	X
10. Representation	X	X	X	X	X	X	X	X	X	X	X	X	X	X	X

Correlation of *Mathematics and Economics: Connections for Life* Lessons with the National Standards for Economics

Economic Standards	Lesson 1	Lesson 2	Lesson 3	Lesson 4	Lesson 5	Lesson 6	Lesson 7	Lesson 8	Lesson 9	Lesson 10	Lesson 11	Lesson 12	Lesson 13	Lesson 14	Lesson 15
1. Scarcity							X					X			
2. Marginal costs/marginal benefits								X	X	X	X	X	X	X	X
3. Allocation of goods and services															
4. Role of incentives															
5. Gain from trade					X										
6. Specialization and trade							X								
7. Markets – price and quantity determination	X	X	X	X	X	X	X								
8. Role of price in market system	X	X	X	X	X	X	X								
9. Role of competition															
10. Role of economic institutions															
11. Role of money															
12. Role of interest rates											X			X	X
13. Role of resources in determining income															
14. Profit and the entrepreneur									X						
15. Growth															
16. Role of government													X		
17. Using cost/benefit analysis to evaluate government programs															
18. Macroeconomy-income/ employment, prices															
19. Unemployment and inflation															
20. Monetary and fiscal policy															

Lesson 1

The Nature of Demand

Mathematics Focus:

Algebra 1

Mathematics Prerequisites:

Prior to this lesson, students should be able to:

- Make a graph using a table of values
- Find slope and vertical intercept
- Write the equation of a line given
  - a) a point and a slope
  - b) two points on the line
  - c) a slope and one intercept
- Define the dependent and independent variables

Lesson Objectives:

To apply prerequisite mathematics concepts and processes to:

- explain why a demand curve has a negative slope
- explain reasons why the law of demand exists
- explain why quantity demanded depends on price

Overview of Mathematics and Economics:

This lesson develops the economic tool of demand. Demand is determined by the value that people attach to a product (a good or a service). A demand curve is a graph with a negative slope that lies in the first quadrant. It illustrates the inverse relationship between the quantity of a product demanded and the price that people are willing and able to pay. A demand curve is most accurately derived from a demand schedule, which is a table of values relating prices to quantities demanded. To make this lesson appropriate for algebra I students, it will be restricted to the study of linear demand curves.

A change in the quantity demanded of a product is caused by a change in the product's price. The demand curve shows the extent to which a change in price causes a change in quantity demanded. A change in quantity demanded can be viewed graphically as a movement along the demand curve. Other factors that influence peoples' desire to buy the product—such as changes in income, tastes, or the prices of substitutes or complements—cause a change in demand as opposed to a change in quantity demanded. A change in demand leads to a new demand curve that is parallel to the original curve. This phenomenon is referred to as a "shift in demand." (See Lesson 4 for further discussion of this concept.)

The demand curve is a graphical representation of the law of demand. The law of demand states that holding everything else constant, there is an inverse relationship between price and quantity demanded. As prices increase, quantity demanded decreases. Some people buy less of an item, thus decreasing the total quantity demanded. As prices decrease, quantity demanded increases because people are willing and able to buy more of the item.

Mathematics and Economics Terms

- Demand curve
- Demand schedule
- Dependent variable
- Independent variable
- Inverse relationship
- Law of demand
- Quantity demanded

Materials

- Straight edge
- Overhead transparencies of Visuals 1.1, 1.2, 1.3, and 1.4 and Activity 1.2
- One copy of Activity 1.2 and 1.3 for each student
- Make one copy of Activity 1.1 on colored paper. Cut the activity slips on the solid lines and place one slip for each student in the class in a paper bag. The following instruction is important:

To ensure that a linear function is produced, leave out the slips that represent the lower prices if you have fewer students than there are slips of paper. In addition, be sure that you use an even number of students. This paper bag will be used in step 3.

Estimated Time

80–100 Minutes

Procedures

1. Warm-Up Activity: Have the students answer the questions in Visual 1.1. Discuss the answers with the class.

COMMENT When discussing the answers to the problems, emphasize the following points:

- In mathematics, the horizontal axis is used for the independent variable and the vertical axis is used for the dependent variable.
- Since the relationship is only valid for positive numbers of lunch charges and a positive balance remaining, the line should be graphed in the first quadrant only.
- Meaningful variables are used. The variables *l* (quantity of lunches charged) and r (remaining balance) are substituted for x and y, respectively, in the equation $y = mx + b$.

Answers to the questions include:

a) $r = -2l + 50$

b) independent—quantity of lunches charged; dependent—remaining balance.

c) See Visual 1.2.

d) $m = -2$ and $b = 50$

e) Nine lunches.

2. Tell the students that today they will be looking at the market for the latest popular CD. Ask the students, "What CD would you most like to buy?" In this activity, they should all imagine that they are studying the market for this CD. They will be looking at the relationship between the number of CDs that people are willing and able to purchase and CD prices.

3. Distribute a copy of Activity 1.2 to each student. Then have each student take a slip of paper at random from the paper bag that you have prepared in Activity 1.1. Tell the students that the number on each slip represents the maximum price that each student is willing and able to pay for the CD. Tell the students, "The number of CDs [or other product] that buyers are willing and able to buy at each and every price is known as the quantity demanded."

4. Tell the students that they will now complete a table of values called a demand schedule. Have the students look at their slips of paper. Ask the students to raise their hands if they are willing and able to pay $32 for the CD. No one should raise his or her hand, so enter a 0 for quantity demanded in your table of values on the projected overhead. Have the students put a 0 in the column "Quantity Demanded of CD" on their copy of Activity 1.2. Ask the students, "In real life, why is no one willing and able to pay $32 for this CD?" Answers will vary but be sure that the reason that the "price is too high" is given. Then ask, "Who is willing and able to pay $30 for the CD?" Two people should raise their hands so write "2" under quantity demanded to correspond with the price of $30. Next ask, "Who is willing and able to pay $28 for the CD?" Four people should raise their hands: the people with $28 on their slips as well as the students with $30 on their slips. Ask the students, "Why would the individuals who would pay $30 also be willing and able to buy the CD for $28?" For each price level, two additional students should raise their hands. Continue this exercise until the table of values is completed and all hands are raised. Work together with the class to fill in the Quantity Demanded column in the table of values in Activity 1.2. As the students fill in the table on their individual sheets, you should complete the table of values on the overhead projector.

Answers are given in Visual 1.3.

Tell the students, "In economics, this table of values is called a demand schedule." Have the students look at the table of values and explain why the quantity demanded decreases as the price increases. Also ask why the quantity demanded increases as the price decreases.

■ **COMMENT** As the price increases, fewer people are willing and able to purchase the item. As the price decreases, more people are willing and able to purchase the item. For example, more people buy items when they are on sale than at a higher regular price.

5. Ask the students to identify the dependent and independent variable in the price/quantity demanded relationship. Remind the students that in mathematics, the independent variable is usually placed on the horizontal axis and the dependent variable on the vertical axis. Economists do the reverse, placing the independent variable (price) on the vertical axis and the dependent variable (quantity demanded) on the horizontal axis. Thus each ordered pair is in the form:

(dependent variable, independent variable) =
(quantity demanded, price).

Students should then complete the ordered pair column of the demand schedule.

Answers are given in Visual 1.3.

6. In Part 2 of Activity 1.2 have the students graph the line from the table of values in Part I. Remind them to label the axes with the appropriate variable. Tell the students that in economics, the line that they have graphed is called a demand curve. Economists and mathematicians often call a linear graph a curve. Have the students label this curve, "Demand." Use Visual 1.4 to demonstrate how the graph should appear.

■ **COMMENT** Tell the students that all demand curves are not linear and even though this curve is a straight line, it is referred to as a "curve."

7. Ask the students to record the characteristics of the graph and the reason why the graph has each characteristic. You may need to use leading questions to help your students identify all of these characteristics. Discuss the students' answers as a class.

The answers should include:

a) The graph is linear because for each $1 increase in price, the quantity-demanded decreases by one.
b) The line has a negative slope because as the price decreases, the quantity demanded increases. Or as the price increases, the quantity demanded decreases.
c) The vertical intercept is $32, or the line intersects the vertical axis at $P = \$32$. This is because no one is willing and able to buy the CD for a price of $32.
d) The line should not intersect the horizontal axis because an infinite number of people would want the CD for a price of zero dollars.
e) The graph lies entirely in the first quadrant because the quantity demanded and the price are never negative.

8. Tell the students,
"In mathematics, the slope of the line is typically viewed as

$$\frac{\text{change in dependent variable}}{\text{change in independent variable.}}$$

Because economists put the independent variable on the vertical axis and the dependent variable on the horizontal axis, we must refer to slope as

$$\frac{\text{change in the variable on the vertical axis}}{\text{change in the variable on the horizontal axis.}}$$

Therefore, in this example, the slope is

$$\frac{\text{change in price}}{\text{change in quantity demanded.}}$$

The students should now calculate the slope. Remind the students that the negative slope means that there is an inverse relationship between price and quantity demanded. The **law of demand** says, holding everything else constant, when price rises, the amount that people are willing and able to buy falls, and when price falls, the amount that people are willing and able to buy rises.

■ **COMMENT** The slope is

$$\frac{\$2}{-2\text{ CDs}} = \frac{-\$1}{1\text{ CD}}$$

9. For Part 3 of Activity 1.2, divide the students into three groups and have each group find the equation of the demand curve using one of the following methods (assign a different method to each group):

Group 1: Point and slope method
Group 2: Two points method
Group 3: Slope and vertical intercept method

■ **COMMENT** The equation of the demand curve is $P = 32 - Q_d$. When the students have found and compared their equations for the demand curve, regroup the students so that in the new groupings each method is represented. Students should share their methods with other members of the group. Have the students record each method on their copy of Activity 1.2. (This method is commonly called the "jigsaw method" in cooperative learning.)

EXTENSIONS

1. Activity 1.3 can be used as an additional assignment.

■ **COMMENT**

Answers to Activity 1.3

1. Figure A
2. A demand schedule shows the quantity demanded of an item at different prices.
3. Price and quantity demanded
4. Quantity demanded is the dependent variable because it is affected by price, which is the independent variable.
5. The **law of demand** states that, holding everything else constant, there is an inverse relationship between price and quantity demanded. That is, as price increases, the quantity demanded decreases. As price decreases, the quantity demanded increases.
6. $P = 70 - \frac{1}{6}Q_d$ or $Q_d = -6P + 420$. Students might write the equation either way. Economists usually write the equation as $Q_d = -6P + 420$. Economists refer to the equation, $P = 70 - \frac{1}{6} Q_d$, as the "inverse demand curve."
7. $P = 69 - \frac{2}{3}Q_d$ or $Q_d = -1.5P + 103.5$. Students might write the equation either way. Economists usually write the equation as
$$Q_d = -1.5P + 103.5$$
Economists refer to the equation, $P = 69 - \frac{2}{3}Q_d$, as the "inverse demand curve."
8. Same answer as problem 7.

9. (a)

Price in cents	Quantity Demanded (Number of People)
75¢	1
70¢	3
65¢	6
60¢	21
55¢	33
50¢	33
45¢	38
40¢	38
35¢	46

9. (b and c)

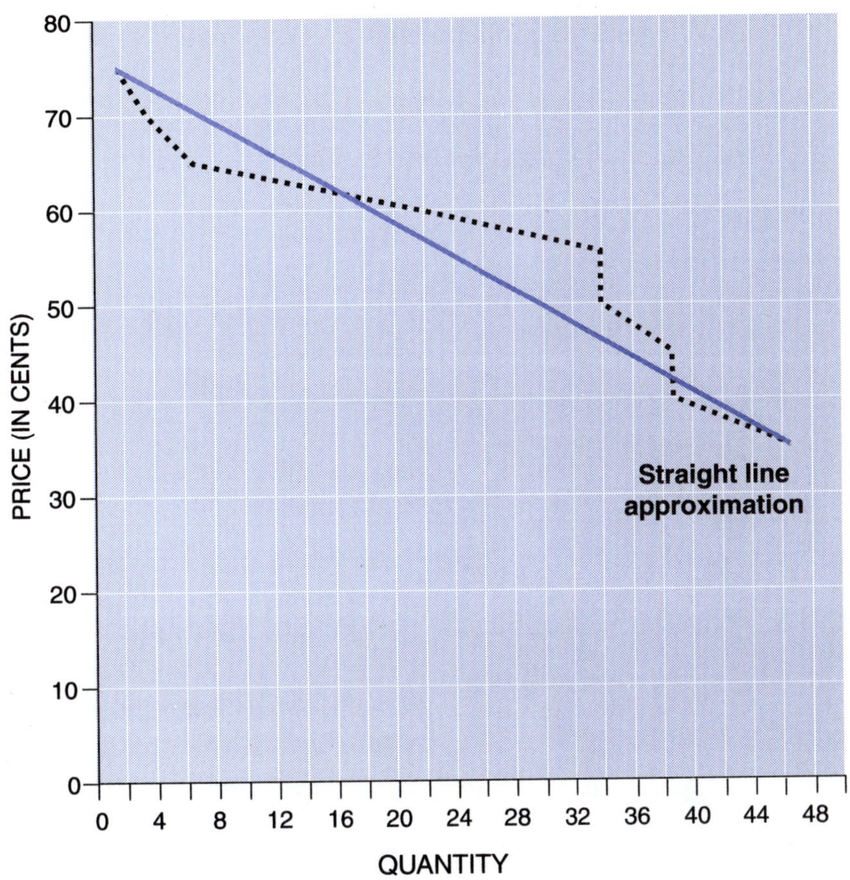

(d) By using the ordered pairs (1,75) and (46,35) to establish our straight line, the slope of the demand curve is $-8/9$. If we assume that no student is willing to pay more than 75 cents for a can of soft drink, then the vertical intercept is approximately 76 cents ($75\ 8/9$).

(e) Since quantity demanded is the dependent variable, economists write the equation of the line of best fit for the demand curve as $Q_d = -9/8P + 85.5$. Some students might write the equation for the "inverse demand curve" which is $P = -8/9\ Q_d + 76$.

VISUAL 1.1 ▲ Warm-Up

A student opens a school lunch account with an opening balance of $50. Lunch costs $2.00 a day, and the student can have the cost charged against the account each day.

ANSWER THE FOLLOWING QUESTIONS:

a) Write the equation for the line representing the balance remaining in the school lunch account in terms of the number of lunches charged.

b) What are your independent and dependent variables?

c) Sketch the graph for 0 to 25 lunches.

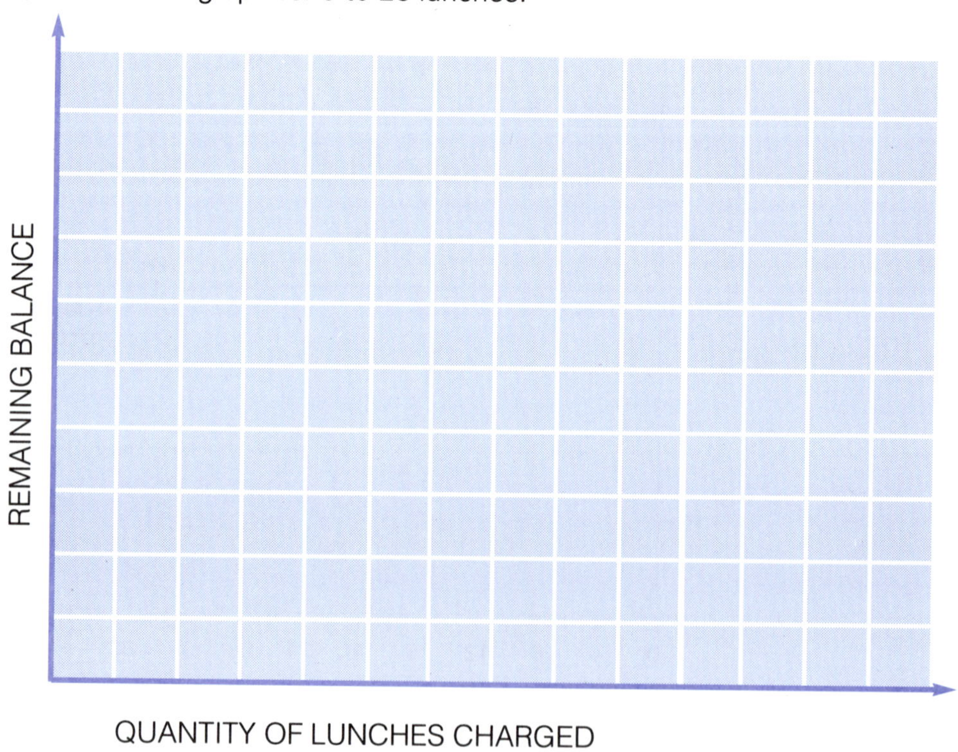

d) What is the slope of the line? (Remember: Slope is the rate of change.) What is the vertical intercept of the line?

e) If the remaining balance is $32, how many lunches have been charged?

VISUAL 1.2 ▲ Schedule from Warm-Up

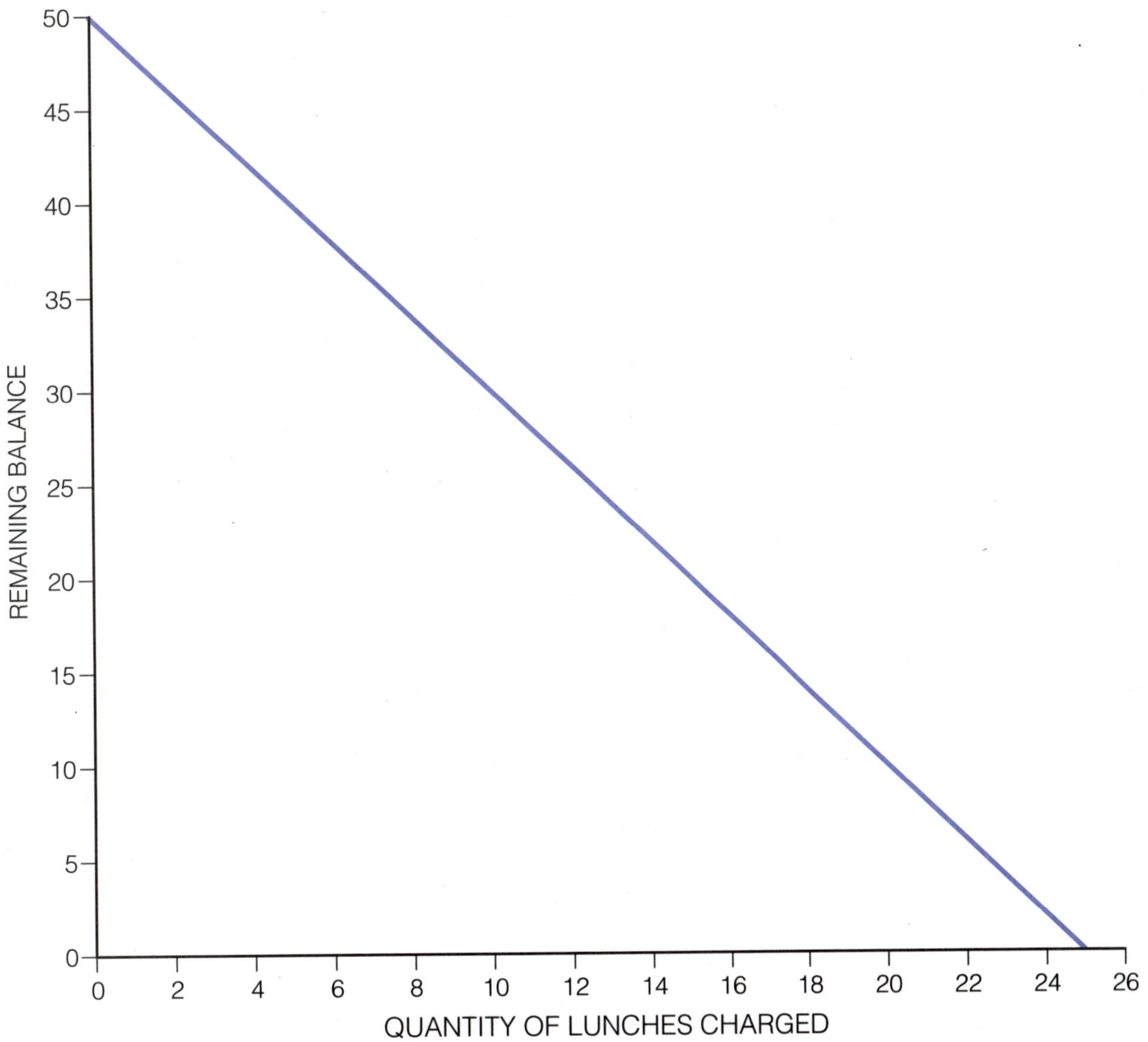

VISUAL 1.3 ▲ Demand Schedule

Price of CD in $ (Independent Variable)	Quantity Demanded of CD (Dependent Variable)	(Dependent Independent Variable, Variable)
32	0	(0,32)
30	2	(2,30)
28	4	(4,28)
26	6	(6,26)
24	8	(8,24)
22	10	(10,22)
20	12	(12,20)
18	14	(14,18)
16	16	(16,16)
14	18	(18,14)
12	20	(20,12)
10	22	(22,10)
8	24	(24,8)
6	26	(26,6)
4	28	(28,4)
2	30	(30,2)

VISUAL 1.4 ▲ Demand Curve for CDs

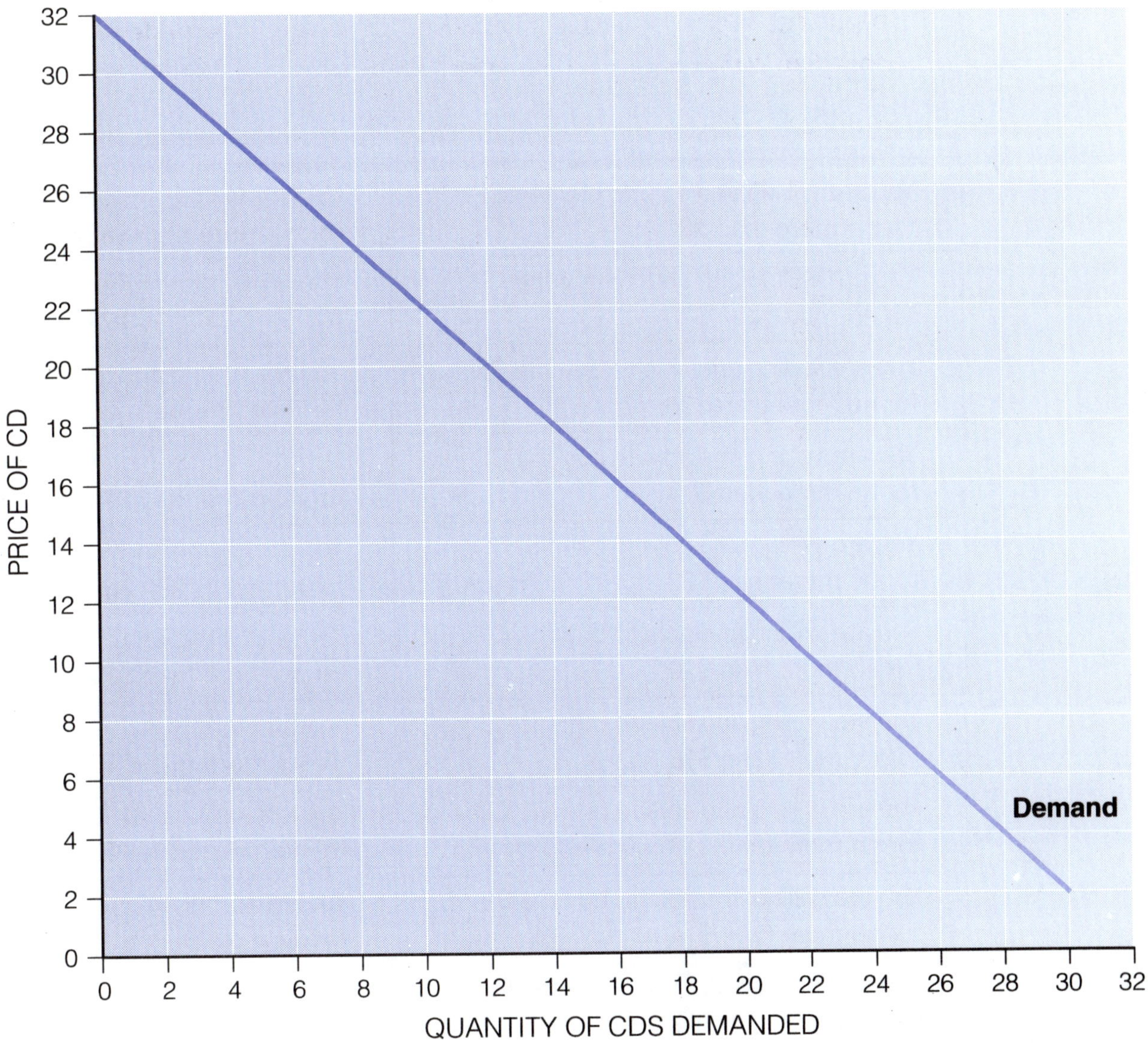

ACTIVITY 1.1

Reproduce this page on colored paper, cut out the slips, and place them in a paper bag. Students will randomly select slips for an activity to create a simulated demand schedule.

You are willing and able to buy the CD for no more than $30	You are willing and able to buy the CD for no more than $30
You are willing and able to buy the CD for no more than $28	You are willing and able to buy the CD for no more than $28
You are willing and able to buy the CD for no more than $26	You are willing and able to buy the CD for no more than $26
You are willing and able to buy the CD for no more than $24	You are willing and able to buy the CD for no more than $24
You are willing and able to buy the CD for no more than $22	You are willing and able to buy the CD for no more than $22
You are willing and able to buy the CD for no more than $20	You are willing and able to buy the CD for no more than $20
You are willing and able to buy the CD for no more than $18	You are willing and able to buy the CD for no more than $18
You are willing and able to buy the CD for no more than $16	You are willing and able to buy the CD for no more than $16
You are willing and able to buy the CD for no more than $14	You are willing and able to buy the CD for no more than $14
You are willing and able to buy the CD for no more than $12	You are willing and able to buy the CD for no more than $12
You are willing and able to buy the CD for no more than $10	You are willing and able to buy the CD for no more than $10
You are willing and able to buy the CD for no more than $8	You are willing and able to buy the CD for no more than $8
You are willing and able to buy the CD for no more than $6	You are willing and able to buy the CD for no more than $6
You are willing and able to buy the CD for no more than $4	You are willing and able to buy the CD for no more than $4
You are willing and able to buy the CD for no more than $2	You are willing and able to buy the CD for no more than $2

ACTIVITY 1.2

Name______________________________ Date__________ Period______

A popular CD has recently been released. You will be collecting data on the maximum price that you and your classmates are willing and able to pay for this CD. These data will be collected and represented in three different ways.

Part 1 DEMAND SCHEDULE

Price of CD in $ **(Independent Variable)**	Quantity Demanded of CD **(Dependent Variable)**	(Dependent Independent Variable, Variable)
32		
30		
28		
26		
24		
22		
20		
18		
16		
14		
12		
10		
8		
6		
4		
2		

ACTIVITY 1.2 (continued)

Part 2 DEMAND CURVE

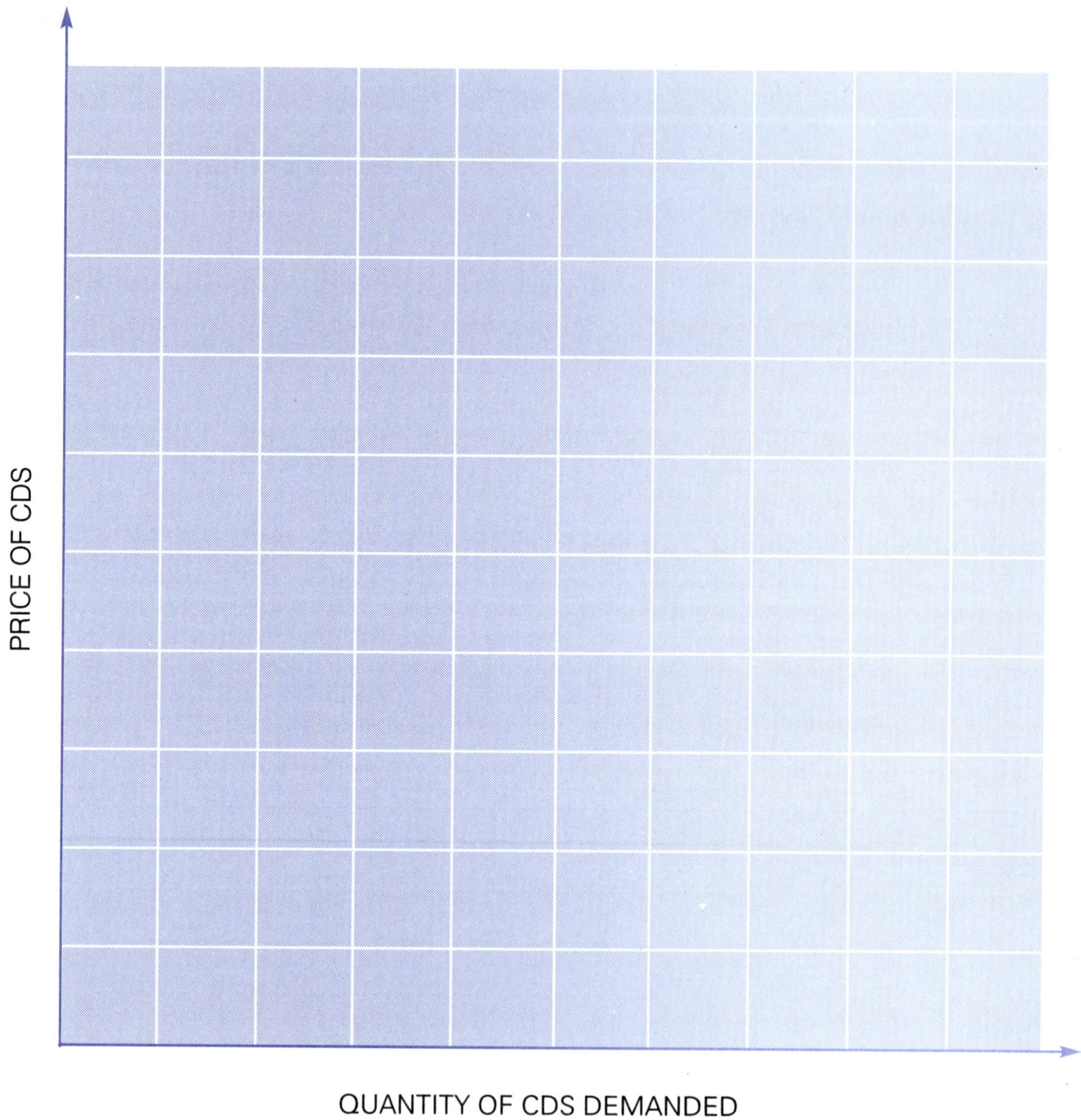

ACTIVITY 1.2 (continued)

Part 3 EQUATION OF THE DEMAND CURVE

Point Slope Method	Slope and Vertical Intercept Method	Two Points Method

ACTIVITY 1.3

Name____ Date_____________ Period______

1. Circle the graph that could be a graph representing a demand curve

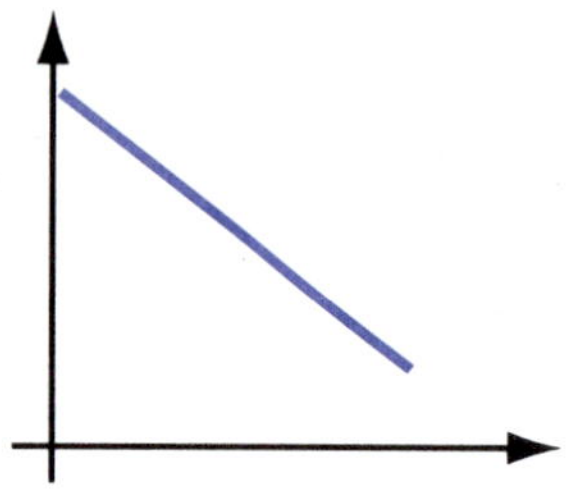

Figure A

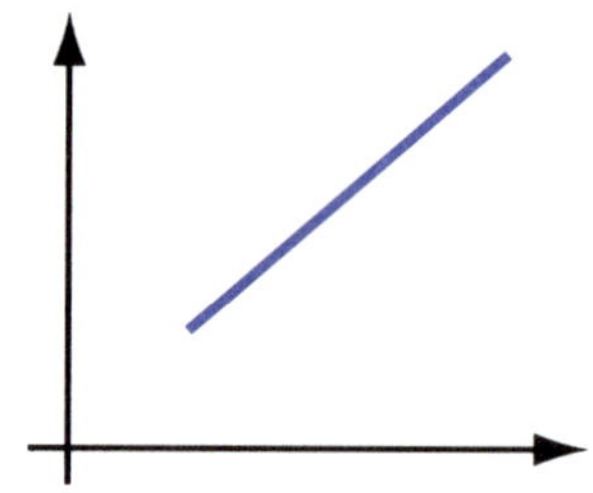

Figure B

2. What is a demand schedule?

3. A demand curve shows the relationship between ______________ and ____________.

4. Explain why quantity demanded is the dependent variable.

5. What is the law of demand?

6. Below is a demand curve for the price and the quantity demanded of designer jeans. Write the equation of the demand curve using the slope intercept method.

Demand Curve for Designer Jeans

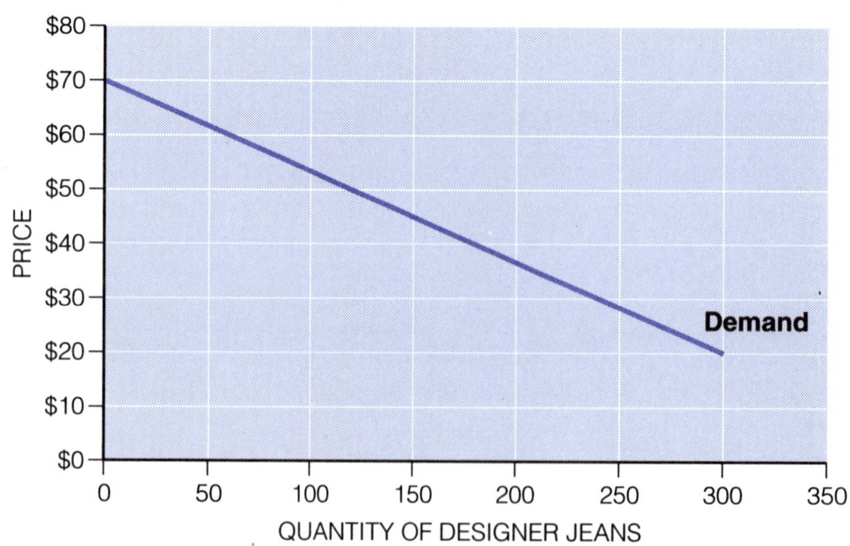

7. Below is a demand schedule for bananas. Use this to write the equation of the demand curve using the point slope method.

Price/lb. in cents	Quantity Demanded
59¢	15
49¢	30
39¢	45
29¢	60
19¢	75

8. Choose two points from the demand schedule for bananas in problem 7 and find the equation of the demand curve using these two points.

9. Before a soft drink machine is installed in your school, the student government surveyed a sampling of students. The survey asked each student, "What is the most you would be willing to pay for one can of soft drink?" Use the data to complete the following tasks:

a) make a demand schedule
b) plot and connect the points from the demand schedule as an economist would
c) draw the linear demand curve that best represents the points plotted
d) write the slope and vertical intercept of the demand curve
e) write the equation of the demand curve

Maximum Price in cents	Number of People
75¢	I
70¢	II
65¢	III
60¢	~~IIII~~ ~~IIII~~ ~~IIII~~
55¢	~~IIII~~ ~~IIII~~ II
50¢	
45¢	~~IIII~~
40¢	
35¢	~~IIII~~ III

Lesson 2 The Nature of Supply

Mathematics Focus:

Algebra I

Mathematics Prerequisites:

Prior to this lesson, students should be able to:

- Make a graph using a table of values
- Find slope and vertical intercepts
- Write the equation of a line given
  - a) a point and a slope
  - b) two points on the line
  - c) a slope and one intercept
- Define the dependent and independent variables

Lesson Objectives:

To apply prerequisite mathematics concepts and processes to:

- Explain why a supply curve has a positive slope
- Explain the reasons for the existence of the law of supply
- Explain why quantity supplied depends on price

Overview of Mathematics and Economics:

This lesson develops the economic tool of supply. Supply is determined by the willingness and ability of producers to sell a product (a good or a service) at different prices. A supply curve is a graph with a positive slope in the first quadrant. It illustrates the direct relationship between the price of a product and the amount of product available for sale at each price. A supply curve is most accurately derived from a supply schedule, which is a table of values relating prices and quantities supplied. To make this lesson appropriate for algebra I students, it will be restricted to the study of linear supply curves.

A change in the quantity of a product supplied is caused by a change in the product's price. The supply curve shows that a change in price causes a change in quantity supplied. Note that a change in price is the only thing that can cause a change in quantity supplied. This can be viewed graphically as a movement along the supply curve. Other factors that influence the producers' desire to sell the product—such as changes in wages and salaries, energy costs, materials costs, technological change, or shocks caused by adverse weather—cause a change in the amount supplied at each and every price. This is graphically represented by a shift in the supply curve. This shift, also known as a change in supply (as opposed to a change in quantity supplied) leads to a new supply curve that is parallel to the original curve. (See Lesson 4 for further discussion of this concept.)

The supply curve shows the law of supply, which states that, holding everything else constant, there is a positive relationship between movements in price and quantity supplied. As price increases, the quantity supplied increases. It is perhaps simplest for students at this level to realize that at higher prices, producers are willing and able to provide more items because of increased profitability. As price decreases, the quantity supplied also decreases. Fewer units will be offered for sale at these lower prices because production is less profitable.

Mathematics and Economics Terms:

- Dependent variable
- Direct relationship
- Independent variable
- Law of supply
- Quantity supplied
- Supply curve
- Supply schedule

Materials:

- Straight edge
- Overhead transparencies of Visuals 2.1, 2.2, 2.3, and 2.4 and Activity 2.2
- One copy of Activity 2.2 and 2.3 for each student
- Make one copy of Activity 2.1 on colored paper. (Use a color different from that used in Lesson 1.) Cut the activity slips on the solid lines and place a slip in a paper bag for each student in the class.

To ensure that a linear function is produced, leave out the slips that represent the higher prices if you have fewer students than there are slips of paper. In addition, be sure that you use an even number of students. This paper bag will be used in step 3.

Estimated Time:

80–100 minutes

Procedures:

1. Warm-Up Activity: Have the students answer the questions on Visual 2.1. Discuss the answers with the class.

COMMENT When discussing the answers to the problems, emphasize that:

- In mathematics, the horizontal axis is used for the independent variable and the vertical axis is used for the dependent variable.
- Since the relationship is only valid for positive numbers of hours worked and a positive total payment, the line should be graphed in the first quadrant only.
- Meaningful variables are used. The variables h (hours) and p (payment) are substituted for x and y, respectively, in the equation y = mx + b.

Answers to the questions include:

1. $p = 3h$
2. independent—hours; dependent—payment
3. Show Visual 2.2.
4. $m = 3$
5. 3 hours, or 3.33 hours, or 3 hours and 20 minutes

2. Ask the students to imagine that they are investigating the possibility of opening a business to sell CDs. Studying some economic characteristics of a currently top-selling CD will give them a good idea whether they can run their business profitably. They will be looking at their willingness to sell the CD at various prices. That is, they will be investigating the quantity supplied. In this analysis, they will be using some of the mathematical concepts that they have been studying.

3. Distribute a copy of Activity 2.2 to each student. Then have each student take a slip of paper at random from the paper bag that you have prepared in Activity 2.1. Tell the students that the number on each slip represents the lowest price at which each student would be willing to sell the CD. The number of people willing to sell the CD at a given price is the quantity supplied.

4. Ask the students to look at their slips of paper. Ask them to raise their hand if they would be willing to sell the CD for $0. No students should raise a hand, so enter a 0 for quantity supplied in your table of values for the price of $0 on the overhead transparency. Have the students complete the form with you. Ask the students, "In real life, why is no one willing to sell the CD for $0?" Answers will vary but make sure that the reason that "since the CD is costly to produce, no one is willing and able to give away the CD" is given.

Then ask, "Who is willing and able to sell the CD for $2?" Two people should raise their hands so write "2" under quantity supplied to correspond with the price of $2. Next ask "Who is willing to sell the CD for $4?" Four people should raise their hands: the people with $4 on their slips as well as those with $2 on their slips. Ask the students, "Why would the individuals who would sell the CD for $2 also be willing to sell it for $4?" For each price level two additional students should raise their hands. Work together with the class to fill in the Quantity Supplied column in the table of values in Part I of Activity 2.2. Continue this exercise until the table of values is completed and all hands are raised. The completed supply schedule is shown in Visual 2.3.

Tell the students, "In economics, this table of values is called a supply schedule." Have the students look at the table of values and explain why the quantity supplied increases as the price increases. Also ask why the quantity supplied decreases as the price decreases.

COMMENT As the price increases, suppliers are willing and able to sell more CDs. There are two phenomena which generally happen here. Existing producers want to increase their production in response to the increased price because the increase generally means more profitability. Also, new producers may find it beneficial to start producing the items because the higher price makes this option more profitable than other ways to use their resources. The converse happens when the price decreases: existing producers may switch some or all of their resources to produce something else because other options are more profitable. This, in turn, lowers the number of units that are produced at the lower price.

5. Ask the students to identify the dependent and independent variable in the price/quantity supplied relationship. Remind the students that in mathematics, the independent variable is usually placed on the horizontal axis and the dependent variable on the vertical axis. Tell the students that economists do the reverse, placing the independent variable on the vertical axis and the dependent variable on the horizontal axis. Thus each ordered pair is in the form

(dependent variable, independent variable) = (quantity supplied, price).

Students should then complete the ordered pair column of the supply schedule. Answers are found on Visual 2.3

6. In Part 2 of Activity 2.2, have the students graph the line from the table of values in Part 1. Remind them to label the axes with the appropriate variable. Tell the students that in economics, the line they have graphed is called a supply curve. Have the students label this curve "Supply." Visual 2.4 shows how the graph should appear.

COMMENT Tell students that not all supply curves are linear and even though this curve is a straight line, it is referred to as a curve.

7. Ask the students to record the characteristics of the graph and the reason why the graph has each characteristic. You may need to use leading questions to help your students identify all of the characteristics. Discuss these answers as a class. The answers should include:

a) The graph is linear because for each $1 increase in price, the quantity supplied increases by one unit.
b) The line has a positive slope because as the price increases, the quantity supplied increases. Or as the price decreases, the quantity supplied decreases.
c) The vertical intercept is $0. That is the line intersects the vertical axis at $P = \$0$. This is because no one is willing and able to sell the CD at a price of zero dollars.
d) The graph lies entirely in the first quadrant because the quantity supplied and the price are never negative

8. Tell students,

"In mathematics, the slope of the line is typically viewed as

$$\frac{\text{change in dependent variable}}{\text{change in independent variable.}}$$

Because economists put the independent variable on the vertical axis and the dependent variable on the horizontal axis, we must refer to slope as

$$\frac{\text{change in the variable on the vertical axis}}{\text{change in the variable on the horizontal axis.}}$$

Therefore, in this example, the slope is $\frac{\text{change in price}}{\text{change in quantity supplied}}$."

The students should now calculate the slope.

Remind the students that the positive slope means that there is a direct relationship between price and quantity supplied. The law of supply says that, holding everything else constant, when price rises, producers are willing and able to increase the quantity supplied, and when the price falls, producers decrease the quantity supplied.

■ **COMMENT** The slope is $\frac{\$2}{2\ CDs} = \frac{\$1}{1\ CD}$

9. For Part 3 of Activity 2.2, divide students into three groups and have each group find the equation of the supply curve using one of the following methods (assign a different method to each group):

Group 1: Point and slope method
Group 2: Slope and vertical intercept method
Group 3: Two points method

COMMENT The equation of the supply curve is $P = Q_s$. When the students have found and compared their equations for the supply curve, regroup the students so that in the new groupings each method is represented. Students should share their methods with other members of the group. Have each student record each method on his or her copy of Activity 2.2. (This method is commonly called the "jigsaw method" in cooperative learning.)

Extension Activities:

Activity 2.3 can be used as an additional assignment.

COMMENT Answers to 2.3

1. Figure B
2. A supply schedule shows the quantity supplied of an item at different prices.
3. Price and quantity supplied.
4. Quantity supplied is the dependent variable because it is affected by price, which is the independent variable.
5. The law of supply states that, holding everything else constant, there is a direct relationship between price and quantity supplied. That is, as price increases, the quantity supplied increases. As price decreases, the quantity supplied decreases.
6. $P = 0 + 0.5Q_s$
7. $P = 0 + 0.00725Q_s$
8. Same as #7 above
9. a)

Supply schedule

Hourly Pay	Number of People
$3.50	1
4.00	4
4.50	9
5.00	19
5.50	22
6.00	32
6.50	41
7.00	48

b) and c)

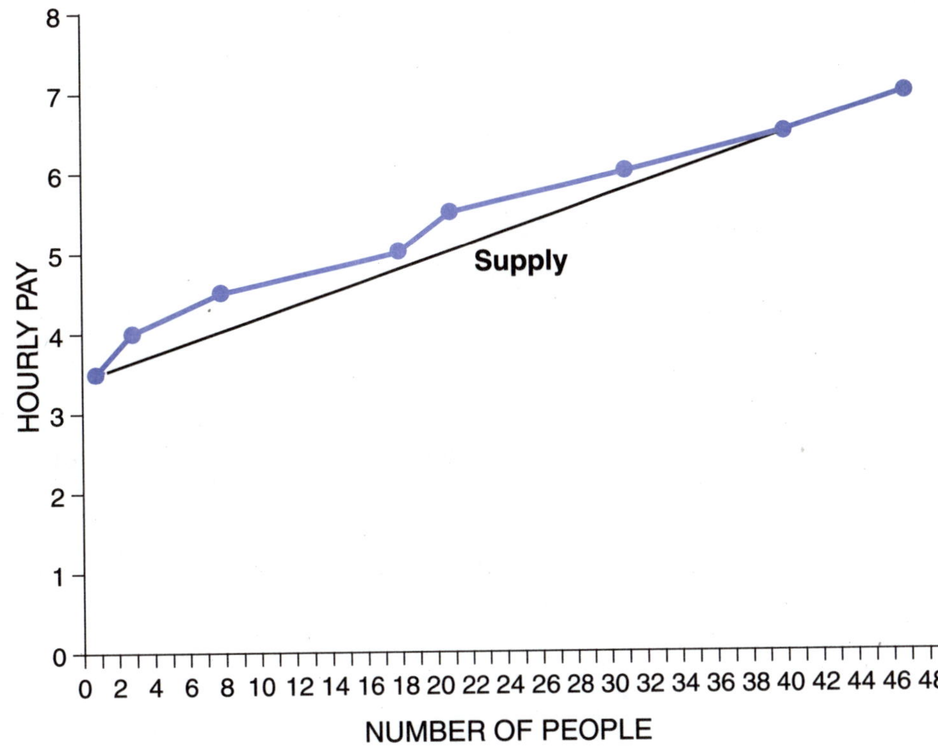

d) In this answer, the estimated slope and vertical intercept depend on how the points are fitted. For example, using the first and last ordered pairs the slope is 3.5/47 = 0.0745, and the vertical intercept is ≈ 3.43.

e) The equation of the line joining the points (1,3.5) and (48,7) is y = (3.5x)/47 + 3.43 where y represents hourly pay and x represents number of people. This provides a good linear approximation of the points in the supply schedule.

VISUAL 2.1 ▲ Warm-Up

Ian charges $3 an hour to babysit.

ANSWER THE FOLLOWING QUESTIONS:

1. Write the equation for the line representing the total amount a customer pays Ian in terms of the number of hours he babysits.

2. What are your independent and dependent variables?

3. Sketch the graph for 0 to 5 hours.

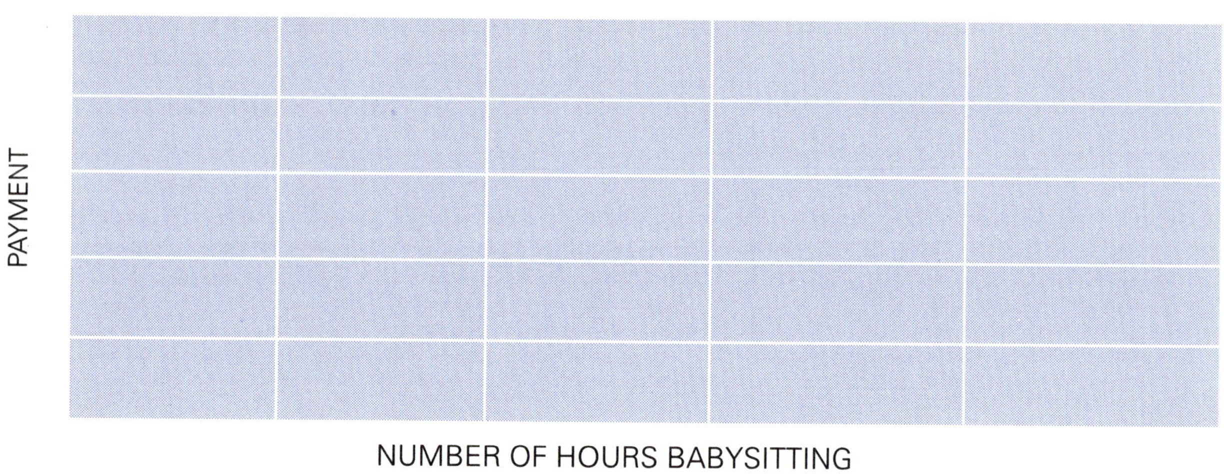

4. What is the slope of the line? (Remember: Slope is the rate of change.)

5. If Ian's customer has $10, how many hours can the customer stay out?

VISUAL 2.2

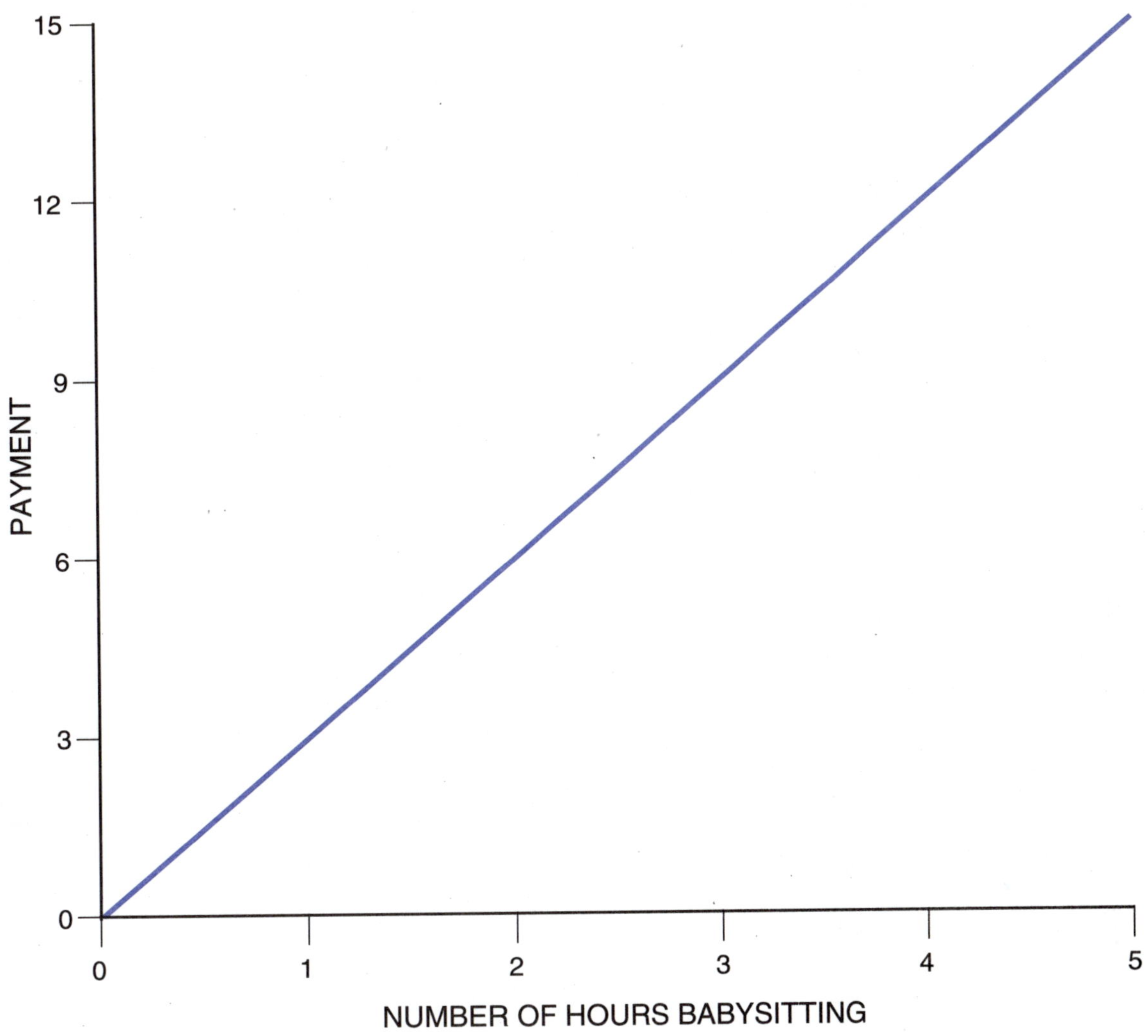

VISUAL 2.3 ▲ Supply Schedule

Price of CD in $ (Independent Variable)	Quantity Supplied of CDs (Dependent Variable)	(Dependent Variable, Independent Variable)
0	0	(0,0)
2	2	(2,2)
4	4	(4,4)
6	6	(6,6)
8	8	(8,8)
10	10	(10,10)
12	12	(12,12)
14	14	(14,14)
16	16	(16,16)
18	18	(18,18)
20	20	(20,20)
22	22	(22,22)
24	24	(24,24)
26	26	(26,26)
28	28	(28,28)
30	30	(30,30)

VISUAL 2.4 ▲ The Supply Curve

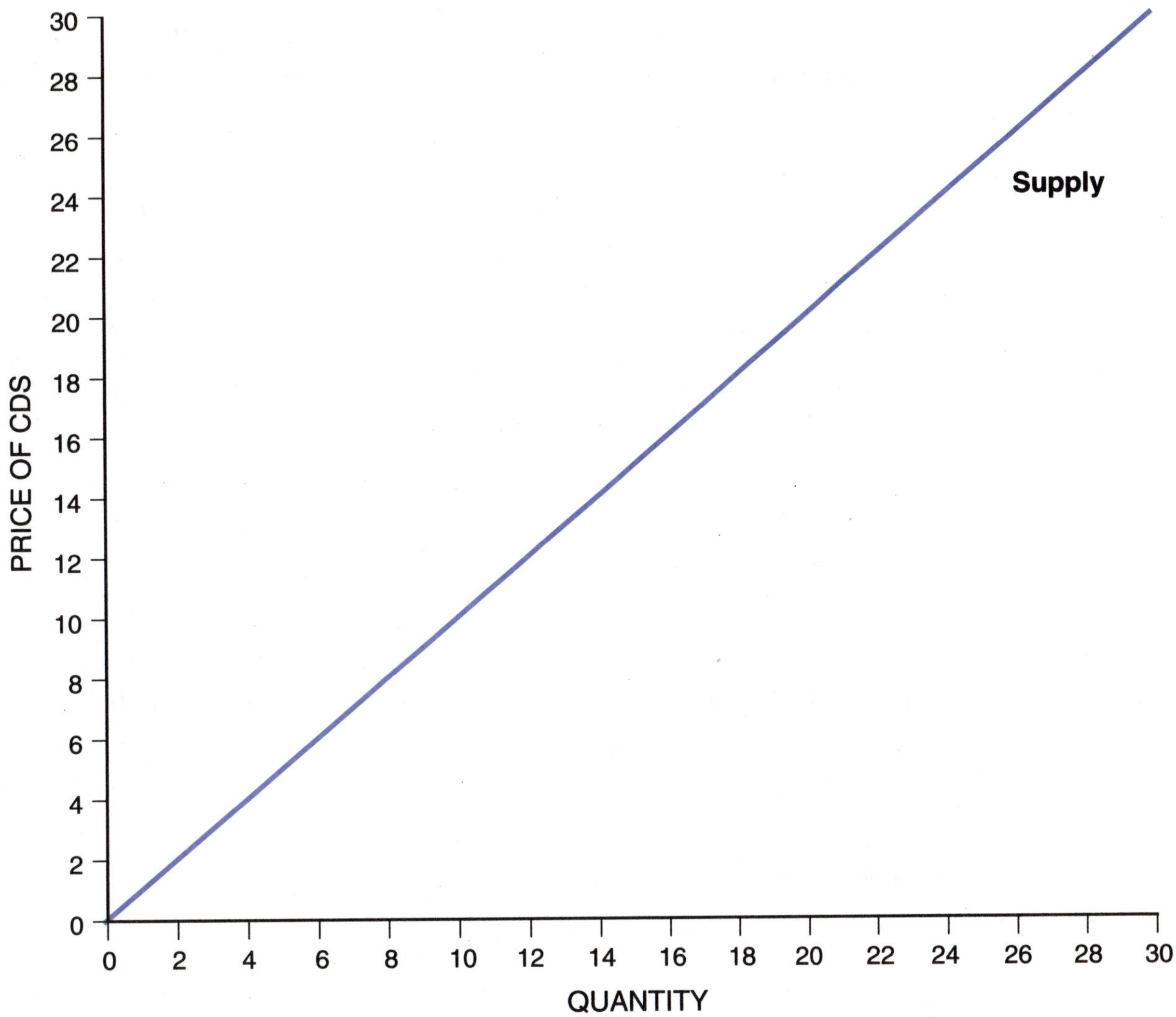

ACTIVITY 2.1

Reproduce this sheet on colored paper (a different color than Activity 1.1). Cut out the slips and place them in a paper bag. Students will randomly select slips to simulate a supply curve.

You are willing and able to sell the CD for no less than $30	You are willing and able to sell the CD for no less than $30
You are willing and able to sell the CD for no less than $28	You are willing and able to sell the CD for no less than $28
You are willing and able to sell the CD for no less than $26	You are willing and able to sell the CD for no less than $26
You are willing and able to sell the CD for no less than $24	You are willing and able to sell the CD for no less than $24
You are willing and able to sell the CD for no less than $22	You are willing and able to sell the CD for no less than $22
You are willing and able to sell the CD for no less than $20	You are willing and able to sell the CD for no less than $20
You are willing and able to sell the CD for no less than $18	You are willing and able to sell the CD for no less than $18
You are willing and able to sell the CD for no less than $16	You are willing and able to sell the CD for no less than $16
You are willing and able to sell the CD for no less than $14	You are willing and able to sell the CD for no less than $14
You are willing and able to sell the CD for no less than $12	You are willing and able to sell the CD for no less than $12
You are willing and able to sell the CD for no less than $10	You are willing and able to sell the CD for no less than $10
You are willing and able to sell the CD for no less than $8	You are willing and able to sell the CD for no less than $8
You are willing and able to sell the CD for no less than $6	You are willing and able to sell the CD for no less than $6
You are willing and able to sell the CD for no less than $4	You are willing and able to sell the CD for no less than $4
You are willing and able to sell the CD for no less than $2	You are willing and able to sell the CD for no less than $2

ACTIVITY 2.2

Name____ Date____________ Period_____

A popular CD has recently been released. You will be collecting data on the minimum price at which you and your classmates are willing and able to sell this CD. These data will be collected and represented in three different ways.

Part 1 SUPPLY SCHEDULE

Price of CD in $ **(Independent Variable)**	Quantity Supplied of CDs **(Dependent Variable)**	(Dependent Variable, Independent Variable)
0		
2		
4		
6		
8		
10		
12		
14		
16		
18		
20		
22		
24		
26		
28		
30		

Part 2 SUPPLY CURVE

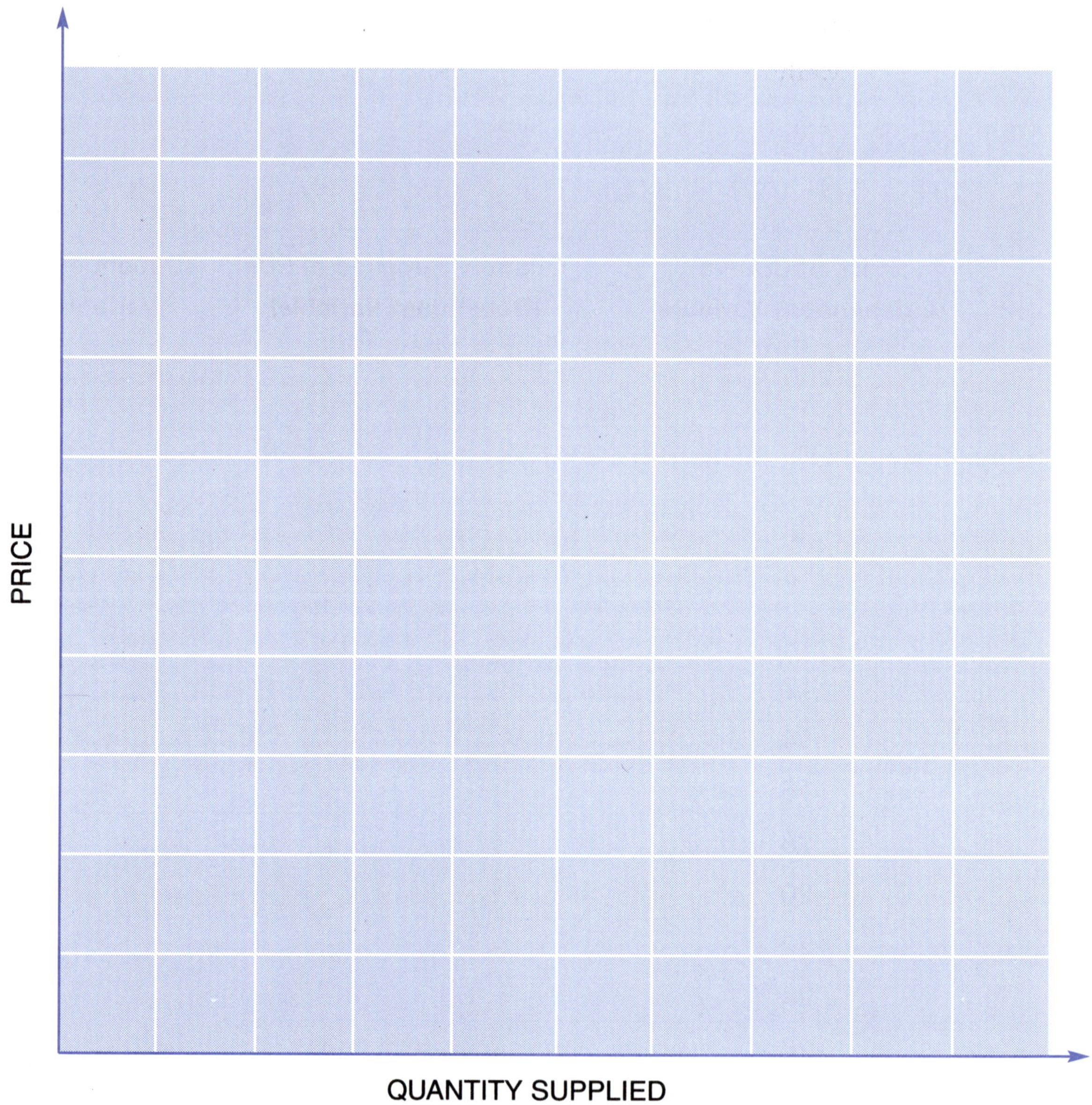

ACTIVITY 2.2 (continued)

Part 3 EQUATION OF THE SUPPLY CURVE

Point Slope Method	Slope Vertical Intercept Method	Two Point Method

ACTIVITY 2.3

Name______________________________ Date__________ Period_____

1. Circle the graph that could be a graph representing a supply curve.

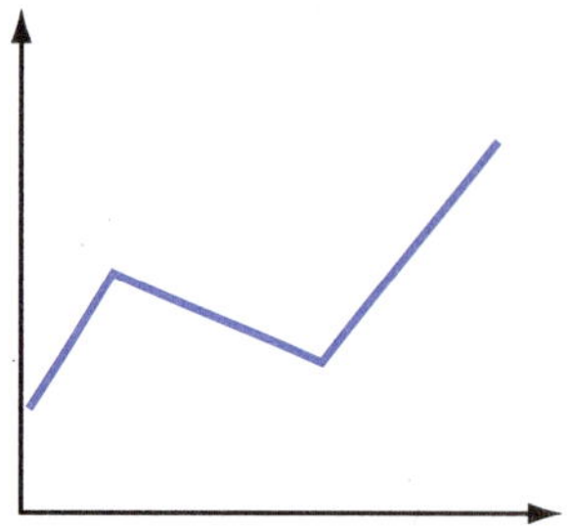

Figure A

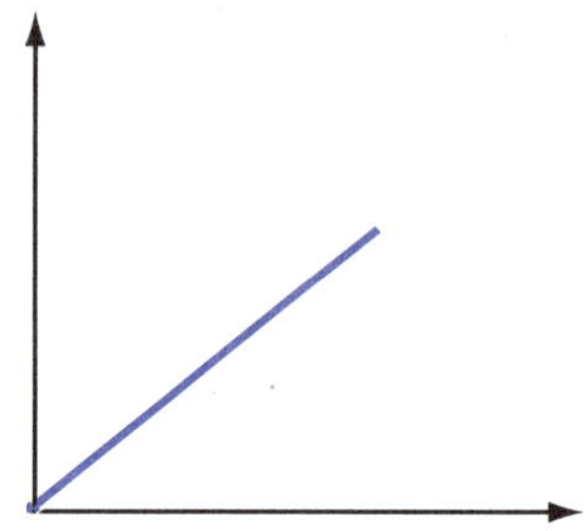

Figure B

2. What is a supply schedule?

3. A supply curve shows the relationship between ____________ and __________.

4. Explain why quantity supplied is the dependent variable.

5. What is the law of supply?

6. Below is a supply curve for the price and the quantity supplied of basketball shoes. Write the equation of the supply curve using the slope intercept method.

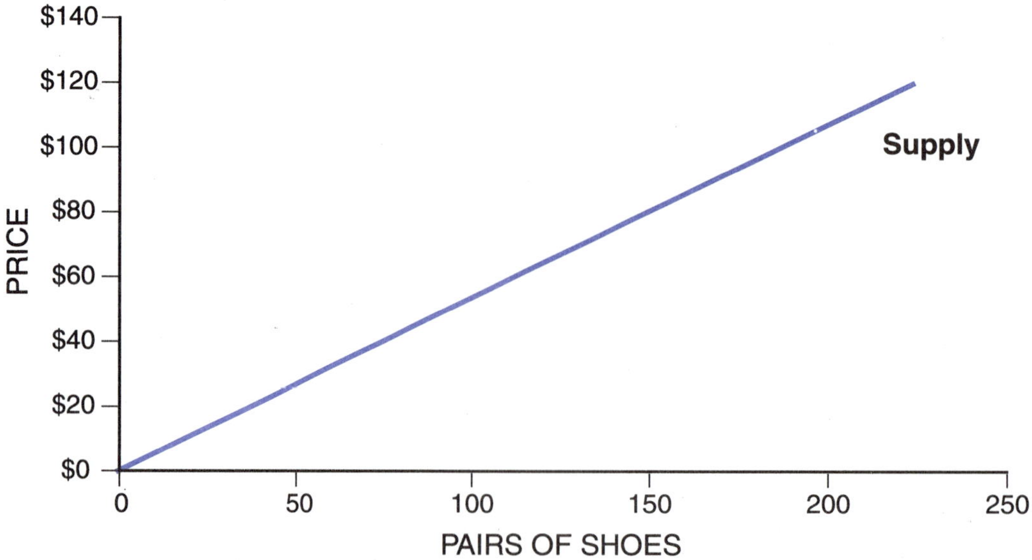

ACTIVITY 2.3 (continued)

7. Below is a supply schedule for peaches. Use this to write the equation of the supply curve using the point slope method.

Price/lb.	Quantity Supplied
$0	0
$0.29	40
$0.58	80
$0.87	120
$1.16	160

8. Choose two points from the supply schedule for peaches in problem 7 and find the equation of the supply curve using these two points.

9. A school wanted to hire students to do grounds work on the school campus. Before doing so, the administration surveyed students to find out how much the venture would cost the school. The survey asked each student, "What is the lowest hourly pay you would accept for doing grounds work?" Use the data to complete the following tasks:

a) make a supply schedule
b) plot the points from the supply schedule as an economist would
c) draw a linear supply curve that best represents the points plotted
d) using the line of best fit of the plotted points, find the slope and vertical intercept of the supply curve
e) write the equation of the supply curve

Hourly Pay	Number of People
$3.50	I
$4.00	III
$4.50	𝍸
$5.00	𝍸 𝍸
$5.50	III
$6.00	𝍸 𝍸
$6.50	𝍸 IIII
$7.00	𝍸 II

Lesson 3

Equilibrium: Determining Prices and Quantities

Mathematics Focus:

Algebra 1

Mathematics Prerequisites:

Prior to using this lesson, students should be able to solve a system of linear equations by using:

- The graphing method
- The substitution method
- The elimination/linear combination method

Economics Prerequisites:

Prior to using this lesson, students should be able to generate and explain both the demand curve and the supply curve. See Lessons 1 and 2.

Lesson Objectives:

To apply prerequisite mathematics concepts and processes to linear supply and demand curves to:

- Find the equilibrium price and quantity exchanged by solving a system of linear equations
- Differentiate between situations of equilibrium and disequilibrium
- Explain that shortages arise when quantity demanded is greater than quantity supplied at a given price
- Explain that surpluses arise when quantity supplied is greater than quantity demanded at a given price

Overview of Mathematics and Economics:

Supply and demand affect the prices people pay and the quantities they exchange in a market economy. Equilibrium is said to occur at the point at which quantity supplied equals quantity demanded. This point is at the intersection of the supply and demand curves. The point can also be found by solving the equations of the demand and supply curves simultaneously.

If prices are below equilibrium, then quantity demanded is greater than the quantity supplied and a shortage exists. When prices are above equilibrium, quantity supplied exceeds quantity demanded and a surplus arises. As long as market forces are allowed to operate, prices tend to increase in response to a shortage and decrease in response to a surplus. Adjustments occur until equilibrium is restored. Therefore, disequilibrium should not persist for a long period of time in an ordinary market setting.

Mathematics and Economics Terms:

- Dependent variable
- Disequilibrium
- Elimination method
- Equilibrium
- Independent variable
- Intercept
- Quantity demanded
- Quantity supplied
- Shortage
- Slope
- Substitution method
- Surplus
- System of linear equations

Materials:

- Overhead transparencies of Visuals 3.1, 3.2, and 3.3
- One copy of Activity 3.1 for each student
- Straight edge
- Graphing calculator (optional-used in the extensions only)
- Colored pencils

Estimated Time:

80–100 minutes

Procedures:

1. Warm-Up Activity: Have the students answer the questions in Visual 3.1.

COMMENT When discussing the answers to the problems, emphasize that the different methods of solving simultaneous equations all produce the same solution. Make sure the students relate the solution obtained numerically (by the substitution method, for example) to the point at which the two curves intersect. Answers to the questions include:

◆ 1. (1.) $y = \frac{1}{3}x + \frac{7}{3}$ (2.) $y = -\frac{1}{4}x + \frac{7}{2}$

2. Show Visual 3.2
3. (2,3)
4. (2,3) The solution found by the substitution method gives the point where the curves intersect. Indeed, that is what it means to solve two equations simultaneously.
5. Answers may vary. Students might use linear combinations to solve the equations, and some might even use matrices. Whatever method they use, it should yield the same solution as found in #3 and #4.

2. Tell the students, "You are going to help me decide whether our consumer electronics company should begin making and selling miniature TVs." Have the students complete Activity 3.1, number 1. Remind them that P, Q_d, and Q_s represent price, quantity demanded and quantity supplied, respectively. Also remind them that this exercise is confined to the first quadrant because price and quantity are always positive. After the students have completed graphing the equations, tell them, "Labels D and S represent the demand curve and the supply curve, while Q_d and Q_s represent quantities demanded and supplied at a particular point on their respective curves." See Visual 3.3 for example.

3. Ask the students to describe the characteristics of the graph. You may have to give some leading questions in order to gain the appropriate responses.

■ **COMMENT** Students' answers should include:

- The demand curve has a negative slope and the supply curve has a positive slope.
- The two curves intersect at one point.
- The quantity demanded and quantity supplied depend on price. Price is the independent variable. Economists reverse the placement of the dependent and independent variables on the graph. (See Lessons 1 and 2 for more information on this placement of variables.) The independent variable price (*P*) is graphed on the vertical axis and the dependent variable quantity (*Q*) is on the horizontal axis.
- Since price, quantity supplied, and quantity demanded are always greater than zero, the entire graph is confined to the first quadrant.

4. Have the students complete number 2 on Activity 3.1.
Ask the students, "What is the slope of the demand curve? What information does this tell us about miniature TVs?"

Answer: The slope of the demand curve is –3. For every $3 decrease in the price, one additional person will be willing and able to purchase a miniature TV.

Ask the students, "What is the slope of the supply curve? What information does this tell us about miniature TVs?"

Answer: The slope of the supply curve is 2. For every $2 increase in the price, producers will be willing and able to supply one additional miniature TV.

Ask the students, "What is the vertical intercept of the demand curve? What information does this tell us about miniature TVs?"

Answer: The vertical intercept of the demand curve is $600. No one is willing and able to purchase a miniature TV for a price of $600 or greater. The horizontal coordinate of this vertical intercept is 0.

Ask the students, "What is the vertical intercept of the supply curve? What information does this tell us about miniature TVs?"

Answer: The vertical intercept of the supply curve is $200. No one is willing and able to supply a miniature TV for a price of $200 or less. The horizontal coordinate of this vertical intercept is 0.

5. Have the students use their results to complete number 3 on Activity 3.1.

Answer: The equations of the curves are:

Demand Curve: $P = -3Q_d + 600$

Supply Curve: $P = 2Q_s + 200$

6. Have the students do number 4 on Activity 3.1. Discuss with the students how they might verify the coordinates where the graphs intersect.

Answer: The demand and supply curves intersect at Price (P) = $360 and Quantity ($Q$) = 80 TVs. Students might suggest putting the coordinates into each equation to verify that the coordinates represent the solution of each equation. Others might suggest solving the equations simultaneously.

7. Tell the students that the point of intersection represents the equilibrium point. If 80 miniature TVs are available for $360 each, then all of the TVs on the market will be purchased and no additional people will be willing and able to buy a TV for that price. The equilibrium point represents a situation at which there is neither a shortage nor a surplus.

8. Next have the students do number 5 on Activity 3.1. Divide the class into two groups. Tell one group to solve the system of equations using the substitution method and the other group to use the elimination/linear combination method. Have the students record their work in the table; then they should check their answers with one another. Remind them that they can also confirm their results by checking with that which has been previously found on their graph.

9. Ask the students, "What will happen at prices lower than $360?" Next ask "What will happen at prices greater than $360?"

Answer: At prices lower than $360 a shortage will develop and prices will ultimately rise. At prices greater than $360 a surplus will occur and this will ultimately force prices down.

10. Tell the students, "When quantity demanded is greater than quantity supplied at an existing price, a shortage exists. When quantity supplied is greater than quantity demanded at an existing price, a surplus exists. Both of these situations are called *disequilibrium* in the market. Price and quantity exchanged will eventually adjust to restore equilibrium in a well-functioning market. This will occur naturally without any need for government intervention.

11. Ask the students to do number 6 on Activity 3.1. Answers include:

1. At a price of $360, the quantity supplied and the quantity demanded will be the same. There won't be additional consumers who are willing and able to buy a miniature TV at that price. Also, producers will have sold all of their miniature TVs at that price.
2. Students can show by their graph (see Visual 3.3 as an example) that the quantity demanded is greater than the quantity supplied at a price of $300. Alternatively, they can substitute P = $300 into each equation and find that quantity demanded is 100 and quantity supplied is 50. A number of consumers will be unable to buy a miniature TV at that price because not enough are supplied. There is a shortage of 50 miniature TVs at that price level.
3. Again, students can show by their graph (Visual 3.3) how the quantity supplied is greater than the quantity demanded at a price of $420. Alternatively, they can examine the results of substituting P = $420 into each equation. All of the miniature TVs will not be sold at that price level. There will be a surplus of 50 miniature TVs at the $420 price level.

Extension Activities:

1. Use a graphing calculator to solve the following system of equations using matrices; then answer the following questions:

$P = 300 + 4Q$

$P = 900 - 6Q$

Answer: The solution to the system is (60, 540).

a) In the system above, which equation represents the demand curve? Explain how you know this.

Answer: The equation $P = 900 - 6Q$ is the demand curve because this curve has a negative slope. We know that a demand curve must have negative slope, because price and quantity demanded are inversely related.

b) At what rate does the quantity demanded change as the price changes?

Answer: The slope of the demand curve is -6. For every \$6 decrease in price, there is a 1 unit increase in quantity demanded.

c) At what rate does the quantity supplied change as the price changes?

Answer: The slope of the supply curve is 4. For every \$4 increase in price, quantity supplied rises by 1 unit.

d) If the price were set at \$600, there would be disequilibrium. Would this situation represent a shortage or surplus, and by what amount?

Answer: At a price of \$600, the quantity demanded would be 50 and the quantity supplied would be 75. This situation represents a surplus of 25.

e) What must happen to price for a state of equilibrium to occur?

Answer: The price must come down to \$540 to regain equilibrium.

f) Give an example of coordinates of a point on the demand curve where there will be a shortage?

Answer: Answers will vary. Any point with a price coordinate of less than \$540 and a quantity demanded coordinate greater than 60 represents a shortage.

VISUAL 3.1 ▲ Warm-Up

For this activity, you will work with the following two equations:

1. $x - 3y = -7$
2. $x + 4y = 14$

ANSWER THE FOLLOWING QUESTIONS

1. Rewrite both equations in the slope-intercept form.

2. Carefully graph both of these equations on the same coordinate axes.

3. At what point do the lines intersect?

4. Use the method of substitution to solve these equations simultaneously. Is your solution the same as your answer to #3? Why or why not?

5. Use at least one other method to solve the two equations simultaneously. Compare your answer to your answers for #3 and #4.

VISUAL 3.2

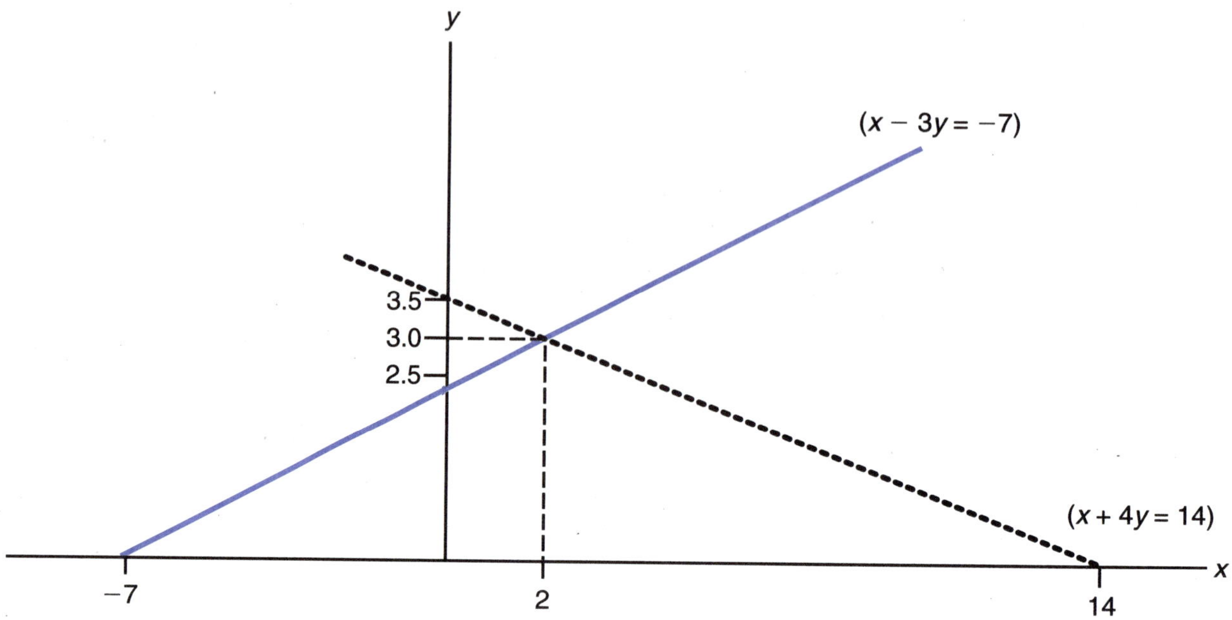

VISUAL 3.3 ▲ Supply and Demand Curves

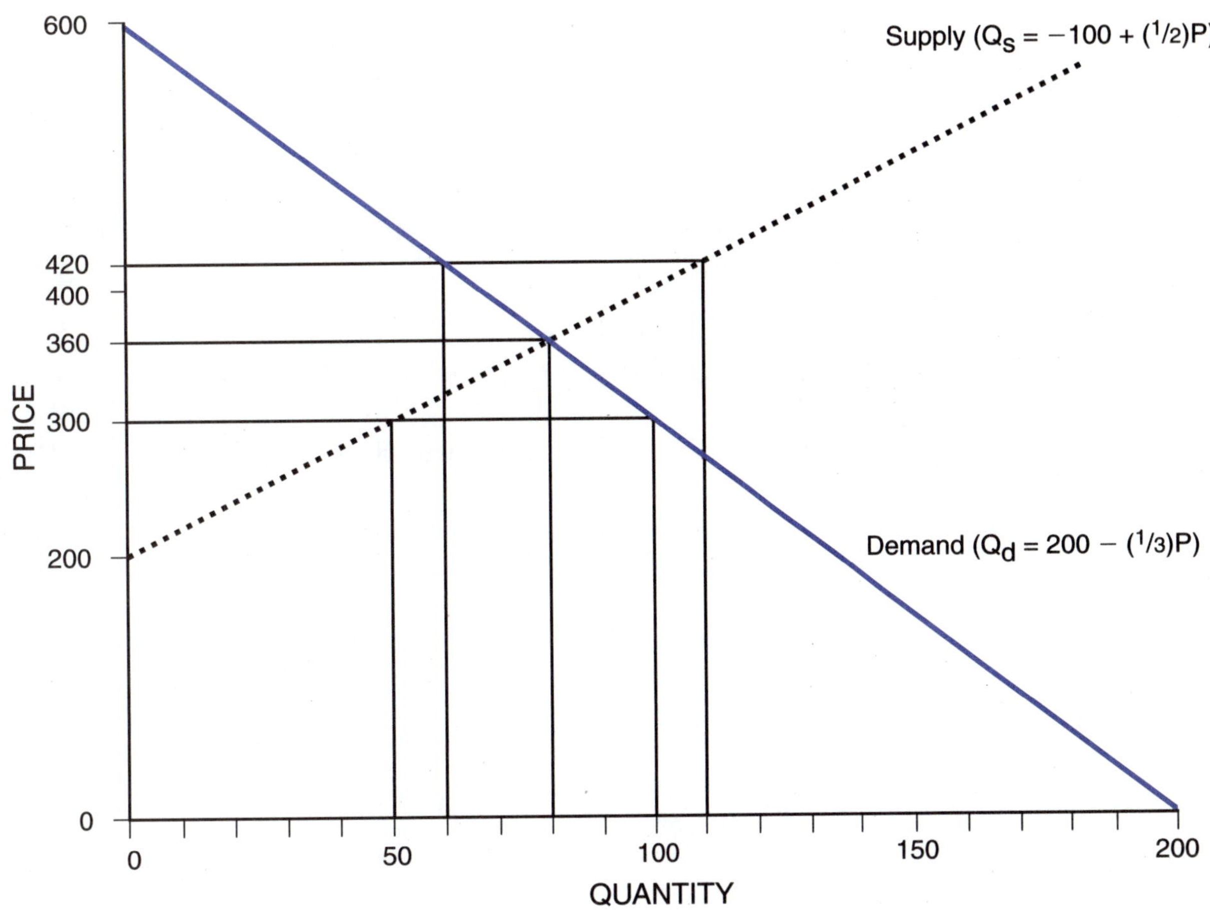

ACTIVITY 3.1

Name ______________________________ Date __________ Period _____

A REPORT ON THE MARKET FOR MINIATURE TVs

You have been asked by your supervisor to analyze the market for miniature TVs. Your report will help your company decide whether or not to enter this new market. The only information your supervisor has given you is the following set of equations. Notice that the equations are not in slope-intercept form:

Demand curve: $Q_d = 200 - (1/3)P$
Supply curve: $Q_s = -100 + (1/2)P$

1. Graph both of the equations on the coordinate plane below. The variable *P* should be on the vertical axis and *Q* on the horizontal axis. Note that your graph should be confined to the first quadrant only. Label the Demand Curve, "D," and the Supply Curve, "S." Use one color for *D* and another color for *S*. Show all your work.

2. Use your graphs and the equations given above to fill in the blanks:
   a) The slope of the demand curve is ____________.
   b) The slope of the supply curve is ____________.
   c) The vertical intercept of the demand curve is ____________.
   d) The vertical intercept of the supply curve is ____________.

3. Use the information you just found to solve for P and write the equations of the supply and demand curves in slope-intercept form.

   Demand Curve: ______________________

   Supply Curve: ______________________

4. At the equilibrium point, the quantity demanded is the same as the quantity supplied ($Q_d = Q_s$) and the price along the demand curve equals the price along the supply curve. Look at your graph to find the coordinates of the equilibrium point: ___________.
How can you check this information before you turn in your report to your supervisor?

5. Your teacher will divide the class into two groups. You will be asked to solve the system represented by the demand curves and the supply curves. Use the method your teacher asks you to use, and record your work carefully in the appropriate column of the table below.

Substitution Method	Elimination/Linear Combination Method

ACTIVITY 3.1 (continued)

6. You now enthusiastically report to your boss that you have discovered the price and quantity that your company can expect to observe in the market for miniature TVs. If you can produce these items at an average cost that is less than the equilibrium price, and if you can produce as many units as the equilibrium quantity, then the company might be able to make a go of it. Pleased, you go home for the evening, content that you have helped your company reach its goal of increased profitability. But when you get into the office the next morning, your boss has laid a piece of paper on you desk that reads as follows:

   In preparation for my meeting with the board of directors, I need to make sure that I can answer all questions that might arise. Please answer questions two and three by using both equations and graphs. Thank you.

   1. *What is the significance of P = $360?*
   2. *If we set a price of $300, what will happen?*
   3. *What happens if we set a price of $420?*

Lesson 4

Understanding the Mathematics of Changes in Supply and Demand

Mathematics Focus:

Algebra 1

Mathematics Prerequisites:

Prior to using this lesson, students should be able to

- Solve a system of linear equations by using the graphing method and an algebraic method
- Determine the equation of a line drawn parallel to a given line
- Recognize when two lines are parallel to one another

Economics Prerequisites:

Prior to using this lesson students should be able to generate both the demand curve and the supply curve and explain how their interaction brings about an equilibrium price. See Lessons 1, 2, and 3.

Lesson Objectives:

To apply prerequisite mathematics concepts and processes to supply and demand curves to:

- Explain that a change in supply is represented by a translation (a parallel shift) in the supply curve
- Explain that an increase in supply decreases price and increases quantity exchanged while a decrease in supply increases price and decreases quantity exchanged
- Explain that a change in demand is represented by a translation (a parallel shift) in the demand curve
- Explain that an increase in demand increases price and quantity exchanged while a decrease in demand reduces price and quantity exchanged

Overview of Mathematics and Economics:

This lesson asks students to look at the factors that cause a change in supply and/or a change in demand. Many factors influence the amount of a product that people are willing and able to purchase at each and every price. Such factors as income, tastes and preferences, the prices of related goods, the number of buyers, and expected future prices influence the demand for a product. When we observe a change in any of these factors, we normally expect to experience a change in demand for the product. A change in demand causes a **parallel shift** (or translation) of the demand curve. This is distinct from a movement along the demand curve, which (as noted in Lesson 1) is called a change in quantity demanded. A change in quantity demanded can only be caused by a change in the price of the product.

An increase in demand is represented by a **rightward** shift (a translation to the right) in the demand curve. This can be caused by an increase in income, an increase in the prices of substitute goods, a decrease in the prices of complementary goods (those goods that are consumed jointly), higher expected future prices, an increase in the number of buyers, or a favorable change in tastes and preferences. When everything else is held constant, an increase in demand leads to higher prices and greater quantities exchanged. A decrease in demand is represented by a **leftward** shift (a translation to the left) in the demand curve. This might be caused by a decrease in income, a decrease in the prices of substitute goods, an increase in the prices of complementary goods (those goods that are consumed jointly), lower expected future prices, a decrease in the number of buyers, or an unfavorable change in tastes and preferences. A decrease in demand usually causes a decrease in price and quantity exchanged.

The supply of a product is affected by the factors influencing the amount of a product that people are willing and able to sell at each and every price. Such factors include the prices of productive inputs (such as capital, labor, energy, and materials), expectations of future prices, technology, or the number of sellers. Changes in any of these factors cause a **parallel shift** (or translation) of the supply curve, also known as a change in supply. This is to be distinguished from a change in quantity supplied, which is caused by a change in the price of the product and is represented by a movement along the supply curve (as noted in Lesson 2).

An increase in supply is represented by a **rightward** shift (a translation to the right) in the supply curve. This can be caused by a decrease in input prices, a technological advance, an increase in the number of sellers, or producer expectations of lower future product prices. When everything else is held constant, an increase in supply leads to lower prices and greater quantities exchanged. A decrease in supply is represented by a **leftward** shift (a translation to the left) in the supply curve. This might be caused by rising input prices, technological regress, a decrease in the number of sellers, or producer expectations of higher future product prices. A decrease in supply leads to higher prices and lower quantities exchanged.

Changes in demand and supply are restricted to the first quadrant because price and quantity (which are respectively measured on the vertical and horizontal axes) must both be positive numbers. An increase in demand is therefore represented by an increase in the vertical intercept while a decrease in demand leads to a decrease in the value of the vertical intercept. Likewise, an increase in supply leads to a decrease in the value of the vertical intercept and a decrease in supply increases the vertical intercept.

Mathematics and Economics Terms:

- Change in demand
- Change in supply
- Demand
- Equilibrium
- Intercept
- Parallel lines
- Slope
- Supply
- Translation

Materials:

- One copy of Activity 4.1 for each student
- One copy of Activity 4.2 for each student (optional)
- Overhead transparencies of Visuals 4.1 – 4.9
- Graph paper for each student
- Straight edge
- Graphing calculator (optional)

Estimated Time:

60 – 80 minutes

Procedures:

1. Warm-Up Activity: Put Visual 4.1 on the overhead and have the students answer the questions.

Answers:

1) and 2) See Visual 4.2

3) See Visual 4.2 and $y = \frac{1}{3}x + 4$

4) $m_{L1} = \frac{1}{3}$

5) $m_{L2} = \frac{1}{3}$

COMMENT The important idea in this warmup activity is for students to recognize that parallel lines have equal slopes

2. Tell the students that in this lesson they will look at forces that change supply and demand and thus cause variation in prices and quantities. Review the point that in the previous lessons (1–3), the students have learned that quantity supplied and demanded depend upon the price of the good or service (movements along the supply and demand curves, respectively). The supply and demand curves show what happens to the quantity supplied and quantity demanded at different price levels.

Factors other than price can also have a strong effect on the purchasing and selling desires of consumers and producers. If something other than the price changes, it can result in a new supply or demand curve that is parallel to the original supply or demand curve. When a non-price-related factor influences either the supply or demand curve, this is said to cause a *change in supply* or a *change in demand*. A change in supply is represented by a shift, or *translation*, in the supply curve while a change in demand is represented by a shift, or *translation*, in the demand curve.

COMMENT This lesson extends economic ideas that were developed in Lessons 1, 2, and 3. Students need an understanding of supply curves, demand curves, and equilibrium in order to complete this lesson.

3. Ask the students to consider the following scenarios:

- Everyone in your school decides to take a part-time job. What will happen to the students' incomes, and how might this change in income affect the demand for miniature TVs?
- Answer: Since income is a primary determinant of spending, demand will likely increase. When people have more income, they are better able to purchase additional goods and services.
- What if the price of computers suddenly quadrupled? What would this change likely do to the demand for computer software?
- Answer: Computers and software are complementary goods; that is, these two items are consumed jointly. With everything else being equal, people will now purchase fewer computers because of the higher prices. This would lead to a decline in the demand for software, a complementary good for computers.
- What would happen to the demand for apples if the Surgeon General determined that eating an apple a day prolongs your life by five years?
- Answer: Demand will likely increase. Because of the promise of longer life, more people will buy more apples.
- What will happen to the demand for health care services in Florida when the population increases and becomes more aged in that state?
- Answer: Demand will increase for two reasons: There will be more people living in Florida, and senior citizens generally use more health care services.
- What would happen to the demand for Titleist golf balls if the price of Top Flite golf balls were cut in half?
- Answer: Since the two goods are substitutes, the demand for Titleist golf balls would fall.

These scenarios are all examples of factors that cause demand curves to shift. They reflect factors not directly related to the change in the product's price that determine the amount of the good or service that people are willing and able to buy at each and every price. In mathematical terms, the demand for an item determines the location of the demand curve in the first quadrant.

The effect of an increase in demand is to raise price and quantity exchanged. Conversely, a reduction in demand causes price and quantity exchanged to fall. A translation of a curve leads to a change in the vertical and horizontal intercept terms, but leaves the slope unchanged.

4. Ask the students to consider the next set of scenarios:

- Suppose that energy prices increase. Higher energy prices would increase the cost of manufacturing blue jeans. What would this increase do to the supply of blue jeans?
- Answer: As the cost to produce jeans increases, the supply will fall, since fewer suppliers would be willing and able to sell the jeans at each and every price.
- What would happen to the supply of fast-food restaurants if a foreign fast-food merchant chooses to expand into the United States?
- Answer: The supply would increase because of the appearance of another fast-food franchise.
- What would happen to the supply of day-care providers if the local government decides to impose strict licensing requirements on providers?
- Answer: The supply would decrease because some providers may not meet the new requirements or may not be willing to comply with the new regulations.
- What would happen to the supply of hand-held calculators if new information technologies are invented that allowed the user to store and retrieve digital calculations?
- Answer: The supply would increase.

These scenarios are all examples of factors that cause supply curves to shift. They reflect factors not directly related to the change in the product's price that determine the amount of the good or service that firms are willing and able to sell at each and every price. Changes in supply alter the location of the supply curve in the first quadrant by causing a translation of the line. An increase in supply is reflected by a rightward shift of the supply curve, which causes a decrease in price and an increase in quantity exchanged. Likewise, a decrease in supply causes a leftward shift of the supply curve, which leads to an increase in price and a decrease in quantity exchanged. The slope of the supply curve remains unchanged in response to a change in supply.

5. Distribute a copy of Activity 4.1 to each student. Tell the students that this lesson focuses on changes in supply and/or demand. They will examine what happens to equilibrium price and quantity exchanged when some outside factor influences the location of the supply or demand curve.

■ **COMMENT** The equations in the solution have been written with quantity, the variable on the horizontal axis, appearing on the left-hand side of the equation. You may wish to solve each equation for P. If the equations are solved for Q, you should remind students that the coefficient of P is not the slope of the curve on the graph. The slope is the reciprocal of the coefficient of P. These issues arise because P is the independent variable, yet economists place it on the vertical axis.

6. Indicate to the students that Activity 4.1 involves looking at four situations to consider the effect on *P* and *Q* of changes in supply and demand. Students are asked to graph each situation using the same piece of graph paper. This allows them to see how prices and quantities exchanged vary in the real world. They will also be asked to determine the equilibrium price and quantity exchanged at the point of intersection of the supply and demand curves.

Have the students complete steps 1 and 2 of Activity 4.1. See Visual 4.3 as an example of the graph.

◆ Answer to question 2: The equilibrium price is $24 and the quantity exchanged is 110.

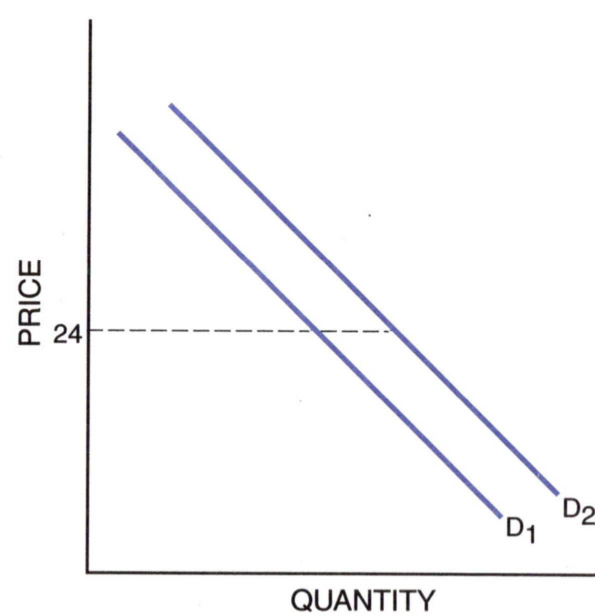

After the students have completed graphing the introductory task, have them look at situation 1. This is an example of an increase in demand, which appears on the graph as a translation of the graph to the right, from D_1 to D_2. One way to illustrate this as an increase in demand is to extend a dotted horizontal line from the vertical axis until it intersects both D_1 and D_2. This line can help the students see that an increase in demand means that there is an increase in quantity demanded at each and every price.

Make sure that your students graph the new curve using the same coordinate grid that they used in the first part of the activity. Using the same grid helps them see that an increase in demand leads to an increase in price and an increase in quantity exchanged. These increases are also apparent when they calculate the new equilibrium *P* and *Q* by solving the new system of equations. After the students have graphed the new curve, instruct them to label it D_2. Show Visual 4.4 of the completed graph. If the students are looking for an explanation of why price increases when demand increases, you can tell them to look at the new graph. The increase in demand has caused a shortage at the original equilibrium price of \$24. This can be seen by drawing a horizontal line that touches both D_1 and D_2 at $P = \$24$. At D_1, there is equilibrium at a price of \$24. But on the curve D_2 there is a disequilibrium at the \$24 price, since $Q_d > Q_s$ at this price. Since a shortage naturally leads to an increase in price, prices eventually rise when there is an increase in demand.

■ **COMMENT** A shortage occurs when the amount that consumers are willing and able to purchase—this is measured along the demand curve—is greater than the amount that sellers are willing and able to offer for sale—this is measured along the supply curve—at an existing price.

Answers to Situation 1, Questions 2–4:

2. In this situation, the demand for oil changes has increased. The new demand graph has been translated to the right. The vertical intercept has increased. The slope of the demand curve is unchanged; there has been a change in demand, which is a shift in the curve.
3. In writing equations for supply and demand curves, economists often write the equations with quantity on the left-hand side of the equation. This is because the amount that people are willing and able to purchase depends on price. Therefore Q_d is the dependent variable. Similar statements can be made regarding quantity supplied. The equations can be solved for P to get $P = 49 - (1/10)\,Q_d$ and $P = 13 + (1/10)Q_s$.

   $Q_d = 490 - 10P$
   $Q_s = -130 + 10P$
   $Q_d = Q_s$
   $P = 31,\ Q = 180$
4. The equilibrium price is \$31 with a quantity of 180 at the equilibrium point.

7. Situation 2 looks at an example of an increase in supply. Have the students graph the new line and label it S_2. An increase in supply leads to a reduction in price and an increase in quantity exchanged. At the old equilibrium price of \$31 we see that $Q_s > Q_d$ for curve S_2. This situation represents a surplus of 80 units at this price.

■ **COMMENT** A surplus occurs when the amount that sellers are willing and able to offer for sale is greater than the amount that buyers are willing and able to purchase at an existing price. Since surpluses eventually cause prices to fall, an increase in supply naturally leads to a price reduction. The increase in supply is graphically represented by a translation of the supply curve to the right. Students sometimes visualize this translation as a downward shift in the supply curve. In that case, they are likely to consider this as a decrease in supply, rather than an increase. For this reason, avoid language such as "upward" and "downward" when talking about shifts in supply and demand curves. To convince students that a rightward translation of the supply curve is indeed an increase in supply, draw their attention to the original and new supply schedules. The quantity supplied at each and every price is now greater than it was before. This increase can also be shown on the graph by extending a horizontal line from the vertical axis that touches both S_1 and S_2. This line helps give a visual representation that quantity supplied is greater at each and every price along S_2 than it is along S_1. Show Visual 4.5 to help explain the concepts.

◆ **Answers to Situation 2, Questions 2–4:**

2. In this situation, the supply of oil changes has increased.The new supply curve has shifted to the right. The vertical intercept has decreased from 13 to 5. Remember that P is on the vertical axis! The slope of the supply curve is unchanged; there has been a change in supply, which is a shift in the curve.
3. As before, the students can set up an algebraic model and solve for P and Q:

   $Q_d = 490 - 10P$
   $Q_s = -50 + 10P$
   $Q_d = Qs$
   $P = 27, Q = 220$
4. The equilibrium price is \$27 with the quantity at the equilibrium point being 220 units.

8. Situation 3 is an example of a decrease in the price and quantity purchased of Aunt Daphne's oil changes: customers have decided to substitute the oil change of the new competitor for the oil change offered by your aunt, causing the demand for her oil changes to decline. This decline is represented by a translation of the demand curve to the left. A decline in demand causes prices and quantities exchanged to fall. After graphing this new curve, have the students label it D_3. Visual 4.6 shows the graph with the addition of D_3.

◆ **Answers to Situation 3, Questions 2–4:**

2. In this situation, the demand for Aunt Daphne's oil changes has now decreased because a competitor offers a reasonable substitute. The

demand curve has shifted to the left. The vertical intercept has decreased. The slope of the demand curve is unchanged; there has been a decrease in demand, which is a leftward shift in the curve.

3. Students can set up an algebraic model and solve for P and Q:

$$Qd = 390 - 10P$$
$$Qs = -50 + 10P$$
$$Qd = Qs$$
$$P = 22, Q = 170$$

4. Equilibrium price is $22 with the quantity at that point being 170.

9. Have the students read Situation 4 and answer the questions. Situation 4 is an example of a decrease in supply. The decrease is seen graphically as a translation of the supply curve to the left, and it leads to an increase in price and a decrease in quantities exchanged. Make sure that the students label this new curve S_3. See Visual 4.7 for the graph with the addition of S_3.

Answers to Situation 4, Questions 2–4

2. In this situation, costs have increased, so the minimum price that Aunt Daphne must receive to offer any given quantity of her product has increased. In other words, supply has decreased. The new supply curve has shifted to the left. The vertical intercept has increased. The slope of the supply curve is unchanged; there has been a change in supply, which is a shift in the curve.
3. The algebraic model and equilibrium price and quantity are:

$$Q_d = 390 - 10P$$
$$Q_s = -110 + 10P$$
$$Q_d = Q_s$$
$$P = 25, Q = 140$$

4. Price at the equilibrium point is $25 with quantity exchanged at that price being equal to 140 units.

10. For the wrap-up, have the students show how the equilibrium price and quantities exchanged has changed over all of the situations that were experienced by Aunt Daphne's business. This will help them understand how the forces of supply and demand impact the prices and quantities exchanged we observe in a dynamic market economy. Visual 4.7 summarizes all of the changes in supply and demand from Activity 4.1.

11. After working through the activity, discuss what you have seen. You have identified a variety of factors that have caused supply and demand curves to shift. Show Visual 4.8, which indicates factors that cause a change in supply and demand. Go over the various factors. Then have the students identify which factors accounted for the changes in supply or demand in each of the four situations.

Answer:

Situation 1. A change in preferences caused a change in demand.
Situation 2. A change in technology caused a change in supply.
Situation 3. A change in the price of a substitute good caused a change in demand.
Situation 4. A change in regulations (taxation) caused a change in supply.

Point out that these factors led to a great deal of variation in prices and quantities exchanged. Such variations happen every day in the real world. For example, there was a large increase in unleaded gas prices in the first half of 2000. Why did this increase happen? The supply and demand tools just developed will help explain what happened to the unleaded gas market. Gas prices rose and quantity exchanged declined. Only one thing could have caused this to happen: a decline in supply (a leftward translation of the supply curve). This is consistent with most economists' views that the abrupt increase in fuel prices could be primarily attributed to oil production cuts by OPEC (Organization of Petroleum Exporting Countries). Increases in the price of gasoline, in turn, caused a reduction in the quantity of gasoline demanded by consumers. This can be seen as a movement upward along the demand curve. When you think in these terms, students should see that service stations are not to blame for higher gas prices. In fact, assuming profit margins are the same at high prices as they are at low prices, service stations prefer to set a low price for gasoline. Why? Because they sell more gas (and perhaps other in-store products) when gas prices are low. This example helps to illustrate the power of economic thinking.

Extension Activities:

The first activity could be used as an assessment activity. All activities here can be used for further study by students.

1. Ask the students to complete Activity 4.2 for homework.

Answers to the questions:

The equations for the supply curve and the demand curve are:

$Q_d = 350 - 10P$ and

$Q_s = -130 + 10P$.

The original equilibrium price and quantity are $P = \$24$ and $Q = 110$. Students might find the new equilibrium price in several different ways. One simple way is to note that since this situation represents an increase in demand, the demand curve should be translated to the right, with the slope remaining constant. Therefore, the new equation can be written:

$$Q_d = (\text{new vertical intercept}) - 10P$$

Substituting P = 45, and Q = 150, you can calculate the new vertical intercept:

$$150 = \text{new vertical intercept} - 10(45)$$
$$600 = \text{new vertical intercept}$$

Thus, the new demand curve is:

$$Q_d = 600 - 10P$$

and since $Q_s = -130 + 10P$

the equilibrium P and Q are determined by solving

$$600 - 10P = -130 + 10P$$
$$20P = 730$$
$$P = \$36.5 \text{ and } Q = 235.$$

2. Ask students to create other examples that could influence the demand and/or the supply of oil changes. Do not allow them to use price changes as an example. A change in the price of oil changes affects the **quantity** demanded and the **quantity** supplied. This causes a **movement along** the demand and supply curves, as opposed to a **change in demand (or supply)**, which is represented by a **translation** of the curve. If your students need a little help thinking about this, you can refer them to Visual 4.8 to provide some guidance.

3. Share with your students Visual 4.9. Ask your students to consider what the papal decree might have done to the demand for tartar sauce and to the demand for meat. It would have decreased the demand for tartar sauce, since it is a complementary good, and increased the demand for meat, since meat is a substitute for fish. Ask the students to draw graphs that might show what happened in the tartar sauce and beef markets. They can also develop accompanying demand and supply schedules, which will allow them to write out a system of linear equations. What (or who) else might have been affected by the Pope's decision? Have your students do some brainstorming. They are likely to come up with several responses including fishermen, shopkeepers in fishing villages, fishing boat manufacturers, etc.

VISUAL 4.1 ▲ Warm-Up

1. On a coordinate grid, graph the equation:

$$x - 3y = -6$$

2. Label this line L_1.

3. On the same grid, graph the line parallel to the line L_1 that passes through the point (6, 6). Label this line L_2, and write its equation.

4. What is the slope of L_1?

5. What is the slope of L_2?

VISUAL 4.2 ▲ Graph for Warm-Up

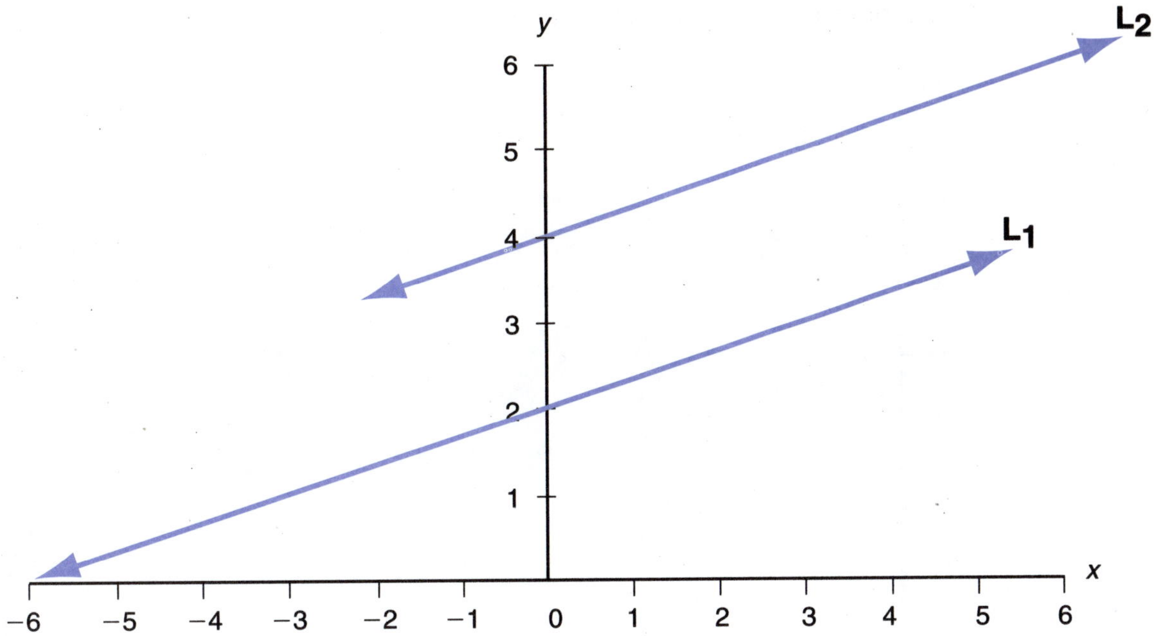

VISUAL 4.3

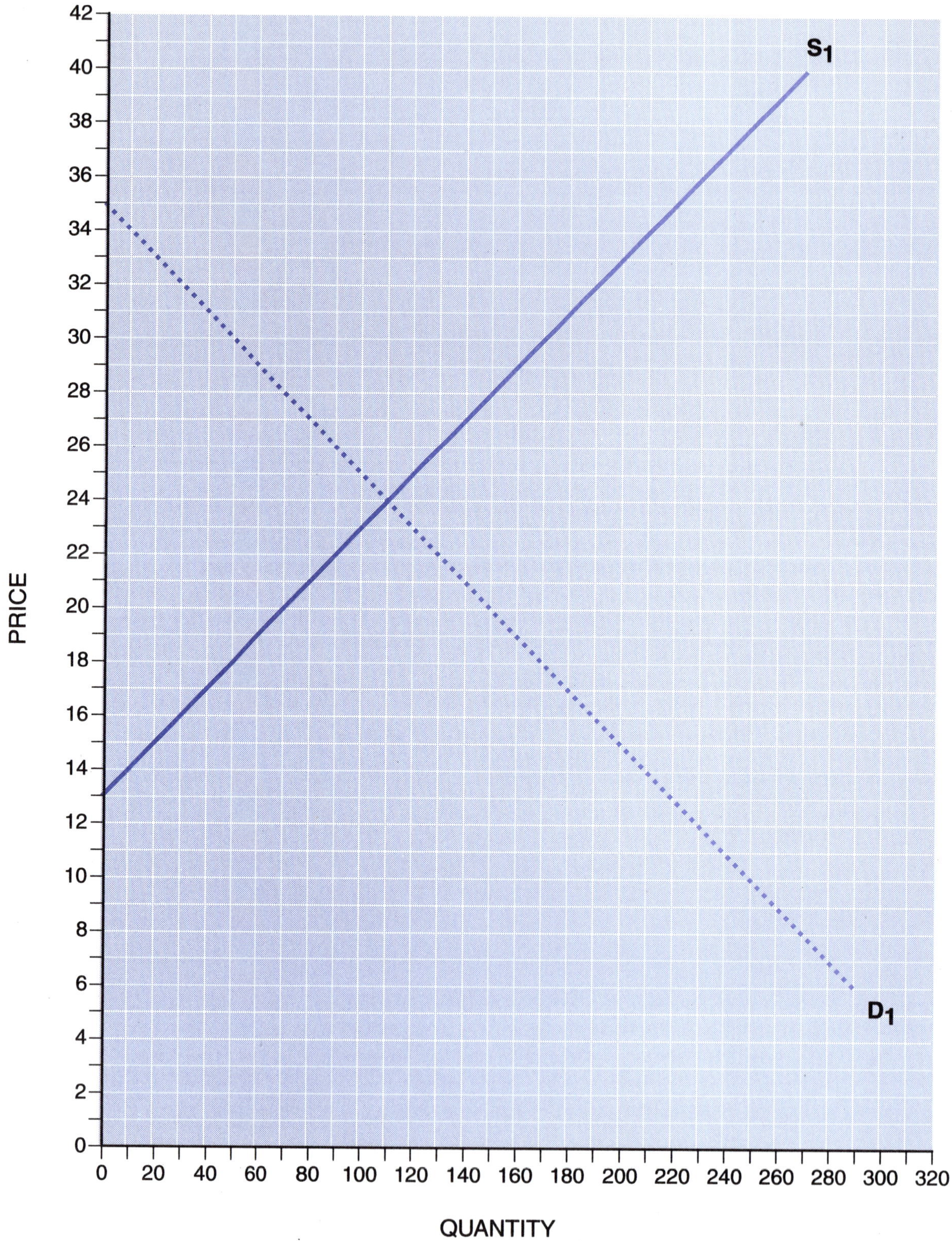

S1
D1
PRICE
42
40
38
36
34
32
30
28
26
24
22
20
18
16
14
12
10
8
6
4
2
0
0 20 40 60 80 100 120 140 160 180 200 220 240 260 280 300 320
QUANTITY

VISUAL 4.4

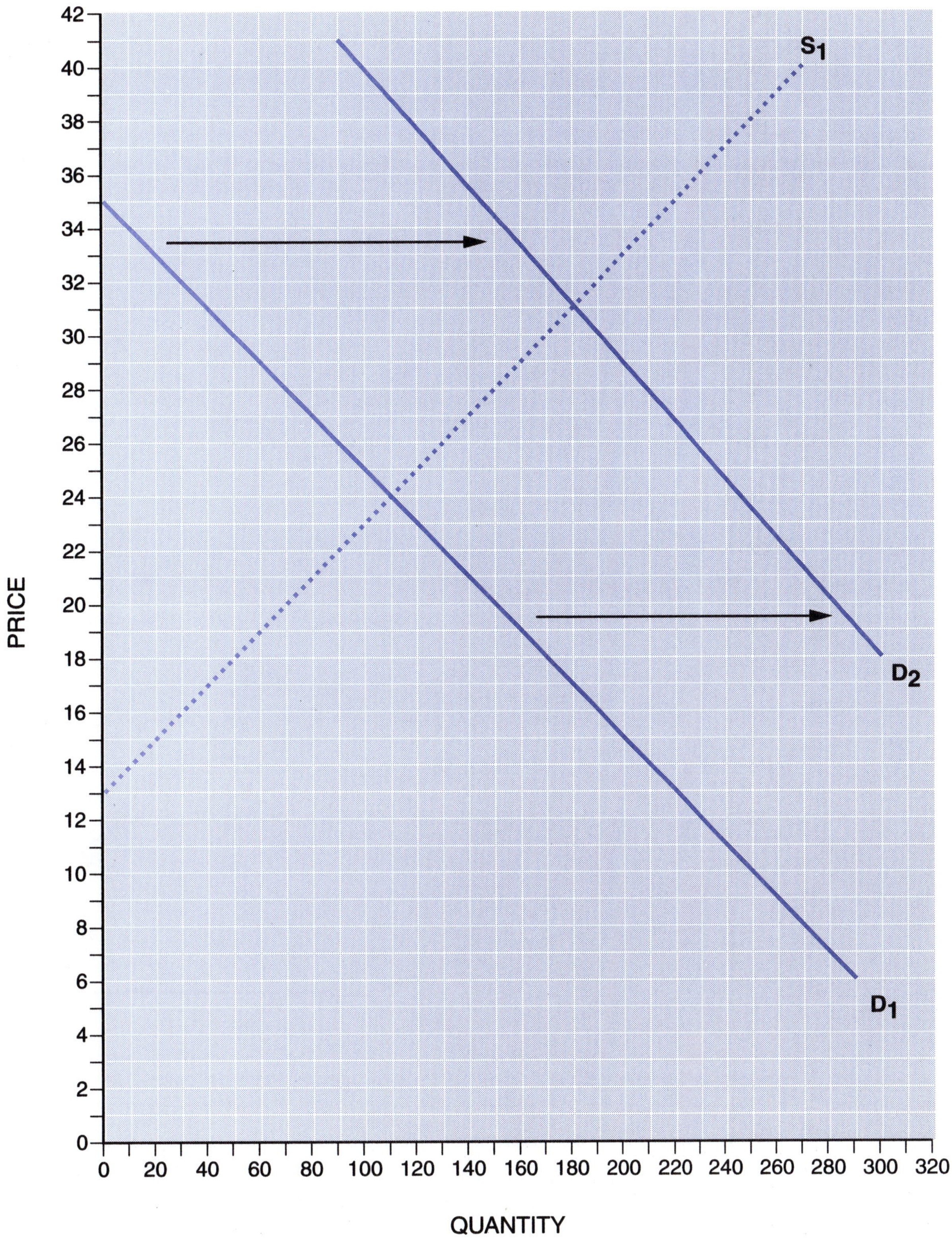
PRICE
QUANTITY
0
2
4
6
8
10
12
14
16
18
20
22
24
26
28
30
32
34
36
38
40
42
0
20
40
60
80
100
120
140
160
180
200
220
240
260
280
300
320
S_1
D_1
D_2

VISUAL 4.5

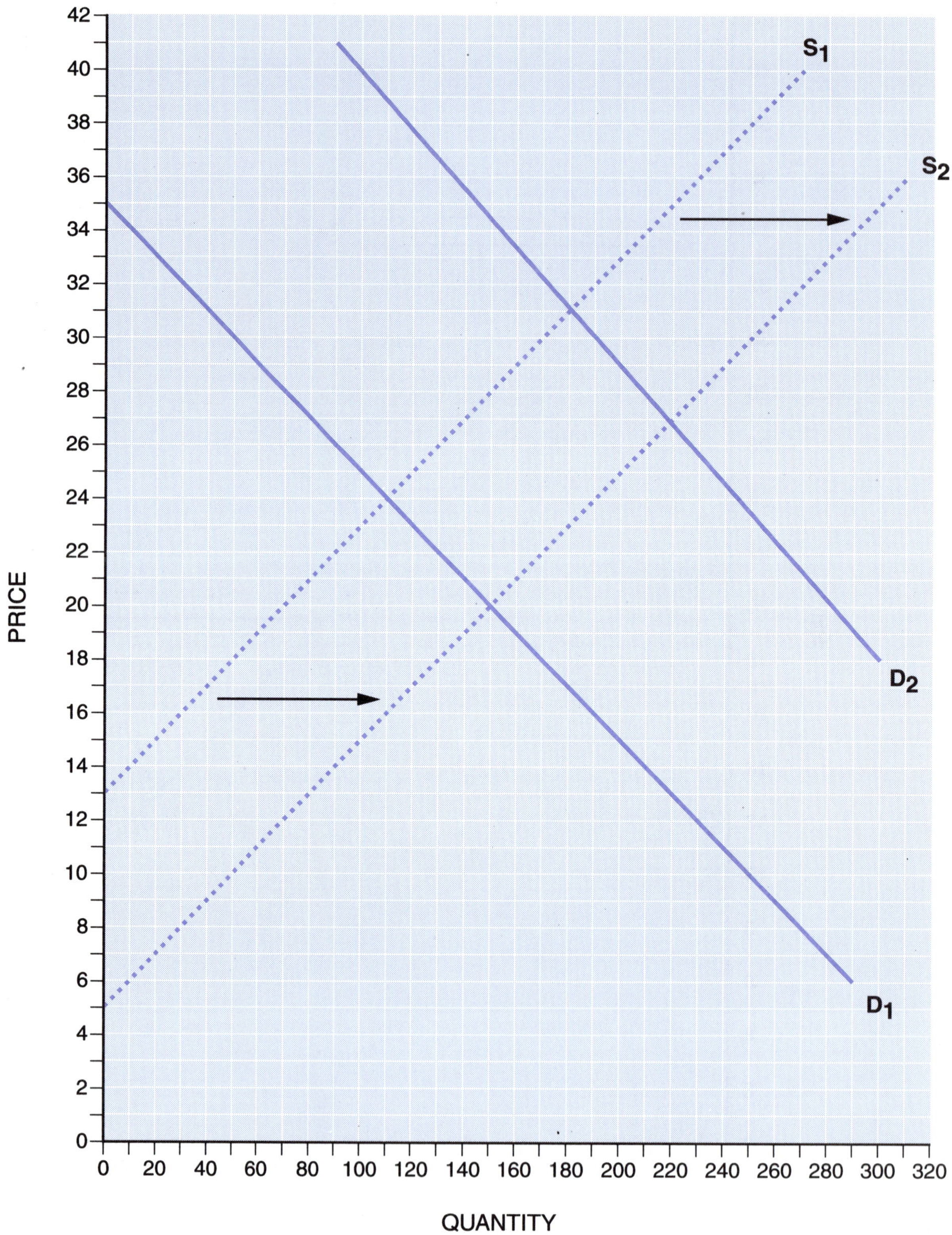
S1
S2
D2
D1
PRICE
QUANTITY
0
2
4
6
8
10
12
14
16
18
20
22
24
26
28
30
32
34
36
38
40
42
0
20
40
60
80
100
120
140
160
180
200
220
240
260
280
300
320

VISUAL 4.6

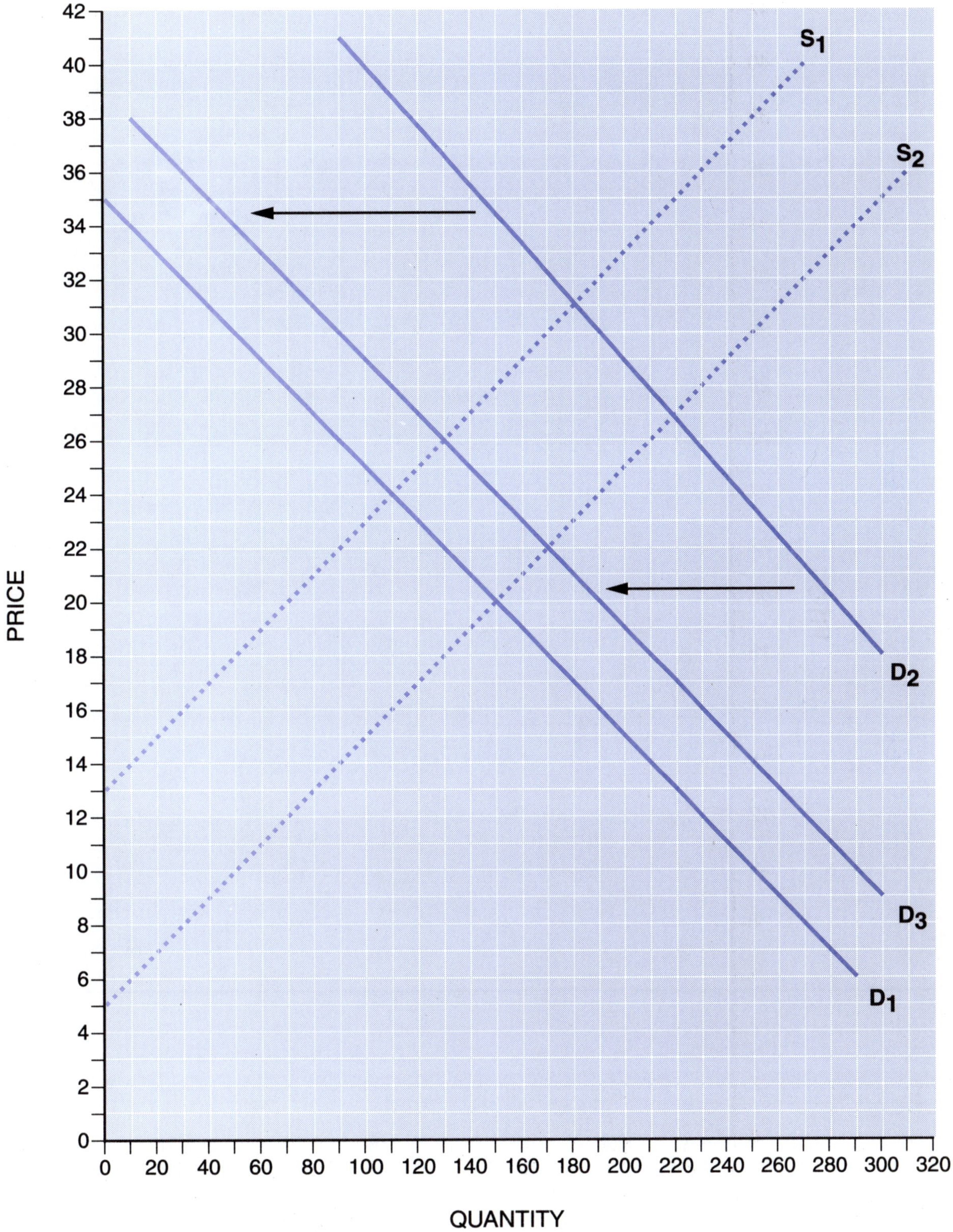

PRICE
QUANTITY
S_1
S_2
D_1
D_2
D_3
0
2
4
6
8
10
12
14
16
18
20
22
24
26
28
30
32
34
36
38
40
42
0
20
40
60
80
100
120
140
160
180
200
220
240
260
280
300
320

VISUAL 4.7

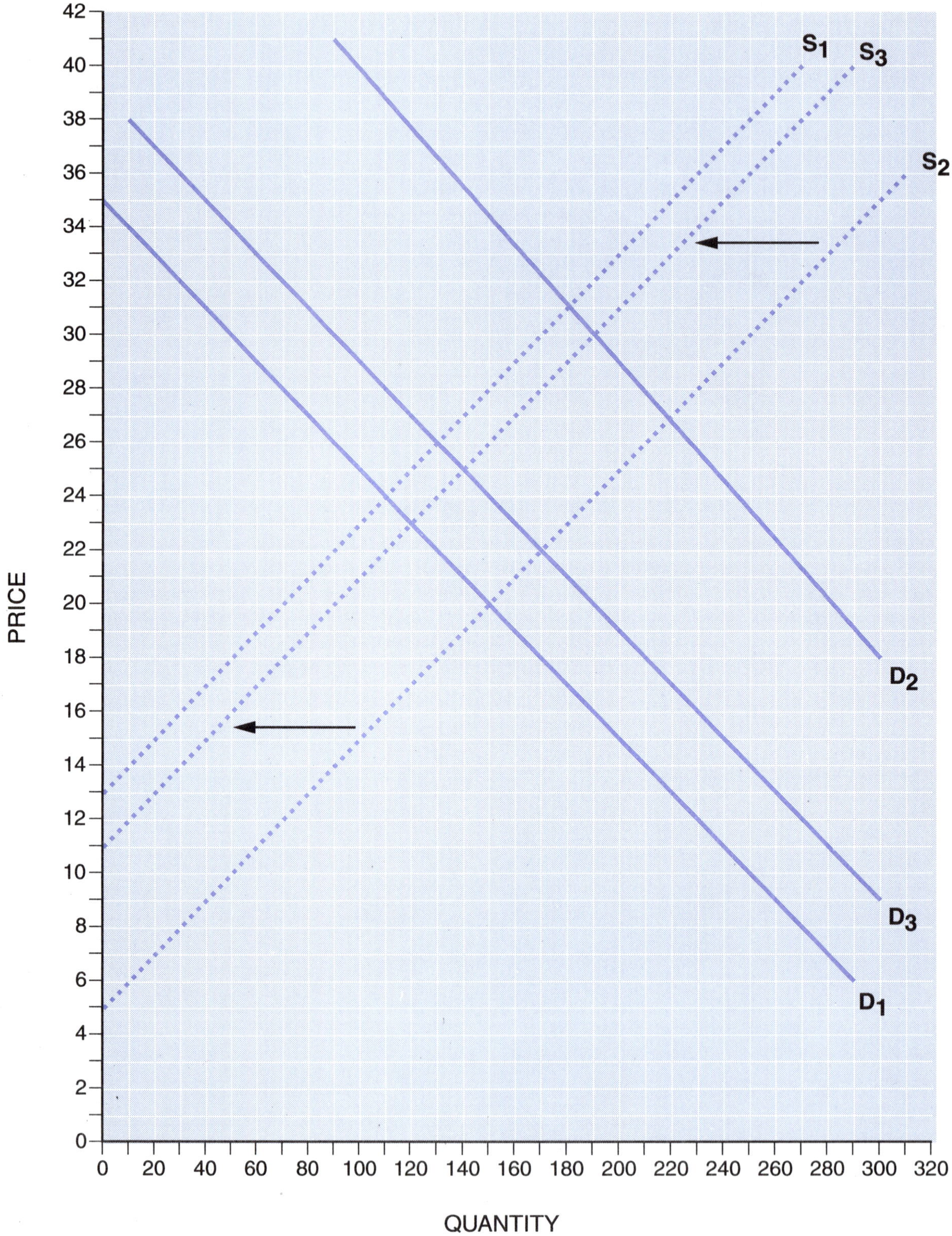

PRICE
QUANTITY
0
2
4
6
8
10
12
14
16
18
20
22
24
26
28
30
32
34
36
38
40
42
0
20
40
60
80
100
120
140
160
180
200
220
240
260
280
300
320
S_1
S_3
S_2
D_2
D_3
D_1

VISUAL 4.8 ▲ Factors that Cause a Change in Demand and Supply

Some Factors that Cause a Change in Demand

1. A change in income
2. A change in the prices of related goods
   a. substitutes
   b. complements
3. A change in the product's expected future price
4. A change in the number of and/or composition of buyers
5. A change in tastes and preferences

Some Factors that Cause a Change in Supply

1. A change in the costs of productive inputs
   a) labor
   b) machinery and equipment
   c) energy
   d) raw materials
2. A change in technology
3. A change in the product's expected future price
4. A change in the number of sellers
5. A random supply shock caused by weather, political events, etc.
6. Legal restrictions such as licensure and regulations

VISUAL 4.9 ▲ A Real World Application of a Decrease in Demand

The Pope and the Price of Fish

In the late 1960s, Frederick W. Bell published an interesting study of the effect of a papal decree on the fish market in New England.* In December 1966, a liberalization of church laws allowed American Catholics to consume meat on Fridays (other than during Lent). Bell hypothesized that this change in church laws would cause a decrease in the demand for fish and would result in a decrease in fish prices and the quantity of fish purchased. After correcting for other factors that could have an outside influence on fish prices, Bell found that fish prices in New England declined on average about 12% following the liberalization.

---

* See Frederick W. Bell, "The Pope and the Price of Fish," *American Economic Review* (December, 1968), p. 1346.

ACTIVITY 4.1

Name ______________________________ Date __________ Period _____

Aunt Daphne's Oil Change Business

Because of some expert advice that you once offered your Aunt Daphne (and because you have a strong background in economics and mathematics), you have been hired as the economic consultant to her oil change business. She consults you frequently for your advice on changing prices as well as what to expect regarding the number of customers that are likely to patronize her business.

Price per Oil Change	Quantity Demanded	Quantity Supplied
$0	350	−130
$15	200	20
$16	190	30
$17	180	40
$18	170	50
$19	160	60
$20	150	70
$21	140	80
$22	130	90
$23	120	100
$24	110	110
$25	100	120
$26	90	130
$27	80	140
$28	70	150
$29	60	160
$30	50	170
$31	40	180
$32	30	190
$33	20	200
$34	10	210
$35	0	220

You have been given the following information about your aunt's business.

1. Graph the relationships on graph paper. Be sure to label the demand curve as D1 and the supply curve as S_1.

2. What price will be charged in equilibrium? How many oil changes will be sold?

Many outside factors have influenced your Aunt Daphne's business lately. Four separate situations stand out. These are outlined below. Graph each of these different situations on the same graph paper, using a different color pencil for each one (four colors). This will allow you to see how the equilibrium price changes as a result of these situations.

Situation 1

A recent independent study commissioned by the federal government was released indicating that people can prolong the life of their cars by five years if they change the oil every two months. Your aunt knows that this report will improve her business. After consulting with you, she believes that the following information now pertains to her business:

Price per Oil Change	Quantity Demanded	Quantity Supplied
$0	490	−130
$15	340	20
$16	330	30
$17	320	40
$18	310	50
$19	300	60
$20	290	70
$21	280	80
$22	270	90
$23	260	100
$24	250	110
$25	240	120
$26	230	130
$27	220	140
$28	210	150
$29	200	160
$30	190	170
$31	180	180
$32	170	190

1. Graph these data on the same piece of graph paper that you used before.
2. Compare the two demand curves. What has happened to the vertical intercept? What has happened to the slope of the demand curve?
3. Set up the new algebraic model and solve for P and Q.
4. Identify the new equilibrium price and quantity.

Situation 2

As a result of a technological advancement, an oil change now takes only 15 minutes, not 30 minutes as it did previously. Aunt Daphne decides to expand the business. She can now offer more oil changes at each and every price. After consulting with you, she believes that the following information now pertains to her business:

Price per Oil Change	Quantity Demanded	Quantity Supplied
\$0	490	−50
\$15	340	100
\$16	330	110
\$17	320	120
\$18	310	130
\$19	300	140
\$20	290	150
\$21	280	160
\$22	270	170
\$23	260	180
\$24	250	190
\$25	240	200
\$26	230	210
\$27	220	220
\$28	210	230
\$29	200	240
\$30	190	250
\$31	180	260
\$32	170	270

1. Graph these new data on the same piece of graph paper that you used before.
2. What has happened to the vertical intercept? What has happened to the slope of the supply curve?
3. Set up the new algebraic model and solve for *P* and *Q*.
4. Identify the new equilibrium price and quantity.

Situation 3

The increase in the demand for oil changes has unfortunately not gone unnoticed by potential business rivals. A competitor has now set up shop across town and has begun to offer discount prices. Some of your aunt's customers are now getting their oil changed at her competitor's business. Your aunt needs your advice. She presents the following information:

Price per Oil Change	Quantity Demanded	Quantity Supplied
$0	390	−50
$15	240	100
$16	230	110
$17	220	120
$18	210	130
$19	200	140
$20	190	150
$21	180	160
$22	170	170
$23	160	180
$24	150	190
$25	140	200
$26	130	210
$27	120	220
$28	110	230

1. Graph these data on the same piece of graph paper that you used before.
2. What has happened to the vertical intercept? What has happened to the slope of the demand curve?
3. Set up the new algebraic model and solve for P and Q.
4. What is the new equilibrium price and quantity?

Situation 4

The Environmental Protection Agency (EPA) has received many complaints about service stations dumping discarded oil and filters from oil changes in their regular garbage cans. Concern has grown about an increase in hazardous wastes in landfills around the country. To pay for establishing separate waste disposal facilities for oil and filters, the EPA imposes a disposal tax on every business that offers oil change service. This tax has the effect of increasing your aunt's cost of doing business. She needs your advice. She presents the following information:

Price per Oil Change	Quantity Demanded	Quantity Supplied
$0	390	−110
$15	240	40
$16	230	50
$17	220	60
$18	210	70
$19	200	80
$20	190	90
$21	180	100
$22	170	110
$23	160	120
$24	150	130
$25	140	140
$26	130	150
$27	120	160

1. Plot these data on the graph that you used before.
2. What has happened to the vertical intercept of the supply curve? What has happened to the slope of the supply curve?
3. Set up the new algebraic model and solve for *P* and *Q*.
4. What is the new equilibrium price and quantity?

Student Graph

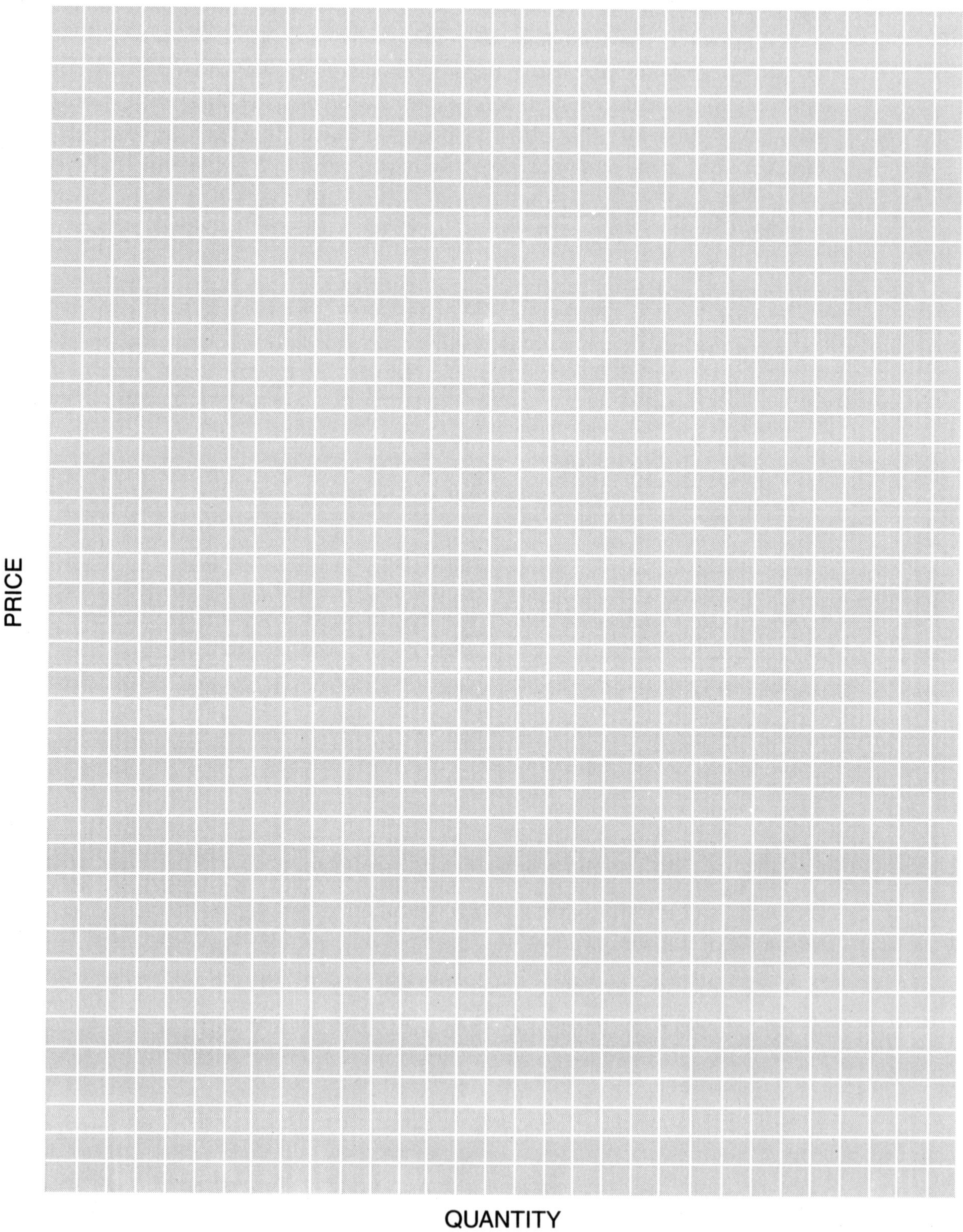

ACTIVITY 4.2

Name ______________________________ Date __________ Period _____

The original table from Activity 4.1 is reproduced below.

Price per Oil Change	Quantity Demanded	Quantity Supplied
$0	350	−130
$15	200	20
$16	190	30
$17	180	40
$18	170	50
$19	160	60
$20	150	70
$21	140	80
$22	130	90
$23	120	100
$24	110	110
$25	100	120
$26	90	130
$27	80	140
$28	70	150
$29	60	160
$30	50	170
$31	40	180
$32	30	190
$33	20	200
$34	10	210
$35	0	220

Write the equations for the supply curve and the demand curve.
Note the original equilibrium price and quantity.

ACTIVITY 4.2 (continued)

You have just been informed that there has been an increase in demand for oil changes, but the only information that you have been given is a single point on the new demand curve: $Q = 150$ and $P = \$45$. Use what you know about changes in demand, as well as the prior information on quantity demanded and quantity supplied, to determine the new equilibrium price and quantity.

Lesson 5 The Gains From Trade

Mathematics Focus:

Algebra I, Algebra II

Mathematics Prerequisites:

Prior to using this lesson, students should be able to

- Graphically solve a system of linear inequalities, and
- Find the areas of quadrilateral and triangular regions using coordinate geometry

Economics Prerequisites:

Prior to using this lesson students should be able to generate both the demand curve and the supply curve and explain how their interaction brings about an equilibrium price. See Lessons 1, 2, 3, and 4.

Lesson Objectives:

To apply prerequisite mathematics concepts and processes to supply and demand curves to:

- Explain the gains that buyers and sellers receive from voluntary exchange
- Explain the concept of economic efficiency
- Explain the efficiency losses that can arise from taxation

Overview of Mathematics and Economics:

This lesson is an application of the supply and demand tools developed in lessons 1-4. In the earlier lessons, models of supply and demand were introduced to show students how (equilibrium) prices are determined in markets. This analysis was also used to help students explain factors that caused a variation in market prices because of shifts in supply and/or demand curves. In this lesson, students learn that voluntary exchange between buyers and sellers results in gains for both. These gains from trade can be interpreted graphically as areas between the supply and demand curves. These regions are triangular when the curves are linear, which means the gains from trade can be calculated by finding the areas of triangles.

A prospective buyer will only agree to purchase a product if she or he values the product at least as much as the product's price. A seller will agree to sell the product only if the price received at least covers the minimum price she or he is willing to accept. This minimum-selling price usually depends upon production costs. If a buyer receives value from a product that exceeds the price paid, then the buyer enjoys a net gain. Economists refer to the cumulative net gain received by buyers as *consumer surplus*. Likewise, sellers who receive a price for their product that exceeds the minimum price they are willing to accept also have net gains that result from voluntary trade. Economists refer to the cumulative net gain received by sellers as *producer surplus*. Overall gains from trade are determined by measuring the net gains that both buyers and sellers receive from exchange.

Economic efficiency is said to arise when all mutually advantageous trades between buyers and sellers have been exhausted. In mathematical terms, economic efficiency occurs when the combined area of net gains from exchange that accrue to consumers and producers is maximized.

Government taxation often reduces the net gains to consumers and producers that are received from economic exchange. Such reduction leads to *economic inefficiency*. Economists use the term *deadweight loss* to describe the efficiency loss that can result from government taxation. In this lesson, students determine the reduction in net gains to consumers and producers that result from taxation by calculating the areas of representative regions. Areas of efficiency loss as well as the total tax revenues that accrue from taxation are also measured.

Mathematics and Economics Terms:

- Area
- Consumer surplus
- Deadweight loss
- Economic efficiency
- Economic inefficiency
- Equilibrium
- Linear inequality
- Parallel lines
- Producer surplus
- Taxation

Materials:

- One copy of Activity 5.1 and 5.2 for each student
- One sheet of graph paper for each student
- One copy of Visuals 5.1 and 5.3 for each student
- Overhead transparencies of Visuals 5.1–5.8
- Straight edge
- Colored pencils
- Graphing calculator (optional)

Estimated Time:

80 minutes

Procedures:

1. Warm-Up Activity: Show Visual 5.1 and hand out copies to students. Have the students complete tasks on graph paper. Answers are as shown on Visuals 5.2 – 5.5.

2. To complete this lesson, students will need to understand the concept of equilibrium. See Lessons 1–3.

3. Distribute a copy of Activity 5.1 and Visual 5.6 to each student.

The answers to the questions are:

a) P = \$5; Q = 50

b–f) Graphing is shown on Visual 5.7

Ask the students to complete parts a – f of Activity 5.1. When they have completed a – f, inform them that the red-shaded region represents the net gains received by consumers who are able to purchase Cheeseburger Super Value Combo meals for less than they are willing to pay for them. Economists refer to this area as *consumer surplus*. This area is the cumulative sum of the difference between the height of the demand curve and the equilibrium price at each and every quantity. To give your students a more detailed explanation of this concept, explain that the height of the demand curve at any given quantity represents the value that consumers attach to the product. Assume that each customer buys one combo. Notice that 10 customers are willing to pay \$13 for the combo (even though each is only charged a price of \$5 for the meal). This comes from measuring P (the height of the demand curve) at Q = 10. This demand curve tells the manager that if the restaurant charged \$13 per combo meal, 10 people would be willing and able to buy it. The first nine people, in fact, value the meal in excess of \$13. If the restaurant charges \$5 per meal, 50 people value the item enough to be willing to make the purchase. Since the same price is usually charged to all the customers, those customers who would have paid more than the equilibrium price receive a gain that can be calculated. The red-shaded area in the graph measures this gain.

4. Tell students that even though consumers sometimes feel like they are getting a good deal at the expense of sellers, it is usually a two-way street. In a voluntary exchange, both parties receive net benefits from trading. To see this, have them look at the blue-shaded area. It represents the cumulative sum of the difference between the price that sellers receive and the price that they were willing to take for each and every quantity. Economists refer to this area as *producer surplus*. The height of the supply curve at any given quantity is the minimum price that a seller must receive to offer another unit of the product. For example, the tenth unit on the graph in Activity 1 is sold for a price of $5 (as are all of the units sold), but the restaurant was willing and able to sell it for $1. The seller therefore gained $4 by being able to sell the tenth unit for more than she was willing to take. It may help students to think of the price that corresponds to the height of the supply curve at any given point as the price that is just sufficient to cover a seller's costs. If the seller gets more than this price for the unit, then she gains. If she is offered less than this amount, she will not make a voluntary exchange.

Ask students to complete this exercise by answering g – i in Activity 5.1. The areas of the red- and blue-shaded portions of their diagrams, when added together, represent the *gains from trade*. You can explain this as the net benefits received by consumers who are able to purchase items for prices which are less than they value them plus the net benefits received by producers who can sell their goods at prices in excess of that which they would be willing to take.

The answers to question g. – i. are:

g) Area = ½ · 10 · 50 = 250 representing $250
h) Area = ½ · 5 · 50 = 125 representing $125
i) Total area = 250 + 125 = 375 representing $375

5. Distribute a copy of Activity 5.2 to each student. Ask your students to answer questions 1 and 2 as well as the questions in part 1 of Activity 5.2.

COMMENT Part 1 of Activity 5.2 is essentially a review of material covered in Activity 5.1.

The answers to Activity 5.2 are:

1. The tax causes producers to reduce the amount that they are willing and able to sell at each and every price. This is known as a decrease in the supply of gasoline.
2. The equation for S_2 is $P = 0.5 + 0.001Q_s$.
   Part 1 Answers:
3. Note that equilibrium occurs where $Q = Q_d = Q_s$. This results in P = $1 and Q = 1000.
4. Triangle FEH. Area = ½ · 1.50 · 1000 =750 representing $750.
5. Triangle EHJ. Area = ½ · 1 · 1000 = 500 representing $500.
6. Triangle EJF. Area = ½ · 2.50 · 1000 = 1250; or
   Area = 750 + 500 = 1250 representing $1250.

6. In the second part of Activity 5.2, students examine the effects of adding a $0.50 per gallon tax on gasoline. Sellers must now send $0.50 in tax collections to the government for every gallon of gas sold. This has the effect of creating a new supply curve of gas represented by S_2. This causes the equilibrium price of gas to increase to \$1.30 and the equilibrium quantity exchanged to decrease to 800 gallons. The seller can't pass the entire \$0.50 per gallon tax increase on to consumers in the form of price increases because the price increase causes consumers to purchase fewer gallons. Taxes of this type drive a wedge between the price that consumers pay for a product and the price that is received by sellers. In this case, consumers pay \$1.30 per gallon, but sellers only receive \$0.80 per gallon after making the \$0.50 per gallon payment to the agency imposing the tax.

7. Students are asked to calculate the post-tax net gains from exchange received by consumers as well as the gains from trade. The net gain received by producers is calculated for them since it is more complicated. Each of these areas has declined. The net gains of consumers decrease because the price increase has caused people to purchase fewer gallons of gas and has caused a reduction in the difference between the consumers' willingness to pay and the price that they actually pay. The net gains of producers decline for similar reasons. Even though gas prices have increased, the amount per gallon that is actually received by producers has fallen. They also are selling fewer gallons of gas. This adds up to a reduction in the realized gains from trade.

A different way for your students to think about this point is to discuss it in terms of economic efficiency. The tax has essentially caused people to not make trades that would otherwise have produced net gains. The efficient quantity of production is Q = 1000 gallons at the equilibrium price of \$1.00 per gallon. Benefits received from the production of each additional gallon of gasoline are measured by the height of the demand curve, D, for each value Q. The cost of providing each additional gallon of gasoline is measured by the height of the supply curve, S, for each Q. For $0 \leq Q \leq 1000$, additional benefits from producing additional gallons of gas exceed or equal the additional cost of these gallons of gas. The tax, however, has caused the market quantity exchanged to fall to 800 gallons. Even though people value gallons 801 through 1000 more than the additional costs of supplying these units, they will not be sold. This is because the tax increase has artificially raised the cost of selling each additional gallon of gas and has caused people to cut back on fuel purchases. Therefore, the tax has caused an economic inefficiency and has reduced the gains from trade.

Part 2a Answers (Use Visual 5.8 to illustrate answers):

1. P = \$1.30 and Q = 800. If sellers raised their price to \$1.50, the supply and demand curves show that there would be a surplus of gasoline.

That is, they would not be able to sell all of their gas. They must therefore charge less than $1.50 per gallon.

2. i) Triangle ACF.
   ii) Area = ½ · 1.20 · 800 = 480 representing $480.
   iii) Net gain for consumers declined from $750 to $480. The tax creates a reduction in the difference between the amount consumers are willing and able to pay and what they actually pay. This represents a reduction in net gain for consumers.

Part 2b Answers (Use Visual 5.8 to illustrate answers):

1. $480 + $320 = $800. The post-tax gains are less than the pre-tax gains.
2. Quadrilateral ACGB has an area of 0.50 · 800 = 400 representing $400.
3. The area of the deadweight loss is ½ · 0.50 · 200 = 50 representing $50
4. Yes.

8. Although the tax has led to fewer trades, it is important to note that the government has increased tax collections that will presumably be distributed in such a way as to benefit some persons. The amount of tax collected is calculated by multiplying the tax by the number of gallons that are sold ($0.50 × 800 = $400). Students can compute this by calculating the area of the quadrilateral ACGB. Because of the redistributive effects of the tax, it is not possible to say whether the tax is "good" or "bad." The well-being of those who receive benefits that are financed by the tax may be measurably greater than (or less than) the losses experienced by those who pay the tax.

9. The final area to be considered is represented by triangle CEG. This is the area that results from the fact that the tax drives a wedge between the price that consumers pay and the money that sellers actually receive. It also results from fewer gallons of gasoline being sold. This area is known as deadweight loss.

Extension Activities:

1. Ask your students to return to Activity 5.1 and imagine that the local city council has decided to impose a $2 tax on the restaurant for each Cheeseburger Super Value Combo meal sold. This has the effect of shifting the supply curve leftward and increasing the vertical intercept of the supply curve from 0 to $2. Ask the students to draw the new graph for this activity and determine the new equilibrium price and quantity (P = $6.33 and Q = 43.33). Now have them calculate the new net gains of consumers and producers, the tax revenue collected, and the deadweight loss. You can also ask them to set up a system of linear inequalities to solve this problem if you wish.

2. Instead of giving your students the equations for the demand and supply curves in Activity 5.2, have them calculate the equations by giving them the vertical intercepts and a point on each curve.

3. Ask the students to do some brainstorming about the net gains that consumers receive from various products. For example, ask them how much a roll of toilet paper costs (usually no more than $0.50). Now ask them how much they would be willing to pay for toilet paper. Chances are that they are willing to pay much more than that. This tells them that they receive a great deal of consumer surplus from toilet paper. But note, producers undoubtedly also receive some gains from trade.

VISUAL 5.1 ▲ Warm-Up

On graph paper supplied by your teacher do the following:

1. Draw the first quadrant of a coordinate plane, labeling the x axis from 0 to 15 and the y axis from 0 to 15.

2. Draw the lines $y = (3/8)x$; $y = -1.5x + 15$; $y = 3$

3. Shade the solution to the following inequalities and find the area of the shaded region. The inequalities are: $y \leq -1.5x + 15$; $y \geq 3$; $x \geq 0$

4. Shade the solution to the following inequalities and find the area of the shaded region. The inequalities are: $y \geq (3/8)x$; $y \leq 3$; $x \geq 0$

5. Shade the solution to the following inequalities and find the area of the shaded region. The inequalities are: $y \geq (3/8)x$; $x \geq 0$; $y \leq -1.5x + 15$

VISUAL 5.2

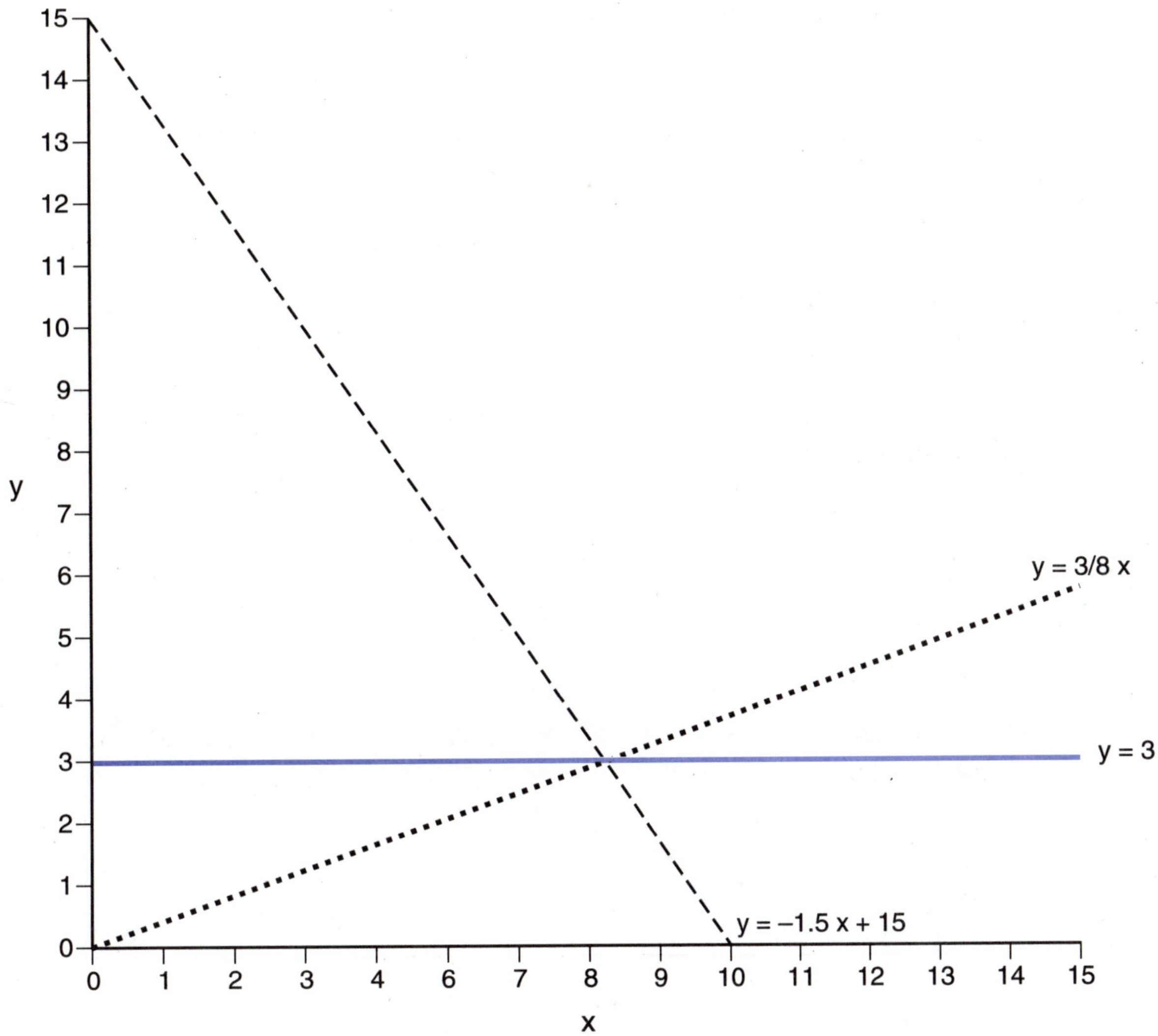

y
15
14
13
12
11
10
9
8
7
6
5
4
3
2
1
0
y = 3/8 x
y = 3
y = –1.5 x + 15
0
1
2
3
4
6
7
8
9
10
11
12
13
14
15
x

VISUAL 5.3

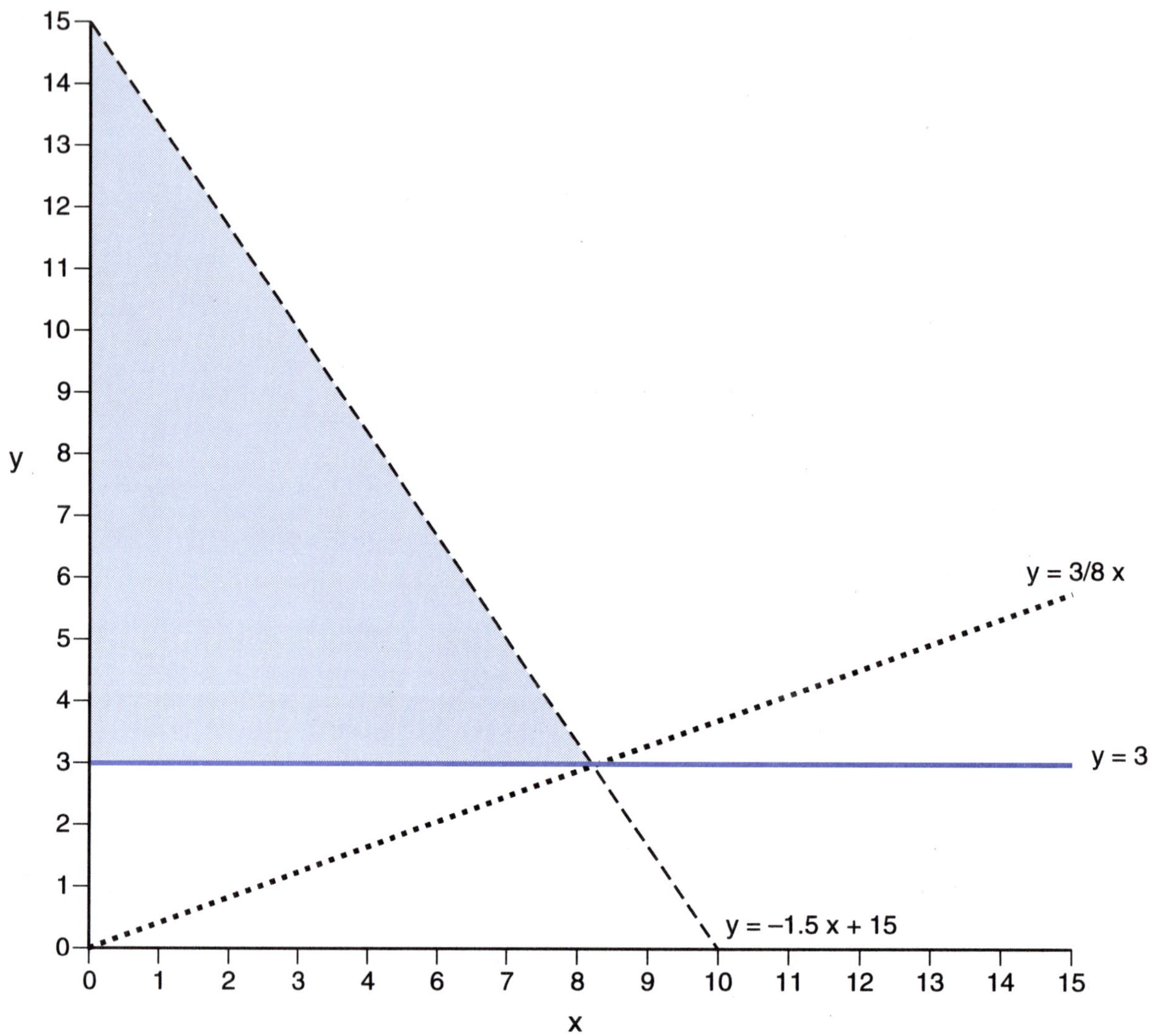

15
14
13
12
11
10
9
y
8
7
6
5
4
3
2
1
0
0
1
2
3
4
6
7
8
9
10
11
12
13
14
15
x
y = 3/8 x
y = 3
y = −1.5 x + 15

VISUAL 5.4

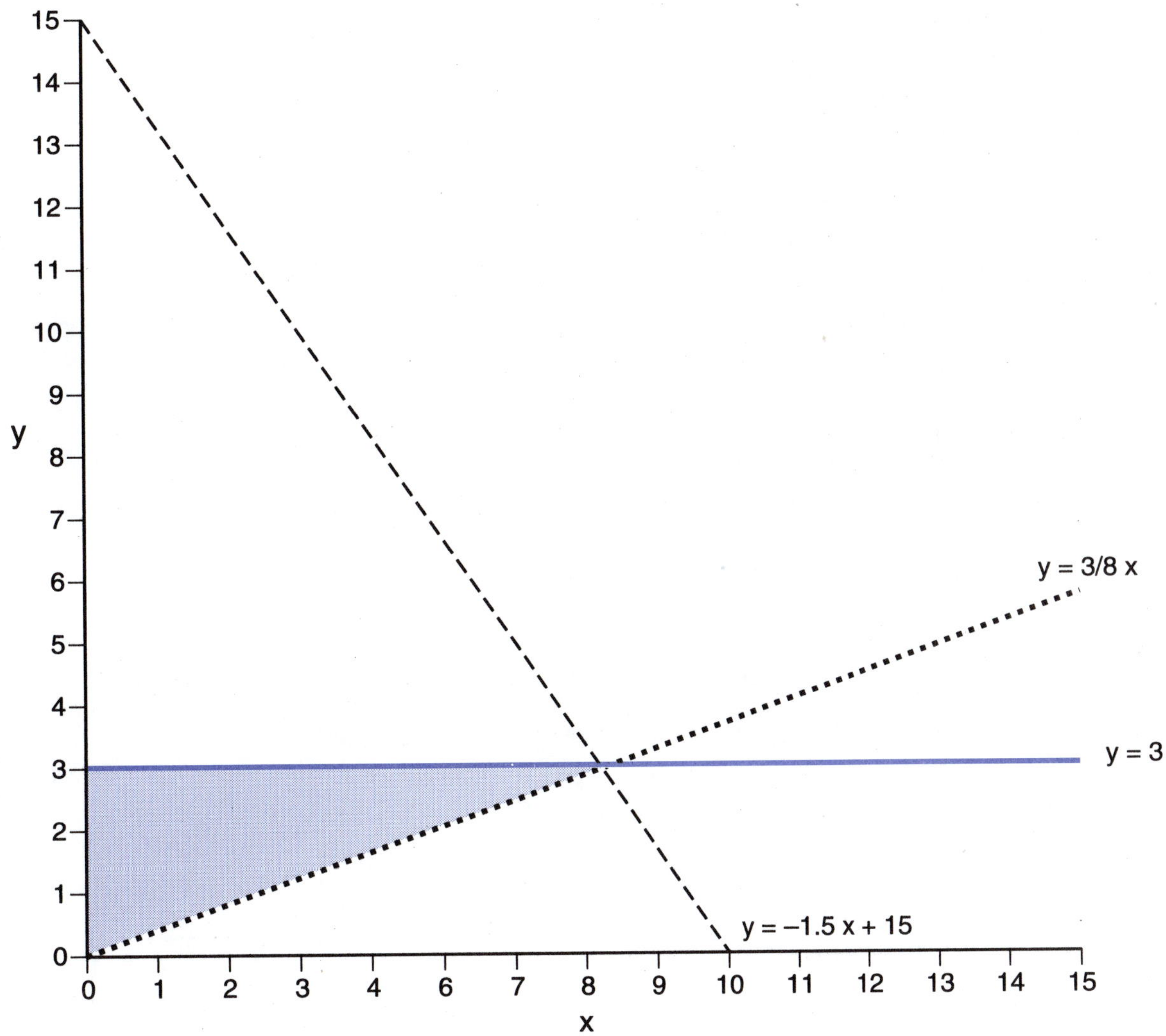

y
x
15
14
13
12
11
10
9
8
7
6
5
4
3
2
1
0
0 1 2 3 4 6 7 8 9 10 11 12 13 14 15
y = 3/8 x
y = 3
y = −1.5 x + 15

VISUAL 5.5

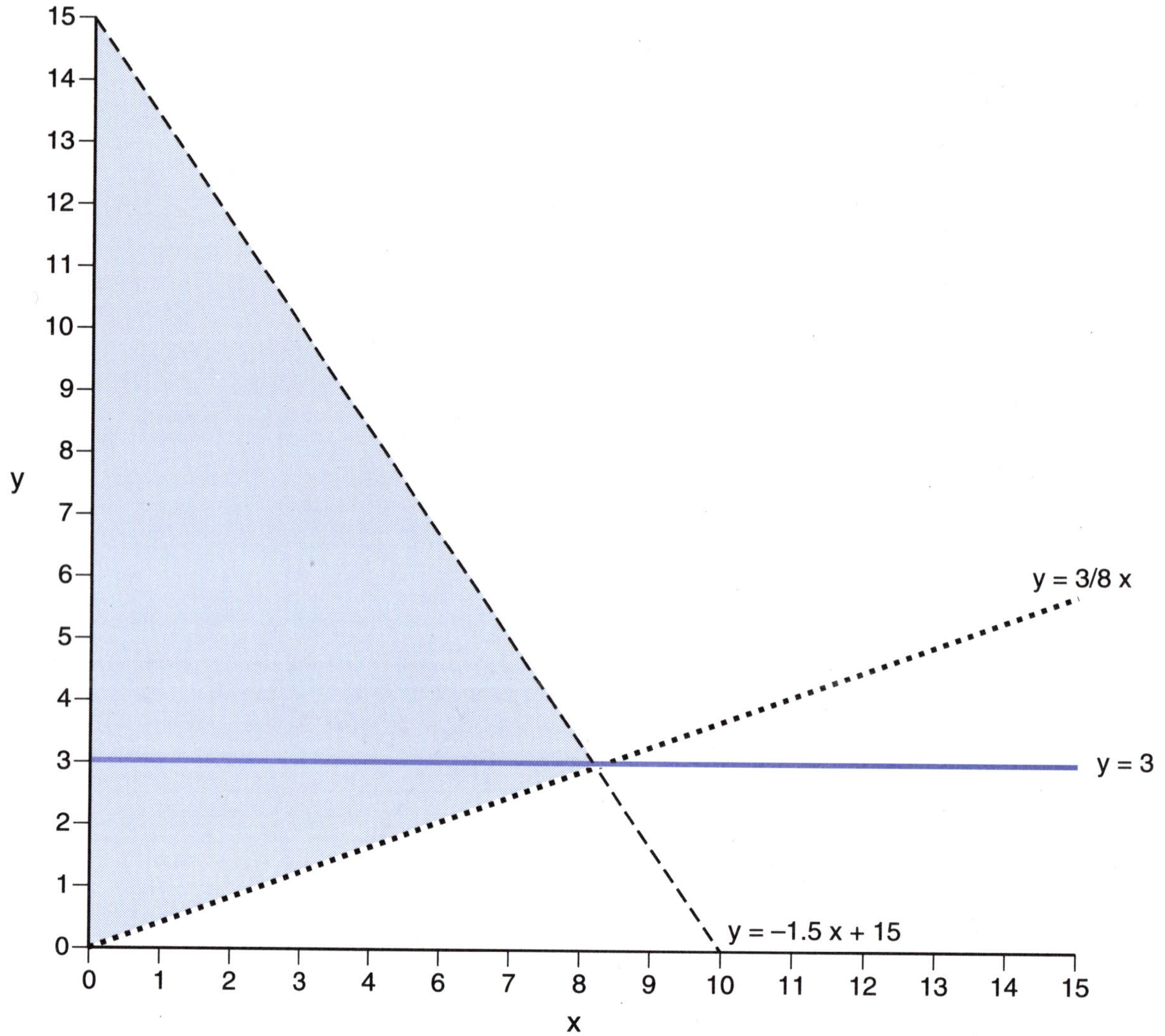
y = 3/8 x
y = 3
y = −1.5 x + 15
y
x
15
14
13
12
11
10
9
8
7
6
5
4
3
2
1
0
0 1 2 3 4 6 7 8 9 10 11 12 13 14 15

VISUAL 5.6 ▲ Super Value Combo Market

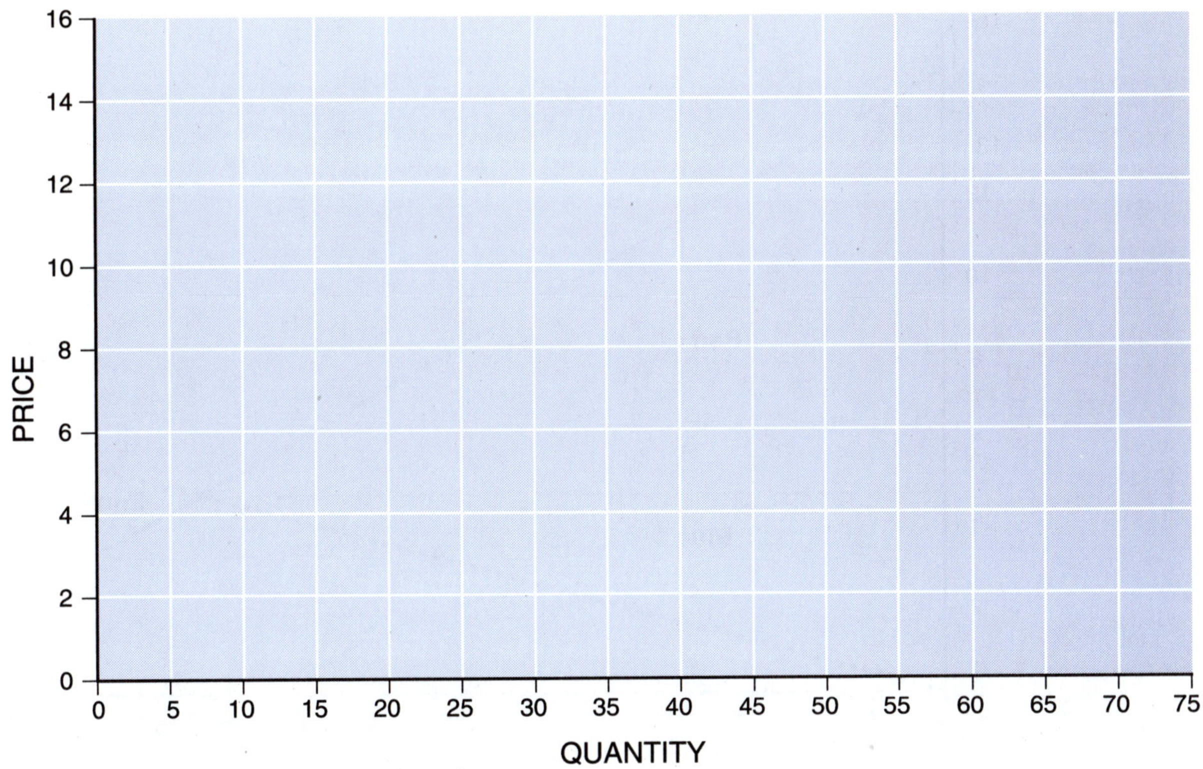

VISUAL 5.7

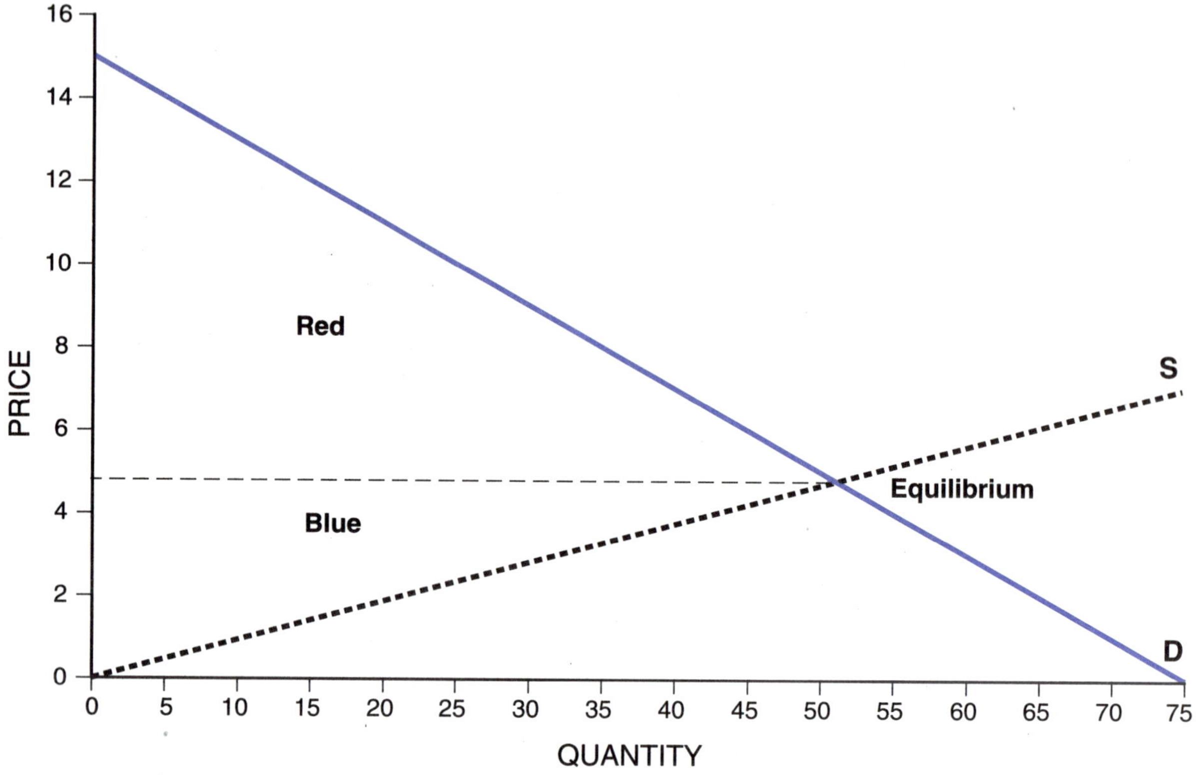

PRICE
16
14
12
10
8
6
4
2
0
Red
Blue
S
Equilibrium
D
0
5
10
15
20
25
30
35
40
45
50
55
60
65
70
75
QUANTITY

VISUAL 5.8

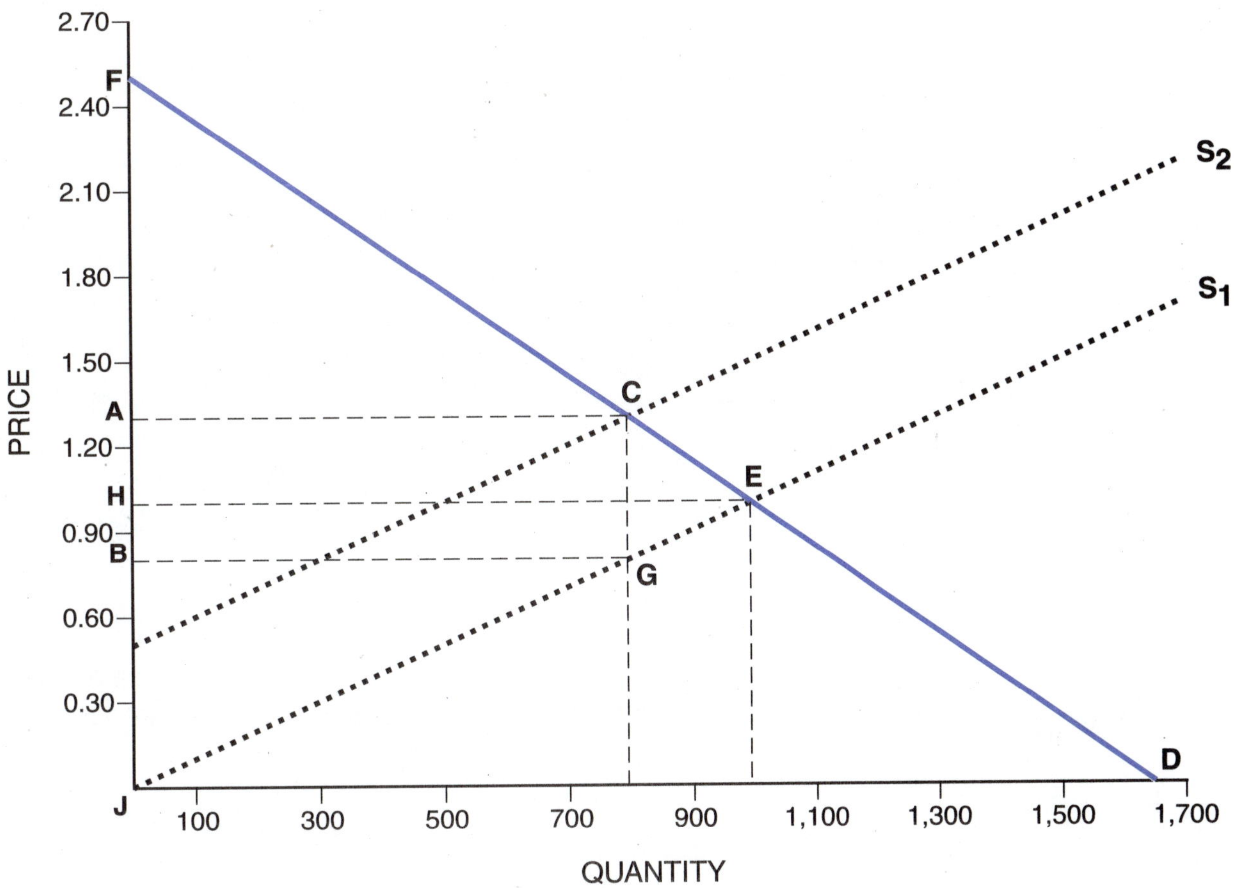
2.70
F
2.40
2.10
1.80
1.50
A
1.20
H
0.90
B
0.60
0.30
PRICE
C
E
G
D
J
S_2
S_1
100
300
500
700
900
1,100
1,300
1,500
1,700
QUANTITY

ACTIVITY 5.1

Name ______________________________ Date __________ Period _____

THE MARKET FOR CHEESEBURGER SUPER VALUE COMBOS

Suppose you are the manager of a local restaurant, and your most popular item is the Cheeseburger Super Value Combo meal. It includes a cheeseburger, fries, milk shake, and mini-pie. To set the price that should be charged for the meal, you need to have some idea about the demand and supply curves for your product. Based on sales in recent years, you determine that you can model the daily supply and demand for your product by using the following linear functions:

$P = 15 - 0.2Q_d$ (Demand) and $P = 0.1Q_s$ (Supply)

a. Recall that at equilibrium, $Q_d = Q_s$. Solve the supply and demand equations and calculate the equilibrium price and quantity of Cheeseburger Super Value Combo meals that you should produce.

b. Using the grid on Visual 5.6, carefully graph the demand curve with a red pencil. Be sure to extend the graph so that it touches both axes. Label this curve "D" (for demand).

c. Carefully graph the supply curve with a blue pencil. Extend the graph all the way back to the origin. Label this curve "S" (for supply).

d. Identify the equilibrium point and draw a dashed line from this point back to the vertical axis. Make sure that this horizontal line is parallel to the horizontal axis and perpendicular to the vertical axis.

e. In red, shade the region on your graph that represents the solution to the inequalities $Q \geq 0$ and $P \leq 15 - 0.2Q$ and $P > 5$.

f. In blue, shade the region on your graph that represents the solution to the inequalities $Q \geq 0$ and $P \geq 0.1Q$ and $P \leq 5$.

g. Calculate the area of the red-shaded region. Be sure to show your work. This area represents the total gains received by consumers who are willing to pay higher prices for Cheeseburger Super Value Combos than is actually charged.

ACTIVITY 5.1 (continued)

h. Calculate the area of the blue-shaded triangle. This area represents the total gains received by the restaurant, which is willing to accept lower prices for Cheeseburger Super Value Combos than is actually received.

i. The sum of the red- and blue-shaded areas represents the total gains from trade. Calculate the total gains from trade.

ACTIVITY 5.2

Name ______________________ Date ____________ Period ______

The Gasoline Market

1. The graph below represents the gasoline market with a tax imposed upon sellers. S_1 is the supply curve without a tax imposed upon sellers and S_2 is the supply curve that exists once the tax has been imposed. What effect does the tax have on the supply of gasoline?

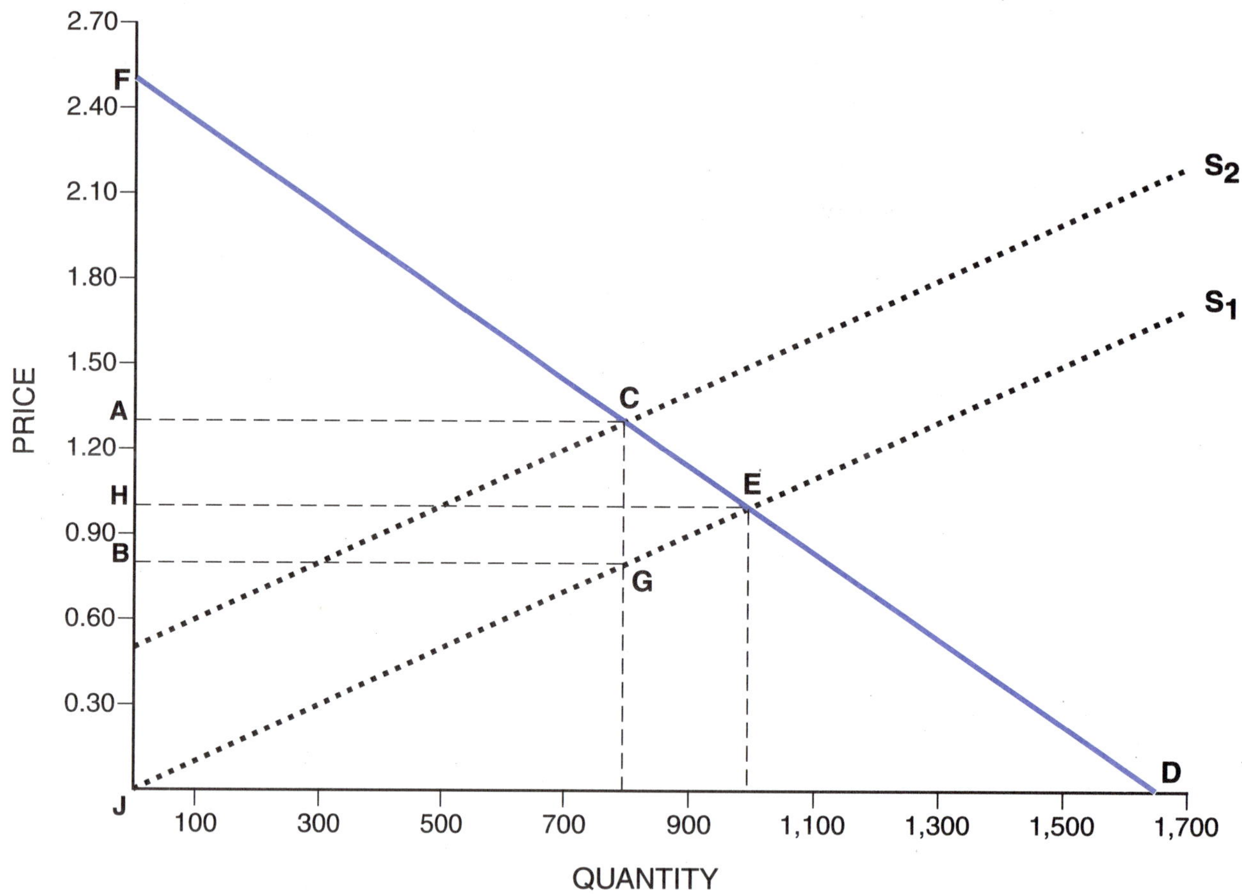

2. The equation for the demand curve is $P = 2.50 - 0.0015Q_d$, and the equation for S_1 is $P = 0.001Q_s$. If S_2 is parallel to S_1 and the vertical intercept of S_2 is 0.5, then the equation for S_2 is P = ____________________ .

Part 1

Answer the following questions. Show your work.

3. What is the pre-tax equilibrium price and quantity exchanged?

4. Using the points labeled on the graph, name the triangle that represents the pre-tax net gains that consumers receive from exchange. Calculate these pre-tax net gains by finding the area of the triangle.

5. Using the points labeled on the graph, name the triangle that represents the pre-tax net gains that producers receive from exchange. Calculate these pre-tax net gains by finding the area of the triangle.

6. Using the points labeled on the graph, name the triangle that represents the pre-tax gains from trade. Calculate the pre-tax gains from trade by finding the area of the triangle. Describe two ways in which this area could be calculated.

Part 2a

Government policymakers have passed a law that requires sellers to send $0.50 to tax collectors for each gallon of gasoline sold. Since the supply curve essentially reflects producer costs, this has the effect of creating a new supply curve for gasoline that is represented by S_2. You may recall from earlier lessons that this is a decrease in supply, since there is now a smaller quantity supplied at each and every price. The supply curve shifts leftward by $0.50 so that the new supply equation is $P = 0.5 + 0.001Q_s$.

1. What is the new equilibrium price and quantity?
Why are gasoline sellers unable to pass the full $0.50 tax on to consumers in the form of higher prices?

2. i) Using the points labeled on the graph, name the triangle that represents the new net gains from exchange received by consumers.
   ii) Calculate the size of these post-tax gains.
   iii) Compare the area to the one that was calculated in part 1 of this activity. What has the tax done to the size of the net gains of consumers?

Part 2b

Gasoline sellers are now paid $1.30 per gallon of gas, although they actually only keep $0.80 per gallon after the tax has been paid. This means the post-tax net gains of producers is represented by the triangle GBJ. The area of this triangle equals ½ · 0.80 · 800 = 320 representing $320. Producers' net gains have declined because fewer gallons of gas are sold and the difference between the price received for gas and the price that sellers were willing to take has been partially eroded.

1. Calculate the post-tax gains from trade. Compare the post-tax gains from trade to the pre-tax gains from trade.

2. Quadrilateral ACGB in your graph represents the total tax collections by the government. This is money that is collected by the government that is redistributed according to the wishes of lawmakers. Calculate the area of this region.

3. Somebody benefits from post-tax gains from trade and from the amount of tax collected: net gains accrue to both consumers and producers, and tax collections are redistributed to the beneficiaries of government programs. Triangle CEG represents the area of the graph that benefits no one. It is referred to as deadweight loss. It occurs because the tax increase causes the amount that buyers pay to be greater than the amount sellers actually receive. In addition, the tax causes fewer gallons of gasoline to be sold. Deadweight loss represents the economic inefficiency that arises from a tax hike. Calculate the area of the deadweight loss.

4. Compare all of the post-tax information with the pre-tax information. Have all of the pre-tax areas been accounted for by the post-tax regions we considered?

Lesson 6

The Mathematics of Linear Economic Shapes: Slopes and Elasticities

Mathematics Focus:

Algebra 1

Mathematics Prerequisites:

Prior to using this lesson, students should be able to:

- Find the slope of a line given two points
- Define slope as a rate of change
- Describe the relationship between the graphical and numerical representation of a slope
- Calculate percent increase and percent decrease

Lesson Objectives:

To apply prerequisite mathematics concepts and processes to a linear demand function to:

- Explain the economic meaning of the terms slope and elasticity
- Explain that altering the units of measurement for a slope calculation does not necessarily imply a change in the fundamental economic relationship between two variables
- Explain that elasticity measures the strength of a relationship between two economic variables and is independent of units of measurement
- Explain that the slope of a straight line is constant
- Define price elasticity of demand

Overview of Mathematics and Economics:

As was noted in Lessons 1–4, a demand curve is used to describe the willingness and ability of buyers to purchase various quantities of goods and services at alternative prices. The visual representation of this relationship is a linear function in the first quadrant with a negative slope. This lesson explores a different way of representing the strength of the economic relationship between changes in price and quantity demanded along demand curves with different slopes.

Since price appears on the vertical axis and quantity appears on the horizontal axis, the slope of a demand curve is measured as the change in P divided by the change in Q_d (where P represents price and Q_d is quantity demanded). Since quantity demanded and price are inversely related, the slope of a demand curve is negative. As long as the demand curve is represented by a linear function, the slope is constant along the straight line.

The slope of a demand curve, while appearing to measure the strength of the relationship between quantity demanded and price, is dependent upon units of measurement. For example, the calculated slope of a hypothetical demand curve for apples is different if it is measured as dollars per pound instead of dollars per ounce. While these slope computations are different, the fundamental economic relationship between the price of apples and their quantity demanded is unchanged when units of measurement are altered. For this reason, when economists wish to gain an understanding of the strength of the relationship between price and quantity demanded, they use a measure that is independent of units of measurement. This measure is known as the *price elasticity of demand.*

The price elasticity of demand is calculated as the percentage change in Q_d divided by the percentage change in P. The larger the number in absolute value, the more responsive quantity demanded is to price changes. Put differently, the larger the absolute value of the price elasticity of demand, the more *elastic* the demand for an item. Students may wish to think of elastic demand as a situation in which quantity demanded stretches (like a rubber band) noticeably in response to a given price change. For example, suppose a 10 percent price increase induces a 30 percent reduction in quantity demanded. In this case, the price elasticity of demand equals –3 (3 in absolute value terms) and demand is said to be elastic. Likewise, the smaller the price elasticity of demand (in absolute value terms), the less responsive is quantity demanded to price changes. This is representative of *inelastic* demand (minimal "stretchability" of quantity demanded in response to a given price change). If a 10 percent increase in price is accompanied by a small 1 percent decrease in quantity demanded, then demand is inelastic, since the calculated price elasticity of demand is –0.1 (an absolute value of 0.1). Note that in all cases, the elasticity calculations do not depend upon units of measurement. Knowledge of the magnitude of the price elasticity of demand is extremely valuable to a firm that is considering a price change.

Mathematics and Economics Terms:

- Absolute value
- Demand curve
- Elastic demand
- Inelastic demand
- Law of demand
- Percent of decrease
- Percent of increase
- Price
- Price elasticity of demand
- Quantity demanded

Materials:

- Straight edge
- One copy of Activities 6.1, 6.2, 6.3, and 6.4 for each student
- Overhead transparencies of Visuals 6.1, 6.2, 6.3, and 6.4
- One copy of Visual 6.1 and Visual 6.4 for each student

Estimated Time:

80–100 minutes

Procedures:

1. Warm-Up Activity: Show Visual 6.1 and distribute a copy to each student. Complete it on the overhead with the students.

Answers are as follows:

1. The slope is 3 feet/board.
2. The slope is 36 inches/board.
3. (a) Both measure the same length of board.
   (b) The units measuring the boards are different and therefore, the numerical values of the slopes are also different.
4. 100% increase
5. 100% increase
6. 100% increase
7. Ratio of 1
8. Ratio of 1
9. No. The percent changes are the same no matter what the unit
10. They cancelled out when the percentage change was calculated in both the numerator and the denominator.

2. Distribute a copy of Activity 6.1 to each student. Indicate that this exercise illustrates the idea that the numerical value of a slope calculation depends upon the units of measurement that are used in graphing the function. Tell them that this activity involves an economic relationship called a *demand curve.* Inform your students that economists and mathematicians call this function a curve even though it is clearly a straight line. This graph maps the relationship between the price of a good or service and the amount that people are willing and able to buy (also known as *quantity demanded*). This is called an inverse relationship because when price increases the quantity demanded decreases. Consequently, the slope is negative. Have the students graph the information in Table 1 on the provided graph paper and label it as D_1. Have the students also answer the two questions associated with Table 1. Visual 6.2 shows how the graph should appear.

Answers to the first two questions follow:

1. This is a straight line.

2. $\frac{\text{change in P}}{\text{change in } Q_d} = \frac{-\$0.04}{\text{1 pound}}$

COMMENT When looking at Visual 6.2, note that P (price) is always on the vertical axis and Q_d (quantity demanded) is on the horizontal axis. You may wish to note that students have graphed a fundamental economic relationship known as the *law of demand*. That is, there is an inverse relationship between the price of a good and its quantity demanded, when everything else remains constant. Put differently, when it is assumed that all other influences on your choices as a consumer are held constant, people prefer paying lower prices to paying higher prices. The law of demand is as simple as that.

3. The range of the curve from P = $1 to $0 has been intentionally omitted from Table 1. Quantity demanded would likely get very large as price approaches $0. This could be graphed as a horizontal asymptote. You can disregard the point where the price is $0 because there is no such thing as universally free economic goods.

COMMENT Have the students convert the slope to a decimal if you wish. Be sure to emphasize the units from this calculation. While the numerical calculation is important, it is also critical that you note that this is in terms of $/pound.

4. Have the students graph the information in Table 2 in Activity 6.1 on the provided graph paper. Have them label this latter curve as D_2. Note that this is shown on Visual 6.3. Then ask them to answer the questions that follow Figure 2.

Answers to the questions include:

1. Yes. It is a straight line.
2. Change in P/change in Qd = –1/400 $/ounce.
3. The slope of the graph from Table 1 has the largest absolute value.
4. The graph from Table 2 is less steep.
5. Dollars per pound
6. Dollars per ounce
7. –1/400 dollars/ounce
8. It is the same as the slope from Table 2. This illustrates that the slope is dependent upon units of measurement. While the numerical value of the slope is different between Tables 1 and 2, the fundamental economic relationship is exactly the same in the two tables. This indicates the need to find a measure that expresses the strength of the rela-

tionship between variables that is independent of units of measurement.

■ **COMMENT** The students are asked to compare the numerical value of the slopes in the two figures. In absolute value terms, the slope of Figure 1 is larger than that of Figure 2. Note, however, that these cannot be directly compared because the units of measurement are different. Simply focusing on the numerical value of a slope calculation, as well as the visual representation of demand curves can be very misleading.

5. Be sure the students understand that the fundamental economic relationship between P and Q_d has not been altered in moving from Table 1 to Table 2. When the units changed from pounds to ounces, the numerical value of the slope decreased in absolute terms. Since changing units can change numerical values, economists use a concept called *elasticity* to measure the strength of the relationship between variables instead of relying on the slope of the function.

6. Tell the students that the *price elasticity of demand* measures the strength of a relationship between price and the quantity demanded of a good. The price elasticity of demand is calculated by dividing the percentage change in quantity demanded by the percentage change in price between two points on a demand curve. A simple general formula for calculating the price elasticity of demand between two points on a demand curve is shown on Visual 6.4. Show Visual 6.4 and explain the formula given on the visual. Indicate that the formula can be revised to $\frac{Q_{d1} - Q_{d0}}{Q_{d0}} \cdot \frac{P_0}{P_1 - P_0} = \frac{Q_{d1} - Q_{d0}}{P_1 - P_0} \cdot \frac{P_0}{Q_{d0}}$. Review finding a percent change, emphasizing that the amount of change is always divided by the original amount. Notice that price elasticity has no units, that is, it is a dimensionless measure because the units cancel out.

7. Distribute a copy of Activity 6.2 to each student. Students may need some help with this exercise, so you may wish to separate them into groups to help each other. Be sure to note that this price elasticity is being evaluated around the point Q_d = 100 pounds and P = \$1 (these correspond to Q_{d0} and P_0 in the formula).

◆ **Answers to the questions include:**

1. a. –25 pounds/\$ b. 1/100 \$/pound c. −1/4 or −.25
2. There are no units—they cancel out.
3. a. −400 ounces/\$ b. 1/1600 \$/ounce c. −1/4 or −0.25
4. It is the same, illustrating that the price elasticity of demand calculation does not change with changes in measurement units. Changes in units do not alter the fundamental economic relationship between variables.

Indicate that a price elasticity of demand of –¼ means that for every 100 percent increase in price, quantity demanded will decrease by only 25 percent. This is potentially very valuable information for a firm. In this case, the firm can double its price from \$1 to \$2 and only see a 25 pound reduction in the quantity of apples demanded.

8. While the slope does not vary along a straight line, the price elasticity of demand does. This can be seen by looking at the revised version of the elasticity formula in Visual 6.4 . The first factor is the reciprocal of the slope of the demand curve, and is thus constant. Since the second factor in the formula, $\frac{P_0}{Q_{d0}}$, is not a constant ratio, the elasticity must change as we move along the demand curve. Have the students complete Activity 6.3 to reinforce this concept.

The answers for the two questions are:

1. It changes from –¼ to –⅔.
2. Since this also equals –⅔, this confirms that the earlier calculation is correct.

9. Indicate that the economic interpretation of an elasticity calculation is straightforward. With a price elasticity equal to –¼, for every one percent increase in price, a seller can expect a decline of 0.25 percent in the quantity of her product that people wish to purchase. You can well imagine that this is extremely important information for a business firm! If everything else remains the same, it is probably a good idea for the firm to raise its price. The loss in sales will be more than offset by the price increase.

When the absolute value of the price elasticity of demand is greater than one, the responsiveness of quantity demanded is greater than the proportional change in price. Demand is said to be *elastic*. When the absolute value of the price elasticity is less than one, changes in quantity demanded are less than the proportional change in price, and demand is said to be *inelastic*. In thinking about the terms *elastic* and *inelastic*, think about the "stretchability" of quantity demanded. When demand is elastic, quantity demanded is highly responsive to price changes (it has a high "stretchability" factor). When demand is inelastic, quantity demanded is very unresponsive to price changes and thus has a low degree of "stretchability."

10. Have each student complete Activity 6.4 as a homework activity. Results should be compared and discussed during the next class period.

The answers are:

1. −1.165
2. They have decreased from $20,970 to $19,975.
3. To increase revenues, reduce the price. The price may not need to be decreased all the way back to $6.99. But this analysis suggests that the $1 increase in price was more than offset by a reduction in quantity demanded. As such, everything else equal, increasing price by $1 was not a particularly good idea.

Indicate that this is an example of the effects of an increase in price on sales revenues when demand is elastic. Since the 14.3% increase in price is offset by a 16.7% decrease in quantity demanded, demand is elastic and the pizzeria's revenues drop as a result of the price hike. You could also ask what would happen if demand were inelastic. In that case, a given percentage increase in price would be incompletely offset by a decline in the quantity demanded. The percentage decrease in quantity demanded would be less than the percentage increase in price. This means that the pizzeria's sales revenues would rise if prices were increased.

Extension Activities:

1. In Activity 6.1, ask the students to consider what would happen to the numerical value of the slope calculation if they were to measure the relationship as cents per pound (or cents per ounce). Have them graph this (these) new relationship(s).

2. Have the students draw both a vertical and a horizontal demand curve. Ask them to identify and comment on the slopes and elasticities of each curve. The vertical curve has no slope—although its slope approaches negative infinity as the change in quantity demanded approaches zero—and an elasticity equal to 0. This is an example of a *perfectly inelastic* demand curve. Large increases in price have no effect on quantity demanded in this extreme case. Insulin for a diabetic, a dialysis machine, or protease inhibitors for a person who is HIV positive, may be examples of items for which the quantity demanded is not sensitive to price increases.

The horizontal curve has a slope equal to 0 and an elasticity of negative infinity. Small increases in price lead consumers to completely eliminate their purchases of items whose demand curve looks like this. This is an example of a *perfectly elastic* demand curve. Items that have a demand structure that appears perfectly elastic are those for which there are a lot of close substitutes. Different brands of homogenized milk, apples of a given variety produced on different farms, and other items that are priced in very competitive markets are examples of items that are highly sensitive to price changes.

VISUAL 6.1 ▲ Warm-Up

Two students, Kelsey and David, are making graphs to show lumber needed for building bird houses. The available lumber is all ¾ inches thick and 6 inches wide. Their plans show that they need 3 linear feet of the available lumber for each birdhouse.

1. Kelsey made the table below to help her create her graph. Each board, x, is 3 feet long. The dependent variable, y, represents total length in feet. Using the slope formula, calculate the slope of the line represented. The slope is ___________

X	y
1	3
2	6
3	9
4	12
5	15

2. David made the table below for his graph. Each board, x, is 36 inches long. The dependent variable, y, represents total length in inches. Calculate the slope of the line represented. The slope is ___________

x	y
1	36
2	72
3	108
4	144
5	180

3. (a) In what ways are these two relationships the same?

____

(b) In what ways are these two relationships different?

____

4. If the number of boards increases from 2 to 4, what is the percent increase in the number of boards? ___________

5. If the total length increases from 6 feet to 12 feet, what is the percent increase in the total length? ___________

6. If the total length increases from 72 inches to 144 inches, what is the percent increase in the total length? ___________

7. In problem #1 what is the ratio of $\frac{\text{percent of increase in x}}{\text{percent of increase in y}}$? ___________

8. In problem #2 what is the ratio of $\frac{\text{percent of increase in x}}{\text{percent of increase in y}}$? ___________

9. Did units make a difference in our percent calculations? ___________

10. What happened to the units in calculating the ratios in problems 7 and 8?

VISUAL 6.2

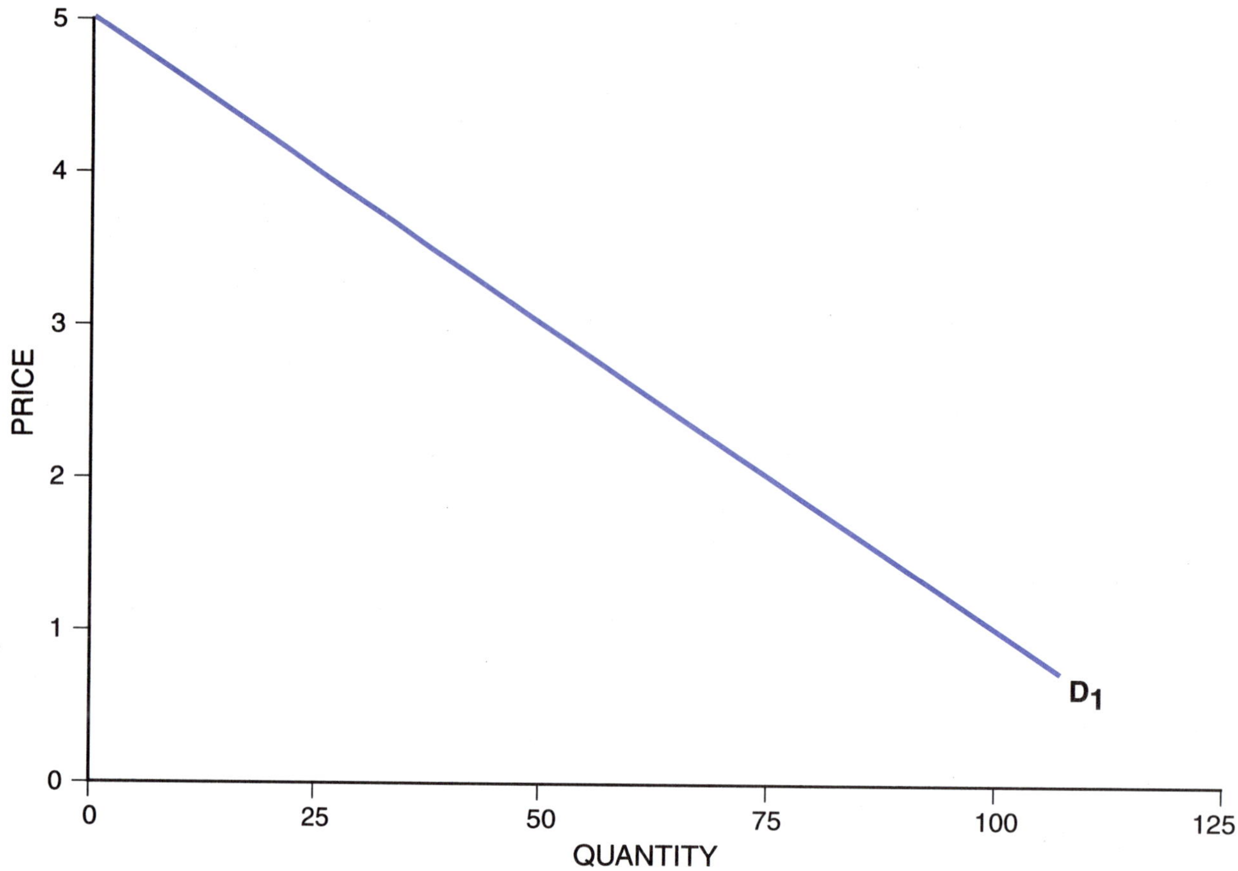

VISUAL 6.3

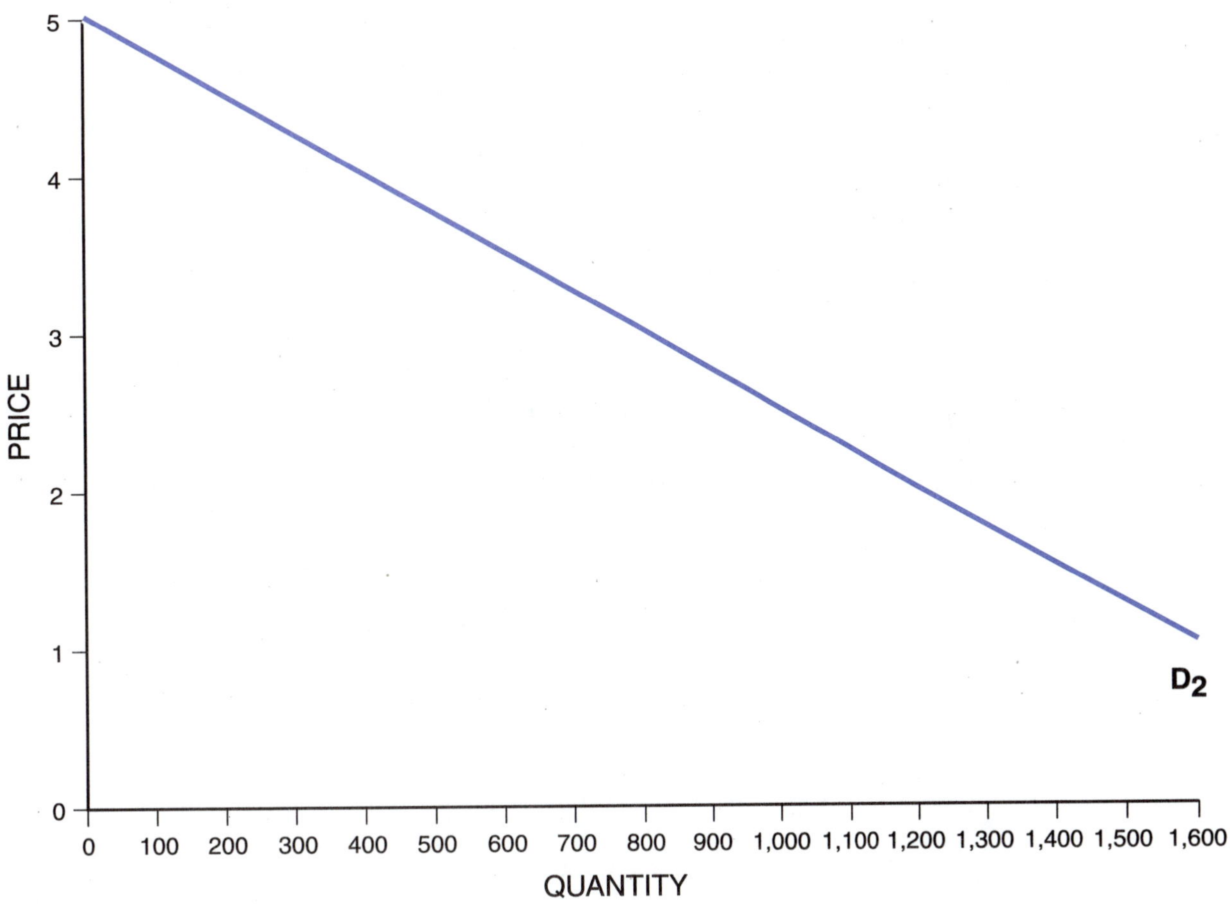

5
4
3
2
1
0
PRICE
D2
0
100
200
300
400
500
600
700
800
900
1,000
1,100
1,200
1,300
1,400
1,500
1,600
QUANTITY

VISUAL 6.4 ▲ The Price Elasticity of Demand

$$\text{Price Elasticity of Demand} = \frac{\text{percent change in } Q_d}{\text{percent change in price}}$$

$$E_d = \frac{\dfrac{Q_{d1} - Q_{d0}}{Q_{d0}}}{\dfrac{P_1 - P_0}{P_0}}$$

This formula can be revised to = $\dfrac{Q_{d1} - Q_{d0}}{Q_{d0}} \cdot \dfrac{P_0}{P_1 - P_0} = \dfrac{Q_{d1} - Q_{d0}}{P_1 - P_0} \cdot \dfrac{P_0}{Q_{d0}}$

Note that $\dfrac{Q_{d1} - Q_{d0}}{P_1 - P_0}$ is the reciprocal of the unchanging slope of the line.

ACTIVITY 6.1 ▲ Slope and the Units of Measurement Along a Demand Curve

Name ______________________ Date __________ Period _____

Part I

You are investigating the demand for apples and are given the following demand schedule:

Table 1

Quantity Demanded (horizontal axis-dependent variable)	Price (in dollars) (vertical axis-independent variable)
Very large (horizontal asymptote)	0
100 pounds	1
75 pounds	2
50 pounds	3
25 pounds	4
0 pounds	5

Using the graph paper below identified as Figure 1, plot the points and draw the graph of the function represented in the above schedule. Let each horizontal increment be 25 pounds.

Figure 1

1. Is this a straight line?

2. Ignoring the portion of the curve between P = $0 and $1, calculate the slope of this function.

Part II

Now use the provided graph paper identified as Figure 2 to plot and draw the graph of the function represented by the following demand schedule; let each horizontal increment be 100 ounces

Table 2

Quantity Demanded (horizontal axis-dependent variable)	Price (in dollars) (vertical axis-independent variable)
1,600 ounces	1
1,200 ounces	2
800 ounces	3
400 ounces	4
0 ounces	5

Figure 2

1. Is this a straight line?

2. Calculate the slope of this function.

3. Compare the numerical value of the slopes obtained from the graphs of Tables 1 and 2. Which slope has the largest absolute value?

4. How do the graphs compare to one another?

5. What are the units of measurement of the slope calculated in Table 1?

6. What are the units of measurement of the slope calculated in Table 2?

7. Recalculate the slope of the data in Table 1 using dollars per ounce.

8. How does this slope compare to the slope in Table 2?

ACTIVITY 6.2 ▲ Calculating the Price Elasticity of Demand

Name ______________________________ Date ____________ Period _____

Instruction: Use the formula for the price elasticity of demand

$$\text{Price elasticity of demand} = \frac{\dfrac{Q_{d1} - Q_{d0}}{Q_{d0}}}{\dfrac{P_1 - P_0}{P_0}} = \frac{Q_{d1} - Q_{d0}}{P_1 - P_0} \cdot \frac{P_0}{Q_{d0}}$$

to do the following:

1. Using Table 1 in Activity 6.1, calculate the following to find the numerical value of the price elasticity in moving from a price of \$1 to \$2:

   a) Calculate $\dfrac{Q_{d1} - Q_{d0}}{P_1 - P_0}$. This is the reciprocal of the slope of the function. For this calculation P_0 = \$1 and Q_{d0} = 100 pounds.

   b) Calculate the ratio P_0/Q_{d0}.

   c) Find the product of the above ratios to determine the numerical value of the price elasticity in moving from a price of \$1 to \$2.

2. What are the units of measurement in this calculation?

Now return to Table 2 in Activity 6.1. Recall the difference between the numerical calculation of the slope in Tables 1 and 2. This occurred although the fundamental economic relationship described in the tables had not changed.

3. Calculate the following to find the numerical value of the price elasticity in moving from a price of \$1 to \$2 in Table 2:

   a) Calculate $\dfrac{Q_{d1} - Q_{d0}}{P_1 - P_0}$. This is the reciprocal of the slope of the function. For this calculation P_0 = \$1 and Q_{d0} = 1600 ounces.

   b) Calculate the ratio P_0/Q_{d0}.

   c) Find the product of the above ratios to determine the numerical value of the price elasticity in moving from a price of \$1 to \$2.

4. How does this compare to the equivalent elasticity calculation in Table 1?

ACTIVITY 6.3 ▲ The Variation of Price Elasticity Along the Demand Curve

Name ______________________________ Date __________ Period _____

1. Using the data from Table 1 in Activity 6.1, calculate the price elasticity of demand in moving from a price of \$2 to \$3. Let P_0 = \$2 and Q_{d0} = 75 pounds.

2. It was suggested earlier that the price elasticity of demand at the same point on the graph expressed in ounces should yield the same result as the one just computed. Check this to make sure your calculation is indeed correct. Use P_0 = \$2 and Q_{d0} = 1200 ounces.

ACTIVITY 6.4 ▲ Pizza Elasticity

Name ____ Date ____________ Period ______

Suppose you work at a local pizzeria. Last month, the pizzeria increased the price of a large cheese pizza from $6.99 to $7.99. As a result of this, the quantity of large cheese pizzas sold declined from 3,000 to 2,500. Assume that a similar pattern of sales was observed for all other items sold by the pizzeria. Your manager is interested in whether or not to continue with the price hike. She recalls that you are learning about mathematics and economics and asks you to determine how strong the relationship is between the change in pizza prices and pizza sales. You recognize that what she really wants is for you to calculate the price elasticity of demand for pizzas.

1. Calculate the price elasticity of demand.

2. What has happened to sales revenues of large cheese pizzas as a result of the price increase?

3. What do you recommend to your manager?

Lesson 7

The Mathematics of Nonlinear Economic Shapes: The Production Possibilities Curve

Mathematics Focus:

Algebra II, Precalculus, and Calculus

Mathematics Prerequisites:

Prior to using this lesson, students should be able to:

- Write the equation of a circle given the center and the radius
- Solve the equation of a circle for one of the variables
- Graph an ellipse centered at the origin given its equation in the form $\frac{x^2}{a^2} + \frac{y^2}{b^2} = 1$
- Write the equation of an ellipse centered at the origin in the form $\frac{x^2}{a^2} + \frac{y^2}{b^2} = 1$
- Understand the meaning of a restricted domain
- Write the domain of a restricted function from its graphical representation

Prior to using this lesson, Calculus students should also be able to:

- Calculate the first derivative of a second degree equation
- Calculate the slope of a function at various points on its curve using the first derivative
- Interpret the concavity of a function by calculating the second derivative

Lesson Objectives:

To apply prerequisite mathematics concepts and processes to the production possibilities curve to:

- Explain the properties of the production possibilities curve
- Explain concepts embodied in the production possibilities curve including scarcity, choice, opportunity cost, increasing opportunity cost, efficiency, and economic growth
- Explain the relationship between specialized resources and increasing opportunity cost

Overview of Mathematics and Economics:

Because the resources (such as raw materials, minerals, energy, labor, equipment, machinery, etc.) that are used to produce goods and services are limited in their availability, we cannot have all that we want. When limited resources come into conflict with unlimited wants, *scarcity* is said to exist. Without scarcity, we could have all that we want, and we would not need to make difficult and costly choices. Because of scarcity, we must make choices, and choices are costly. In economics, cost (also referred to as *opportunity cost*) is defined as the highest valued alternative that must be forgone as a result of making a choice. For example, if one of your students is considering whether or not to join the school drum line, she must weigh the other alternatives that must be forfeited as a result of making this choice. These might include giving up a weekend job, having less time to do homework, or being unable to join the stage crew for the school play. The *highest valued* of these alternatives is the opportunity cost of joining the drum line. So, if the most valued alternative to joining the school drum line is having less time to do homework, then the student's opportunity cost of joining the drum line is giving up time to work on her studies.

A highly useful tool for examining many fundamental economic concepts is the *production possibilities curve*. The production possibilities curve looks at the maximum amount of two goods that can be produced by a nation, region, business, or individual, given a fixed amount of productive resources, with a given level of technology, in a particular time period. This construct helps students visualize the important concepts of scarcity, choice, and costs. It also helps them understand the concepts of economic *efficiency* and economic *growth*. Efficiency in production is said to occur when a producer gets the most out of his or her resources. When efficiency is attained, it is not possible to achieve gains in production of one good without reducing production of other goods. Economic growth occurs when increases in productive resources and/or technological advances lead to an increase in the production of goods and services over time.

Finally, because resources are often specialized (that is, more suitable to one application than another), the production possibilities curve also teaches us about *increasing opportunity costs*. When a country uses its resources more intensively to produce a particular good, such as wheat, additional units of wheat production come at an expense of increasing amounts of other goods (cotton, for example) whose production must be forgone. While wheat is grown quite effectively in Iowa, growing conditions in Georgia tend to favor the production of cotton. To use productive resources in Georgia to grow wheat (which might eventually happen if a country produced wheat more intensively) would cause a country to give up a relatively large amount of cotton production. A much smaller amount of cotton production is forgone when the first few units of wheat are produced. This is because the initial units of wheat production are obtained by using those resources that are best suited to growing wheat. For example, growing wheat in Iowa implies forgoing a modest amount of cotton production since resources in Iowa are not particularly suited to growing cotton. Since an increasing amount of cotton production is forgone when a country produces wheat more intensively, increasing opportunity costs are experienced.

The economic relationships embodied in a production possibilities curve suggest that the curve can be modeled graphically as a segment of a circle in the first quadrant of the coordinate axes. The mathematical properties of this "quarter-circle" help explain the important fundamental concepts referred to above.

Mathematics and Economics Terms:

- Concavity
- Circle
- Cost
- Derivative
- Domain
- Economic growth
- Efficiency
- Ellipse
- Increasing opportunity cost
- Opportunity cost
- Production possibilities curve
- Scarcity

Materials:

- One copy of Visual 7.1 for each student
- One overhead transparencies of Visuals 7.1, 7.2, 7.3, 7.4, and 7.5
- One copy of Activities 7.1 and 7.2 for each student

Estimated Time:

80 – 120 minutes

Procedures:

1. Warm-Up Activity: Distribute a copy of Visual 7.1 to all students and have them complete the questions as follows: questions 1–10 for Algebra II and Precalculus students and questions 1–14 for Calculus students. Show the overhead of Visual 7.2 and cover the answers in class.

The answers are:

1. See Visual 7.2.
2. See Visual 7.2.
3. $(x - h)^2 + (y - k)^2 = r^2$

4. $x^2 + y^2 = 100$
5. $y = \pm \sqrt{100 - x^2}$
6. Only the quarter circle in the first quadrant has positive values for x and y.
7. $y = +\sqrt{100 - x^2}$ Domain = $\{x \mid 0 \leq x \leq 10\}$
8. When the value of x decreases, the value of y increases. When the value of x increases, the value of y decreases.
9. We say x and y are (ANS: inversely) related to each other. This relationship results in a (ANS: negatively) sloped curve.
10. $y' = \frac{1}{2}(100 - x^2)^{-1/2}(-2x) = -x(100 - x^2)^{-1/2}$;
    $y'' = -(100 - x^2)^{-1/2} - x^2(100 - x^2)^{-3/2}$
11. Because the first derivative is negative for $0 < x < 10$ we can say that the slope of the graph is negative.
12. Because the second derivative is negative for $0 < x < 10$ we can say that the function is concave down.
13. The slope at $x = 1$ is –.1005. The slope at $x = 5$ is –.5774. The slope at $x = 9$ is –2.0647.
14. The absolute value is greatest when $x = 9$. This means that the rate of change of the function is increasing. Each increment of x causes larger and larger increments of *y*.

2. Distribute a copy of Activity 7.1 to each student. Ask the students to consider a simple country in which the productive resources can produce two goods—hot dogs and/or butter (note that economists sometimes think of a Robinson Crusoe economy of fish and breadfruit as a different example). What mathematical formula might be used to represent the production potential of this country? What important economic concepts would be embodied in this mathematical formula? What is the graphical representation of this relationship? What mathematical tools can be used to explore the economic properties of this relationship? These are the questions that are answered in this lesson.

Activity 7.1 asks the students to construct a production possibilities curve from the given equation. Be sure to inform your students that they are to confine themselves to the first quadrant in drawing this curve. Why should the analysis be confined to the first quadrant? Because the economic values that we wish to explore are both positive. Negative quantities are unrealistic. Explain to your students that most economists think that a reasonable way to represent a country's production potential of hot dogs and butter is an equation such as that provided in Activity 7.1.

◆ **Answers to Activity 7.1 are in blue print in the following text.**

1. See Visual 7.3

After students have graphed the curve, note that what they have drawn is a production possibilities curve. It looks at the maximum potential production of hot dogs and butter that can be achieved with given technology and resources in a particular time period. For example, Creeperland could produce 30 hot dogs and 0 units of butter, or it could produce 30 units of butter and 0 hot dogs. They could also produce such combinations as 20 hot dogs and 22.4 units of butter or 10 hot dogs and 28.3 units of butter. This exercise is not concerned with the point at which they choose to produce. In a market economy, this is determined by the interaction of supply and demand forces. Instead, this activity is concerned with a country's maximum potential to produce goods.

Make sure the students complete the remainder of Part I of this activity. The questions are designed to address the shape of the curve, vertical and horizontal intercepts, etc. After your students have determined that this is simply a portion of a circle, ask them to determine the area under the curve. Note that this area has an economic meaning. It can be thought of as the feasible set of points of hotdog and butter production that are attainable in the country of Creeperland. Simply put, any point in the first quadrant that is on or below the production possibilities curve is a potential point of production. Any point above the curve is not feasible (although it can become feasible through economic growth, which is explored in Part II of Activity 7.1). While points inside the curve are attainable, economists suggest that these points are representative of *inefficient* production. Why? Because *productive efficiency* occurs when it is not possible for a country to use its given resources and technology to produce more of one good without forgoing some production of the other good. Only when a feasible point of production of hot dogs and butter lies on the curve is this condition met. For example, if Creeperland was currently producing 30 units of butter and 0 hot dogs, the only way for them to produce 10 hot dogs would be to give up 1.7 units of butter production. That is, the only way to achieve gains in the production of hot dogs is to give up some units of butter output. Note that this condition is not met when the production point occurs inside the curve. When production occurs inside the production possibilities curve, resources could be used more efficiently in order to achieve output gains of both hot dogs and butter. Additional hot dog production could be achieved without forgoing butter production. For example, consider a situation in which Creeperland was producing 20 hot dogs and 10 units of butter. This is clearly part of the feasibility set, but it is inefficient. Why? Because Creeperland could use given resources and technology to produce more of both goods. For instance, the point 22 hot dogs and 20 units of butter is a potential point of production. This means that 20 hot dogs and 10 units of butter must be a point of inefficiency. Similar reasoning suggests that the production point 20 hot dogs and 30 units of butter is not feasible and not attainable given current resources and technological capabilities. This is a good time to note that the concept of scarcity is embodied in the production possibilities model because there is an area that is unattainable. In a world without scarcity, everything is attainable.

2. Because quantities produced cannot be negative.
3. 30
4. 30
5. Nonlinear
6. Concave down
7. See Visual 7.4
8. It is a circle.
9. Since the radius is 30, this makes the area equal to 2827.43.
10. It is one-quarter of the total area, therefore equaling 706.9.

3. Part II of Activity 7.1 looks at the effects of an increase in the quantity and/or quality of productive resources on the production possibilities curve. It also looks at how the formula of the circle is affected by economic growth. An increase in resources causes the curve to shift outward and the radius of the circle to increase. This causes the feasibility set to increase, making new points of production attainable. This is the beauty of economic growth. Production possibilities that did not previously exist become attainable through growth in the quantity and/or quality of productive resources. History is replete with examples of the powerful influence of growth on economic prosperity. The Industrial Revolution, U.S. growth in the 1950s, 1960s and the last half of the 1990s, the growth of Japan and other Asian Tigers over the post-World War II period, etc. are all examples of the favorable effects of long-term economic growth.

11. It will increase Creeperland's production potential.
12. It will be represented by an outward shift of the production possibilities curve.
13. You can increase the radius of the circle. This will increase the vertical and horizontal intercepts in the first quadrant. See Visual 7.5.
14. The new graph represents the new production potential of Creeperland. This expansion in production possibilities has resulted from the economic growth that has arisen from an increase in the quantity and/or quality of productive resources in Creeperland.
15. It has expanded Creeperland's feasibility set. Part of the previously unattainable area has now been made attainable.
16. The new area is 1256.6.
17. The area has increased by nearly 78 percent.
18. Yes, this point is now feasible since $25^2 + 30^2 = 1525 < 1600$.
19. This point is not efficient because it lies inside the production possibilities curve.

4. Distribute a copy of Activity 7.2 to each student. Tell students that *opportunity cost* is another important economic concept that is embodied in the production possibilities curve. Opportunity cost is what economists think of when they think of costs. It is easiest to think of opportunity cost as the most highly valued alternative that is forgone as a result of making a choice. This can be calculated along a production possibilities curve because the decision to produce an extra unit of one good implies forgoing the production of an extra amount of the other. In the hot dogs and butter example in Activity 7.2, the cost of the first unit of butter (going from 0 units of butter to 1 unit of butter) is 0.02 units of hot dog production (this is calculated as follows: at $Q_{butter} = 0$, $Q_{hot\ dogs} = 30$; at $Q_{butter} = 1$, $Q_{hot\ dogs} = 29.98$. This means that 30 - 29.98 = 0.02 units of hot dog production are given up to produce the first unit of butter. Similar logic suggests that the opportunity cost of the second unit of butter (going from $Q_{butter} = 1$ to $Q_{butter} = 2$) is 0.05 hot dogs, the cost of the third unit of butter (going from $Q_{butter} = 2$ to $Q_{butter} = 3$) is 0.08 hot dogs, and so on.

As you move down the production possibilities curve in Activity 7.2 (think of this as producing butter more intensively), the opportunity cost of each additional unit of butter production increases. That is, the 30th unit of butter is more costly to produce than the 20th, which is more costly to produce than the 10th, which in turn is more costly to produce than the first unit of butter. Note that this is not saying that 30 units of butter cost more to produce than one unit. This is necessarily true. What this statement indicates is that the incremental cost of additional units of butter production is higher, the more intensively that butter is produced. Note that this result follows from the concavity of the production function.

But why do economists think that a concave production possibilities curve represents real world production possibilities? Because in the real world, we tend to observe *increasing opportunity costs*. Increasing opportunity costs result from specialized resources that are better suited at one productive endeavor than another. At the vertical intercept of the first figure in Activity 7.1, all resources are being used to produce hot dogs. Consequently, when we decide to produce the first unit of butter, we are freeing up resources that are no doubt better suited to butter production (for example, we recommision a butter production facility in Wisconsin that had been converted into a hot dog production plant). This process continues until butter becomes the only good produced. While producing butter more intensively, however, we will no doubt find that we will be forced to use those specialized resources for butter production that are better suited to producing hot dogs. For example, we may be able to convert hot dog processing equipment into dairy containers, but it may not be the best use of this equipment. Likewise, people whose job it is to research new hot dog fillers can probably be employed as butter production analysts, but this may not be a particularly good use of their skills. Economists note that these highly valued hot dog production resources will be very costly to give up--they will thus be the last units to be forgone when additional units of butter are produced. Using these resources to produce butter will be very costly indeed.

Answers to Activity 7.2 are:

1. They are each equal to 30.
2. 30
3. 29.98 hot dogs
4. 0.02 hot dogs
5. 29.98 – 29.93 = 0.05 hot dogs. You may need to remind your students that they are not to calculate the total cost of producing two units of butter. They are only interested in the cost of the second unit.
6. 29.93 – 29.85 = 0.08 hot dogs
7. 0.34 hot dogs
8. 0.86 hot dogs
9. 7.68 hot dogs
10. Opportunity costs are increasing.
11. Specialized resources are more suitable to some productive applications than others. As butter is more intensively produced, we begin employing resources in butter production that are perhaps better suited in producing hot dogs. This is what is referred to as increasing opportunity costs.

5. (Optional calculus exercise). We now know that the concavity of the production possibilities curve implies increasing opportunity costs of production. Note that the measurement of these opportunity costs is obtained by calculating the slope of the curve at any given point. This will illustrate that the slope of a nonlinear function can be measured by drawing a line tangent to the curve at a specific point. It will also remind students that the slope of a nonlinear function varies from one point to the next. Ask your students to calculate the slope of the first figure that they have drawn in Activity 7.1 at various points along the curve (this is Visual 7.3).

Answer: Note that the slope of the function is {change in $Q_{hot\ dogs}$/change in Q_{butter}} which can be approximated by taking the first derivative $dQ_{hot\ dogs}/dQ_{butter}$. To obtain this first derivative solve the production possibilities equation for $Q_{hotdogs}$ as follows:

$$Q^2_{hot\ dogs} = 900 - Q^2_{butter}$$
$$Q_{hot\ dogs} = (900 - Q^2_{butter})^{1/2}$$

and differentiate with respect to Q_{butter}. This yields:

$$dQ_{hot\ dogs}/dQ_{butter} = \{1/2 \cdot (900 - Q^2_{butter})^{-1/2}\} \cdot (-2Q_{butter})$$
$$= -Q_{butter}/(900 - Q^2_{butter})^{1/2}$$

When $Q_{butter} = 1$, the slope is $-1/(899)^{1/2}$
When $Q_{butter} = 2$, the slope is $-2/(896)^{1/2}$
When $Q_{butter} = 3$, the slope is $-3/(891)^{1/2}$
When $Q_{butter} = 17$, the slope is $-17/(611)^{1/2}$

and so on. It is clear that the (absolute value of the) slope is increasing as the quantity of butter produced increases. This is a reflection of the real world notion of increasing opportunity costs.

Extension Activities:

1. Have the students consider what would happen to the production possibilities curve if a new technology was developed (such as a new process for mass producing hot dogs or a new bovine-injected hormone treatment that increases the amount of milk produced by each cow) that affected Creeperland's ability to produce only hot dogs or only butter. What would this do to the production possibilities curve?

◆ Answer: It would rotate outward (increase the radius) for one good only. The intercept term of the good whose production was unaffected by the technological advance would remain fixed. But the intercept of the good whose production was changing would increase.

What would this do to the size of the feasibility set?

◆ Answer: It would increase it. It would now take fewer resources to produce a given quantity of the good for which the technological advance has occurred.

How can this be shown in the equation?

◆ Answer: If the technological advance were in hot dog production, this could be shown by altering the original equation to, say, $\frac{1}{3} Q^2_{hot\ dogs} + Q^2_{butter} = 900$. Note that when $Q_{hot\ dogs} = 0$, the maximum production of butter is 30—the technology has not affected the ability to produce butter. But when $Q_{butter} = 0$, the new vertical intercept is approximately 52. This has the effect of converting the circle into an ellipse).

2. Have the students consider what happens to a country's production possibilities curve when it experiences a war on its soil (examples include western Europe and Japan in WWII, Korea, and Vietnam). Have them consider what this does to the equation of the production possibilities curve as well as how this is shown graphically.

◆ Answer: This has the effect of shifting the curve inward (reducing the radius). This can be shown by altering the equation to, say, $Q^2_{hot\ dogs} + Q^2_{butter} = 400$. This occurs because a war destroys valuable productive resources—especially labor and capital—and perhaps slows technological progress.

3. Ask students what would be implied if the production possibilities curve were concave up.

◆ Answer: Decreasing opportunity costs of production—not likely to happen.

What would be implied if the production possibilities curve was a straight line?

◆ Answer: Constant opportunity costs of production. This might happen in a country that only produced left shoes and right shoes—where resources were not specialized and thus are not favorably suited to one productive application over another.

4. (For calculus students) Have the students determine the concavity of the production possibilities function by calculating the second derivative from the function in part (5) of the procedures above.

◆ The second derivative = $-Q^2_{butter}(900 - Q^2_{butter})^{-3/2} - (900 - Q^2_{butter})^{-1/2}$

VISUAL 7.1 ▲ Warm-Up

1. On the coordinate axes above sketch the graph of the ellipse $\frac{x^2}{9} + \frac{y^2}{36} = 1$

2. On the coordinate axes above sketch the graph of a circle with center at the origin and radius of 10 units.

3. Write the general equation of a circle.

4. Write the equation of the circle in question 2 above.

VISUAL 7.1 (continued)

5. Solve for y in the equation in the previous question.

6. If x and y cannot be negative values, what part of the circle is being considered?

7. What is the equation and domain for the part of the circle considered in question number 6?

8. When x decreases what happens to the value of y in the equation of question 7? What happens when x increases? (Verify your conclusion by looking at the circle.)

9. We say x and y are (directly inversely) related to each other. This relationship results in a (positively negatively) sloped curve. (Circle the correct answers).

10. Optional calculus: Find the 1st and 2nd derivatives of the function found in answer 7.

11. Optional calculus: From the first derivative above, what can be determined about the slope of the graph where $0 < x < 10$?

12. Optional calculus: From the second derivative above, what can be determined about the concavity of the graph where $0 < x < 10$?

13. Optional calculus: Calculate the slope of the curve at $x = 1$, 5, and 9.

14. For which of these values of x is the absolute value of the slope greatest? What does this indicate?

VISUAL 7.2

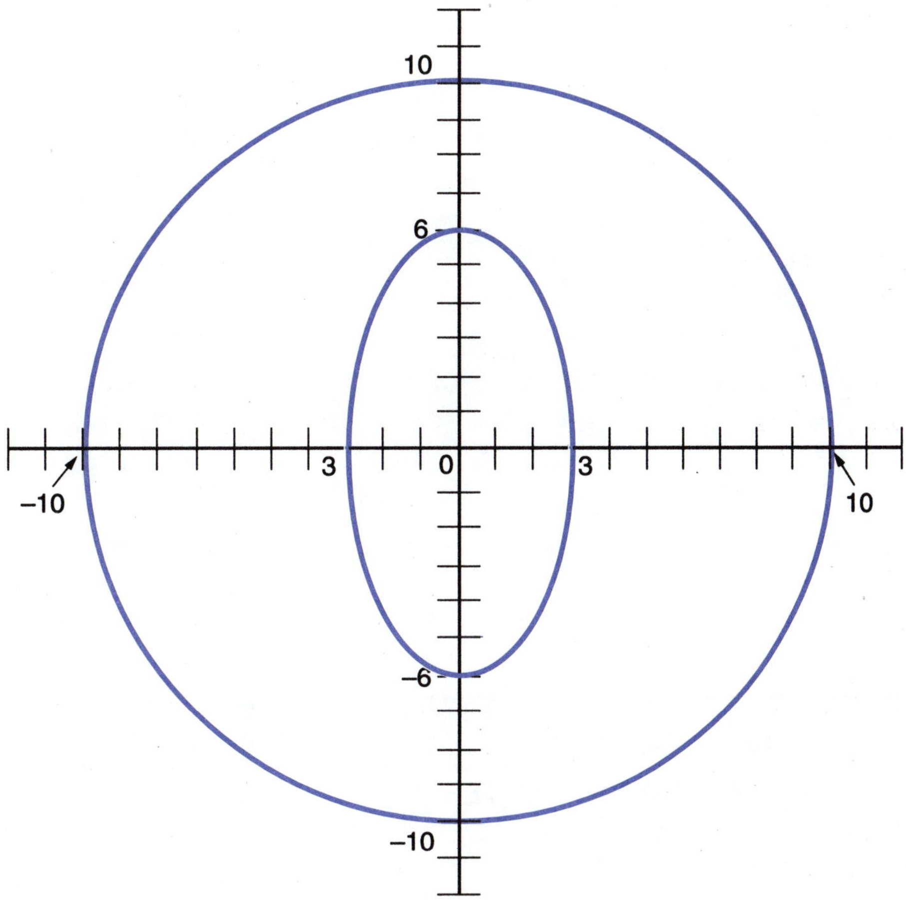

VISUAL 7.3

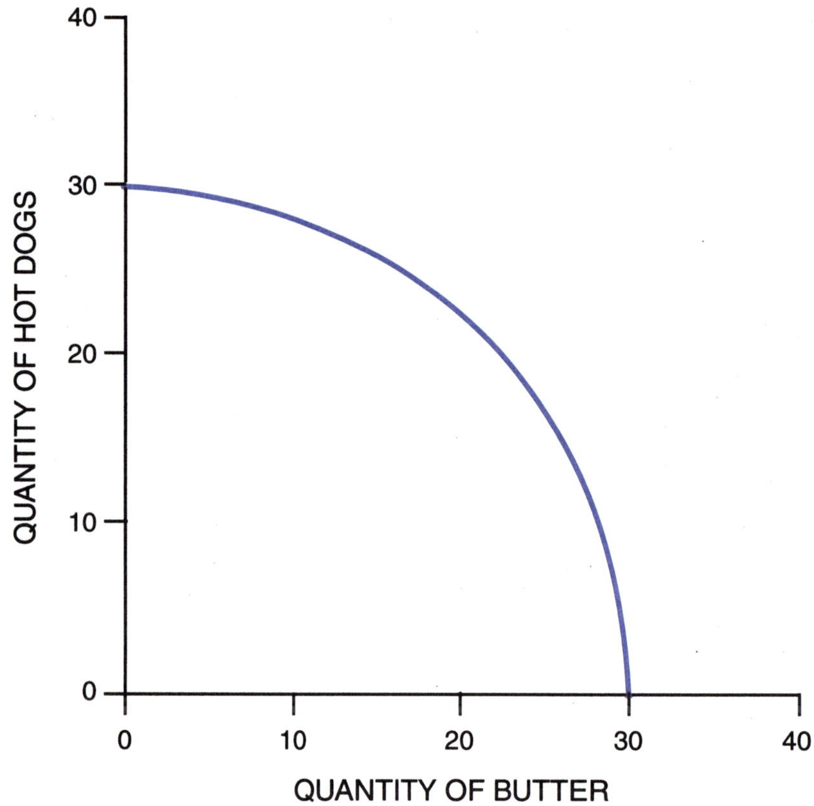
40
30
20
10
0
QUANTITY OF HOT DOGS
0
10
20
30
40
QUANTITY OF BUTTER

VISUAL 7.4

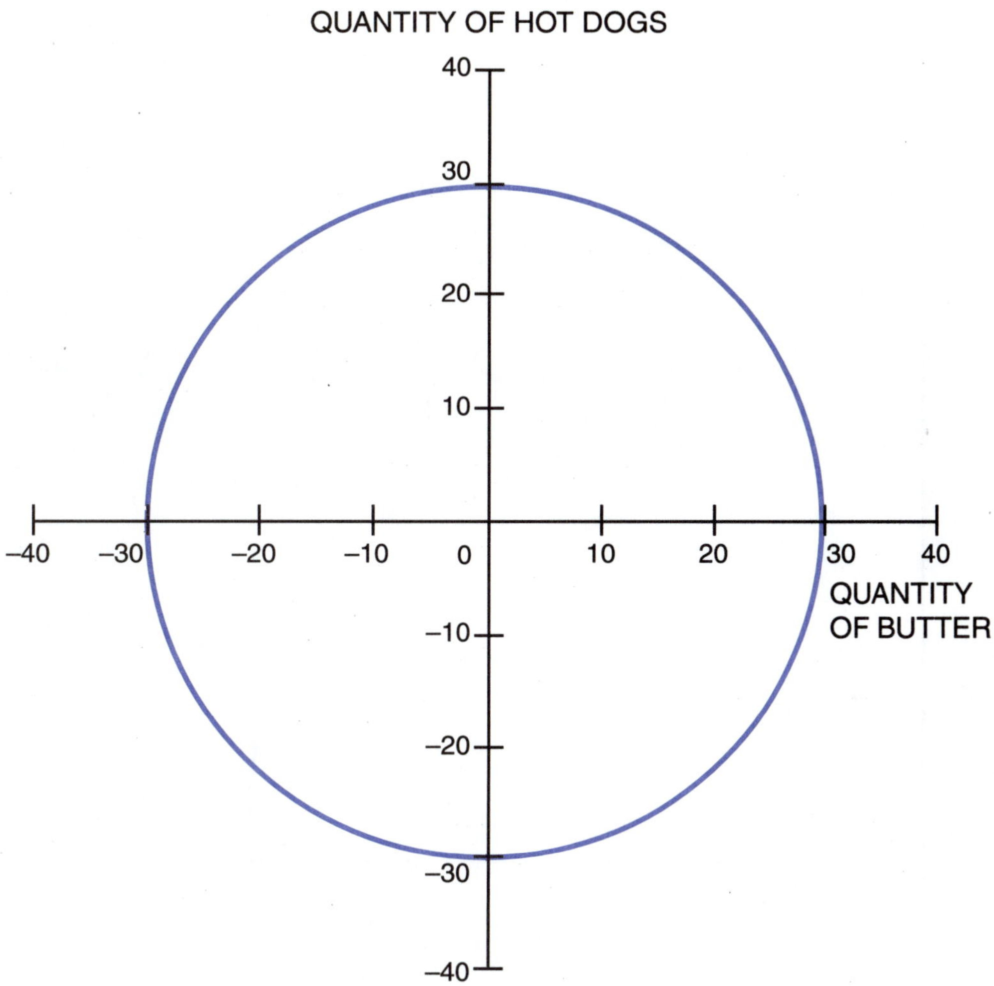

QUANTITY OF HOT DOGS
40
30
20
10
–10
–20
–30
–40
–40
–30
–20
–10
0
10
20
30
40
QUANTITY OF BUTTER

VISUAL 7.5

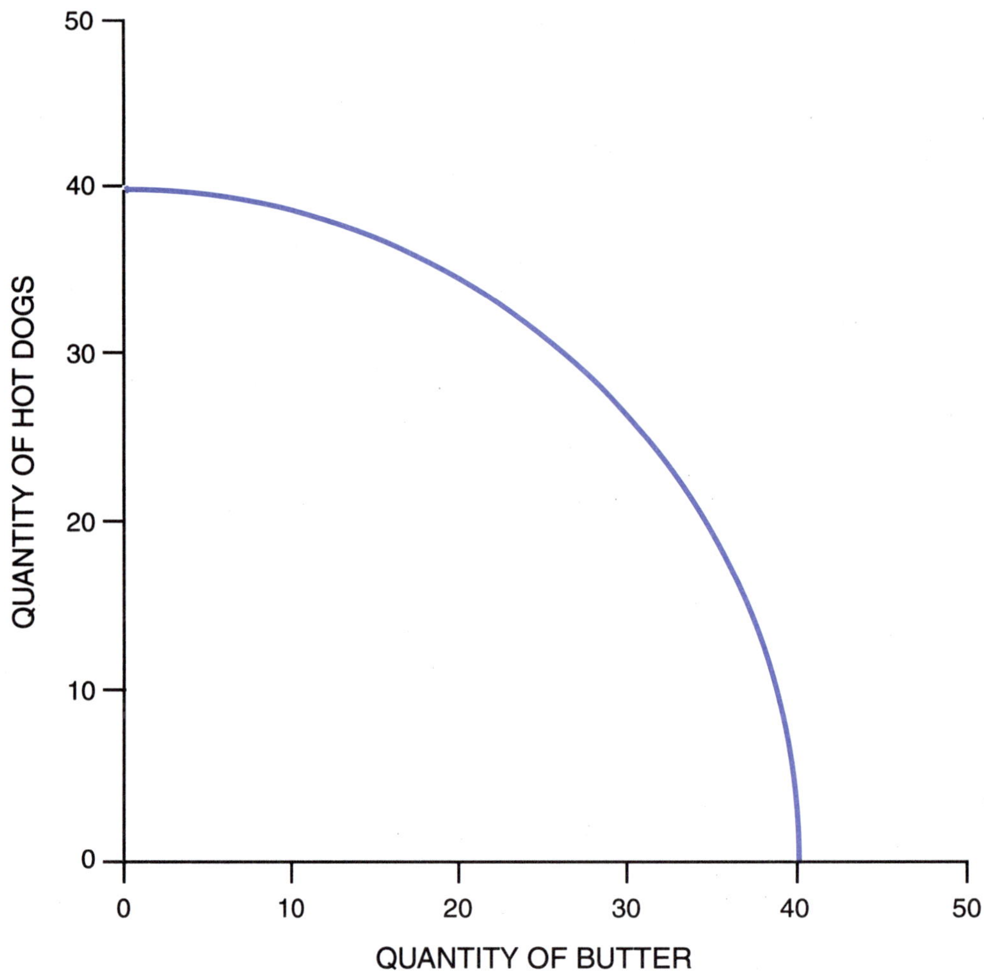

50
40
30
20
10
0
QUANTITY OF HOT DOGS
0
10
20
30
40
50
QUANTITY OF BUTTER

ACTIVITY 7.1 ▲ The Production Possibilities Curve

Part I

The country of Creeperland can only produce two goods—hot dogs and butter. Creeperland's finance minister is interested in the production potential of the country, and has asked you to consider the maximum quantity of these two goods that can be produced assuming the amount of productive resources is unchanged and the state of technological progress is fixed. He has asked the country's best mathematician to devise the formula for Creeperland's production potential. The result is:

$$Q^2_{\text{hot dogs}} + Q^2_{\text{butter}} = 900$$

where $Q_{\text{hot dogs}}$ is the quantity of hot dogs produced and Q_{butter} is the quantity of butter produced.

1. Use the graph below to graph this equation (use $Q_{\text{hot dogs}}$ on the vertical axis and Q_{butter} on the horizontal axis) in the first quadrant only.

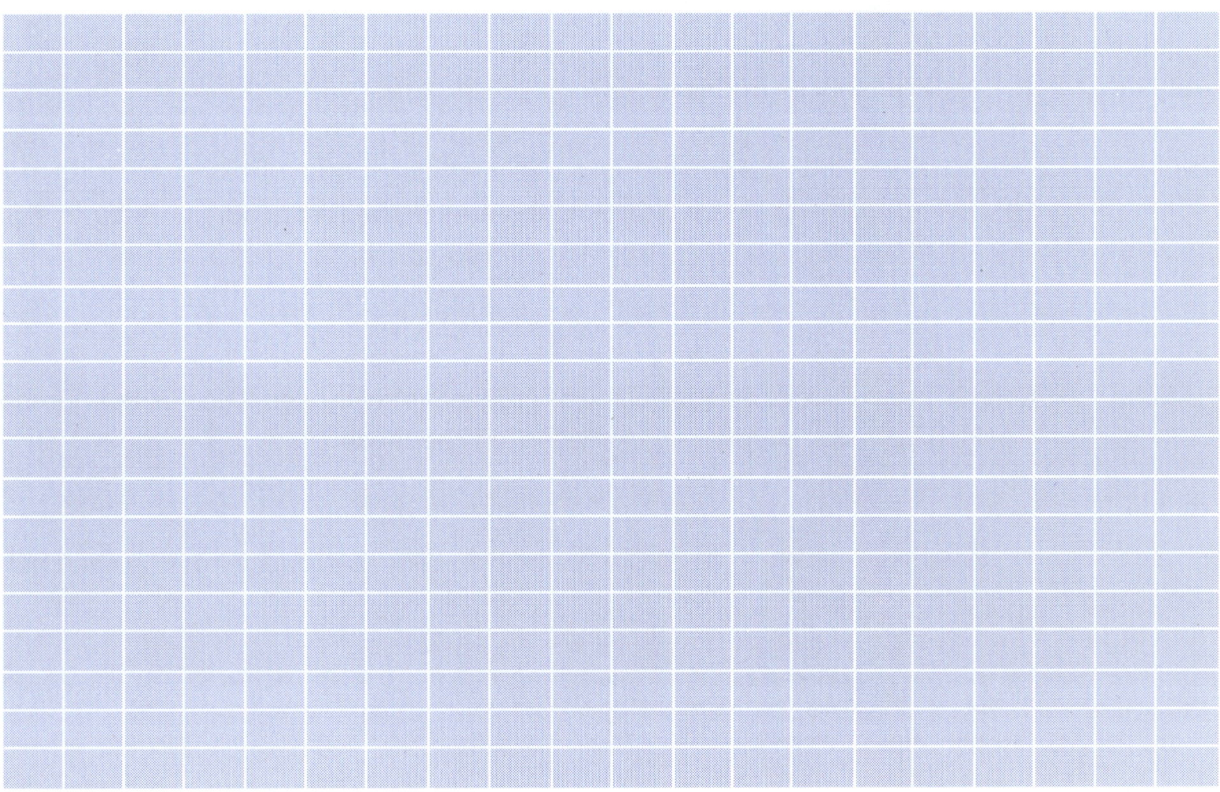

2. Why is your graph confined to the first quadrant?

3. What is the value of the vertical intercept?

4. What is the value of the horizontal intercept?

5. Is this a linear or a nonlinear function?

6. If nonlinear, is it concave down or up?

7. Draw this function in all four quadrants.

8. What does this graph look like?

9. Calculate the area of this figure?

10. Use this information to determine the area in the first quadrant under this curve.

Part II

Suppose the quantity and/or quality of productive resources (such as the number of workers, machinery, and/or equipment) increases in Creeperland.

11. What is this likely to do to Creeperland's ability to produce hot dogs and butter?

12. How would this be shown graphically?

13. How can you alter the equation of the production possibilities curve to represent this growth of resources?

Graph the following function on the paper provided:

$$Q^2_{\text{hot dogs}} + Q^2_{\text{butter}} = 1600$$

14. What does this new graph represent?

15. How has the increase in the quantity and/or quality of productive resources affected Creeperland's feasibility set?

16. Calculate the size of the area under the new production possibilities curve.

17. By what percentage has the area changed as a result of the increase in resources?

18. The point 30 units of butter and 25 hot dogs was not feasible prior to economic growth in Creeperland. Is it now feasible?

19. Is this point efficient? Why or why not?

ACTIVITY 7.2 ▲ Examining the Concavity of the Production Possibilities Curve

Refer to the first graph you drew in Activity 7.1 to help you in completing this activity.

Recall that the equation for this graph is:

$$Q^2_{\text{hot dogs}} + Q^2_{\text{butter}} = 900$$

1. Note the value of the vertical and horizontal intercepts.

2. Suppose Creeperland is producing on its production possibilities curve and has decided to produce 0 units of butter. Use the formula above to calculate the number of hot dogs Creeperland must be producing.

3. Use the equation above to calculate the quantity of hot dogs produced when 1 unit of butter is produced. That is, calculate $Q_{\text{hot dogs}}$ when $Q_{\text{butter}} = 1$. What result do you obtain?

4. Now subtract this number of hot dogs from the number you obtained in question number 2. What number do you get?

This is the amount of hot dog production that was forgone as a result of producing the first unit of butter. This is what economists call the **opportunity cost** of the first unit of butter production. It is called this because the opportunity cost refers to the highest valued alternative that is forgone as a result of making a choice. In this case, Creeperland chose to produce the first unit of butter and therefore gave up 0.02 units of hot dog production. This can also be seen by looking at your first graph from Activity 7.1.

5. What is the opportunity cost of the 2nd unit of butter production? (Hint: compare the number of hot dogs produced when $Q_{\text{butter}} = 2$ to the number of hot dogs produced at $Q_{\text{butter}} = 1$).

6. What is the opportunity cost of the 3rd unit of butter production?

7. What is the opportunity cost of the 10th unit of butter production?
(Hint: you must first calculate the quantity of hot dogs produced at $Q_{butter} = 9$).

8. What is the opportunity cost of the 20th unit of butter production?

9. Finally, what is the opportunity cost of the 30th unit of butter production?

10. What do you observe happening to the opportunity cost of additional units of butter production as more and more units are produced?

11. How might you explain this?

Lesson 8

The Mathematics of Nonlinear Economic Shapes: The Cubic Cost Function

Mathematics Focus:

Algebra II, Calculus

Math Prerequisites:

Prior to using this lesson, students should be able to:

- Use a graphing calculator to graph and interpret a function
- Evaluate and graph cubic and quadratic functions
- (Calculus students) calculate, graph, and interpret the first and second derivatives of a cubic equation

Lesson Objectives:

To apply prerequisite mathematics concepts and processes to a representative firm's cost function to:

- Explain the properties of the cost function by analyzing the graph
- Explain that total cost equals the sum of fixed and variable costs
- Explain the concept of marginal cost and how it is calculated from the total cost function
- Explain the law of diminishing marginal returns

Overview of Mathematics and Economics:

Careful control of total cost is essential for a firm if it wishes to maximize profits. While many firm managers prefer to concentrate on the more glamorous activity of marketing and selling the company's product, many companies have gone bankrupt because of a lack of attention paid to the cost side of the profit-loss statement. In a world or scarcity, it is necessary for firms to economize on their use of precious productive resources. For a given level of production, the reward for success in containing costs in the marketplace is a profit. The penalty for failing to recognize the importance of limiting costs is an economic loss that could lead to bankruptcy.

Economists have reason to believe that the best way to describe the economic behavior of a firm's costs is to use a cubic cost function. A properly specified cost function yields the result that business costs initially increase at a decreasing rate, but then rise at an increasing rate. This functional form captures the important notion that *marginal costs*, the addition to total costs that arise from producing an additional unit of output, first

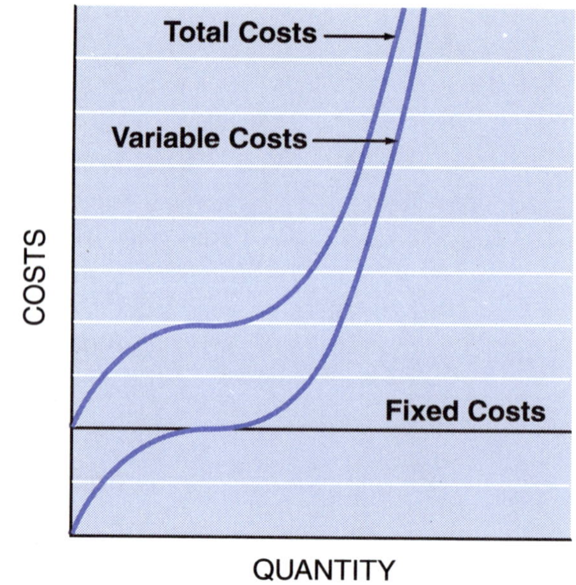

decrease and then increase. Because each additional unit produced requires the use of productive resources (such as workers, machines, materials, energy, etc.) that have a cost, marginal costs are always positive. Those costs that vary with the level of output are called variable costs. In most cases, these include the cost of labor, materials, energy, etc. Firms also face *fixed costs*. These are the costs that do not vary with the level of output. In the short run, the firm faces these fixed costs even when it is not producing any good or service. (Note that for most firms the short run is no longer than a year or two.) Examples of fixed costs include rent, property taxes, and licensing fees. Together, fixed plus variable costs comprise a firm's total costs. When these total costs divided by the firm's level of output (also know as *average total costs*) are kept to a minimum, a firm is said to be achieving productive efficiency by minimizing the per unit costs of production.

That marginal costs are positive and eventually increase when firms expand production is critical to understand the *law of diminishing returns*. This economic "law" basically states that as long as variable resources are combined with some fixed factor of production to produce output, at some point, additional factors must make a lesser contribution to output than did the previous variable factor. Put differently, as long as some productive factors are fixed, it must eventually get more and more costly to obtain additional units of production. That is, marginal costs must eventually increase. What are the mathematical implications

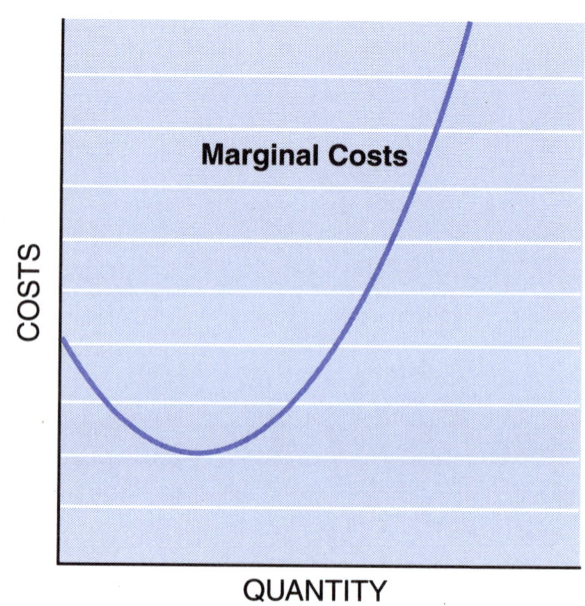

of these observations? Since the slope of a nonlinear function at any point is equal to the slope of a line drawn tangent to the curve at that point, the slope varies along the curve. This slope is approximated by the first derivative of the total cost function—an equation that equals marginal cost. Since the firm's total cost curve is a cubic function, an inflection point can be calculated where the second derivative of the function switches from negative to positive. This is a point at which marginal costs reach a minimum.

Mathematics and Economics Terms:

- Cubic function
- First derivative
- Fixed cost
- Inflection point
- Law of diminishing marginal returns
- Marginal cost
- Quadratic function
- Second derivative
- Total cost
- Variable Cost

Materials:

- Overhead transparencies of Visuals 8.1 through 8.10. Visual 8.11 for calculus classes only.
- Copies of Activities 8.1 and 8.2 for each student
- Copies of Activity 8.3 for each calculus student
- Copies of Activity 8.4 for use as a homework activity
- Graphing calculators for students
- Optional graphing calculator for overhead
- Straight edge

Estimated Time:

80–100 minutes

Procedures:

Part I: For Algebra II and Calculus Students

1. Warm-Up Activity: Show Visual 8.1 and distribute a copy of this visual to every student. Have students answer the questions in Visual 8.1. In questions 1 and 2, assist the students with the graphing calculator. Go over the answers with the class.

The answers follow:

1. Show Visual 8.2.
2. Show Visual 8.3.The equation of the first derivative is $f'(x) = 99x^2 - 500x + 700$.

3. The second function describes the slope of the first function. Draw tangent lines on an overhead sketch to see that the slope is positive, gets smaller and smaller, reaches zero, becomes positive and continues to increase as the f(x) graph becomes steeper.
4. (Give Algebra II students the second derivative: $f''(x) = 198x - 500$.) The answer is $f''(x) = 198x - 500$; $f''(x) = 0$ when $x = 2.5252...$
5. When $x = 2.5252...$ f(x) is changing from a 'concave down function' to a 'concave up function.' Hence $f'(x)$ has its smallest value at $x = 2.5252$. The second derivative is zero when the slope of the first derivative is zero which is at the vertex of the quadratic function $f'(x)$.
6. Show Visual 8.4.
7. $f'(0) = 700$; $f'(1) = 299$; $f'(2.5252...) = 68.69$; $f'(3) = 91$
8. The negative slope means that the rate of change of f(x) is decreasing.

2. Distribute a copy of Activity 8.1. Tell the students, "Today we are going to take a trip with Anna and Milton as it is described on this activity sheet." Remind them that Anna and Milton will be traveling only in the first quadrant.

■ **COMMENT** This is a simple attempt to get students to visualize what a cubic cost function looks like. This is a good time to reinforce the difference between linear and nonlinear relationships. It is also an excellent time to discuss the properties of an inflection point—the point at which the concavity of the graphed function changes. This point occurs between the fourth and fifth stages of the mountain climb.

3. Have the students complete the graph and answer the questions on the activity sheet and then discuss the questions. Visual 8.5 shows the graph that the students will develop. The answers follow:

◆

1. No. The graph of this function is not linear.
2. The graph looks somewhat like a mirror image of an 'S.'
3. The curvature changes between stage 4 and stage 5. This point of curvature change is known as an inflection point.
4. No. They did not find the pot of gold because there is no top on Cost Mountain—it keeps growing.

4. Distribute a copy of Activity 8.2 to each student. Tell the students that economists believe that a cubic function is a valid way to represent total costs faced by companies. This is the same shape of the curve Anna and Milton created. A cubic function of this type has many properties that are very important in economic theories.

5. Ask the students to answer the first question in Activity 8.2. Then ask the students to compare this vertical intercept with the vertical intercept for the graph in Activity 8.1.

Answer: The starting point in the graph for Activity 8.1 was 0. In Activity 8.2, the starting point (the vertical intercept) equals 100.

6. Have the students answer question #2. Tell them that the economic meaning of the vertical intercept in this application is the representation of the firm's *fixed* costs, those costs faced by the firm that do not vary with output and are present even when nothing is produced. Show Visual 8.6, the visual of the fixed cost, variable cost, and total cost graph as shown in the background material above. Fixed costs include items such as rent, licensing fees, and property taxes.

7. After the students have completed #3 and #4, note that total costs increase as output expands. This is because firms must hire more workers and purchase more equipment, machinery, materials, and energy in order to increase production. These costs, which vary with output, are known as *variable costs*. Visual 8.7 shows the total cost figures.

8. When the students have finished #4 of Activity 8.2, tell them that economists are usually quite interested in the behavior of *marginal costs*, the change in total costs when a producer moves from x units to x + 1 units of output. Understanding the behavior of these costs for each additional item produced is extremely important for a firm that is trying to calculate the appropriate amount of output to maximize profits.

9. Ask the students to complete the marginal cost column in Activity 8.2. The marginal cost of the first bike is calculated for them. Note that there is no marginal cost of 0 units of production, since it is unrealistic to produce –1 units. Have the students share their answers with the class. Visual 8.7 shows the marginal costs for the various quantities. Ask the students why they believe that the marginal costs increase after a point. Point out that this shows an economic law at work. It is the law of *diminishing marginal returns*. It occurs when variable resources are combined with some fixed factor of production (resource) to produce output. At some point, additional factors must make a lesser contribution to produce output. Put differently, as long as some productive factors are fixed, it must eventually get more and more costly to obtain additional units of production. That is, marginal costs must eventually increase.

10. Tell the students to graph the marginal cost curve as asked in item #7 of Activity 8.2. This is parabolic in shape, and it reaches a minimum between six and seven units of production. Also, note that marginal costs are always positive. That is, each additional unit of production adds to total cost. Visual 8.8 shows the graph.

11. Show Visual 8.9 and have the class read and discuss it. The example reinforces the principle of diminishing marginal returns.

12. Distribute Activity 8.4 and have the Algebra II students answer the first four questions as a homework exercise. The answers are provided in Part II below. Note that calculus students will receive this activity after completing Activity 8.3.

Part II for calculus students who have completed Part I

1. Indicate to the class that all the economic concepts discussed in the first part of this lesson can be captured by applying calculus to the cubic cost function. Distribute Activity 8.3 to each student and work through the activity with the class.

2. Ask the students to complete the first three questions.

The answers are:

1. $TC' = \frac{3}{2}Q^2 - 18Q + 200$.
2. It is the function that describes the slope of the total cost curve at any particular point. The slope varies along the total cost curve and therefore this is a nonlinear relationship.
3. The first derivative represents the marginal cost of producing an additional unit of output. It is perhaps easiest to think of this as the instantaneous change in total cost divided by the change in output. Note that this is the definition of marginal cost.
4. The graphs are essentially the same.

3. When the students finish their graph, show Visual 8.10 which is the graph of the derivative of the total cost function (marginal cost).

■ **COMMENT** You may wish to note that the values of the marginal cost calculations are slightly different here because calculus techniques implicitly consider the change in output (that appears in the denominator of the MC function) to be infinitesimally small around the point of output that is being evaluated. This makes the slope calculation more precise than that which was used to draw the marginal cost curve in Activity 8.2.

4. Have the students complete the remainder of the questions for Activity 8.3. Encourage a discussion of answers. The rest of the answers include:

5. $TC'' = 3Q - 18$; $0 = 3Q - 18$; $Q = 6$.
6. It is the point at which marginal costs start to increase or said differently, diminishing marginal returns set in.
7. The sign of the second derivative changes.
8. The first derivative is the function which describes the slope of the total cost curve at any given point on the curve. Thus, the first derivative represents marginal costs. The second derivative indicates the point at which the slope of the total cost function switches from decreasing to increasing. This is the point at which marginal cost reaches a minimum and starts to increase. Economists say the inflection point on the cost curve is where diminishing marginal returns begin.

COMMENT The inflection point of the total cost curve occurs when marginal cost begins to rise. This is at six units of bike production. Ask the students to think of this as the point at which the total cost of producing bikes begins increasing at an accelerating rate. To calculate where an inflection point occurs on a total cost curve, compute the second derivative of the total cost curve and set it equal to 0. A different way of thinking of this is to recognize that the second derivative of the total cost function is the first derivative of the marginal cost function. Therefore, the marginal cost curve reaches a point of extrema where the derivative of marginal cost is zero. The derivative or slope of marginal cost = $3Q - 18$. This function is zero at $Q = 6$, which confirms that this is a point of extrema. To confirm that this is a minimum point, students can compute the second derivative of the marginal cost curve (which is the third derivative of the total cost function with respect to Q). Since the second derivative of the marginal cost curve is greater than zero at the point of extrema, this verifies that the marginal cost curve is concave up and the point of extrema is a minimum point. This is also the point at which diminishing marginal returns set in. This is left for your students as an extension exercise. Finally, note that the sign of the second derivative of the total cost function changes from negative to positive at the inflection point. The concavity of the cost function changes at that point.

5. Distribute a copy of Activity 8.4 for completion as a homework review assignment.

The answers are as follows:

1. See Visual 8.11.
2. Marginal cost is the additional cost associated with producing one additional unit of output. Marginal cost begins to rise after its minimum at $Q = 3$ and $Q = 4$ and continues to rise thereafter.
3. Fixed cost equals $625.

4. Answers will vary. Fixed cost includes rent, property taxes, fees, licenses, permits, etc. Fixed costs only apply to the short run.

The remaining questions are for calculus students

5. $TC' = 3Q^2 - 18Q + 196$ $TC'' = 6Q - 18$
6. Marginal costs start to rise at the point where the second derivative of the total cost curve is zero. $TC'' = 6Q - 18 = 0$ when $6Q = 18$ which means $Q = 3$. Check graphs of first and second derivatives on a graphing calculator with window x[–20, 30] and y[–3000,3300].

Extension Activities:

1. The average total cost of output is computed at any given level of Q, quantity produced, by dividing total cost by quantity produced. Therefore, the average total cost (ATC) at Q = 1 bike in Activity 8.2 equals $291.50, equals $234 at Q = 2 bikes ($468/2), is $210.83 at Q = 3 bikes (632.5/3), and so on. Have the students calculate average total cost for all levels of bike production from Q = 1 through Q =10. Ask them to plot this function on the same graph as the marginal cost curve in Activity 8.2. What do they notice is the relationship between marginal cost and average total cost?

Answer: Marginal cost equals average total cost at the minimum point of average total cost. When marginal cost < average total cost, average total cost is falling, and when marginal cost > average total cost, average total cost is rising. Why is this? Because if each additional unit is adding more to total cost than the previous average, it must be pulling up the average. That is, when marginal cost > average total cost, average total cost must be rising. Similar reasoning applies when marginal cost < average total cost. When the addition to total cost is less than the previous average, it must be pulling down the average total cost. This corresponds to average total cost falling. It follows that marginal cost = average total cost $_{min.}$ Intuitively, the relationship between average total cost and marginal cost can be thought of as follows: Suppose you were to calculate the numerical average score for your class on a test. Suppose it equals 70—this is equivalent to average total cost. Now suppose you were to add a grade of 90 to that average—think of this as marginal cost, which is equivalent to marginal cost > average total cost, which increases the average. Similar reasoning suggests that adding a grade of 50 would lower the average total cost. These results can also be shown by using calculus to determine the point at which average total cost reaches a minimum.

2. Suppose you are told that marginal cost is constant at $100. What must this imply about the total cost function?

Answer: It must be an upward sloping linear function with slope equal to 100. There is no point of diminishing returns in this function. An example of a total cost function for which marginal costs are constant at $100 is TC = 100Q + 100, although there are an infinite number of other specifications that can be obtained by varying the fixed cost—or vertical intercept—term.

3. In Activity 8.3, prove that the first derivative of the marginal cost function is zero at Q = 6.

◆ Answer: Set $MC'(Q) = 3Q - 18$ to 0. This yields Q = 6. This is a minimum point since the second derivative of marginal cost is positive ($MC''(Q) = 3$) indicating a function that is concave up.

4. Blunders in Economics: Suppose you were given the following total cost curve:

$$TC = Q^3 - 30Q^2 + 10Q + 100.$$

Show that this equation for total cost yields results that are inconsistent with observations from the real world. Look for errors in what you know to be realistic expectations for marginal cost.

◆ Answer: If we were to write a total cost function in general terms as $TC = aQ^3 + bQ^2 + cQ + d$, then the general parameter restrictions that must be observed in order for this cost function to be well-behaved are a, c, d > 0; b < 0; and $b^2 < 3ac$. Since this latter restriction is violated in this example, the total cost function is misspecified. This can be shown by calculating marginal cost = $TC'(Q) = 3Q^2 - 60Q + 10$. It is easy to show that there are values of Q for which marginal cost < 0, which is in violation of all that is known about the behavior of costs.

VISUAL 8.1 ▲ Warm-Up

1. Using your graphing calculator, graph the function

$$f(x) = 33x^3 - 250\,x^2 + 700x + 300.$$

Graph this function in the first quadrant viewing rectangle of [0, 10] [0, 3000].

2. In the same window find and graph the first derivative. Algebra II students will get this function from their teacher.

3. Explain how the second function relates to the first function.
(Algebra II students: Find a relationship by visually inspecting the graphs.)

4. Calculate the second derivative of f(x) and find the x value that makes it zero.
(Algebra II students: Get this function from your teacher.)

5. What is the meaning of the x value found in question 4 with respect to f(x) and f′(x)?

6. Sketch f(x) and f′(x) on the coordinate axes below. Use only the first quadrant.
Let each unit on the vertical axis represent 300.

Graph of Function f(x) and its 1st Derivative

VISUAL 8.1 (continued)

7. Calculate the slope of the curve f(x) by finding f′(0), f′(1), f′(2.5252. . .) and f′(3).

8. What is the meaning of the negative slope on the graph of f″(x) for 0 < x < 2.52? (Algebra II students: Recall that f′(x) is a function that describes the slope of f(x). Examine your graphs.)

VISUAL 8.2

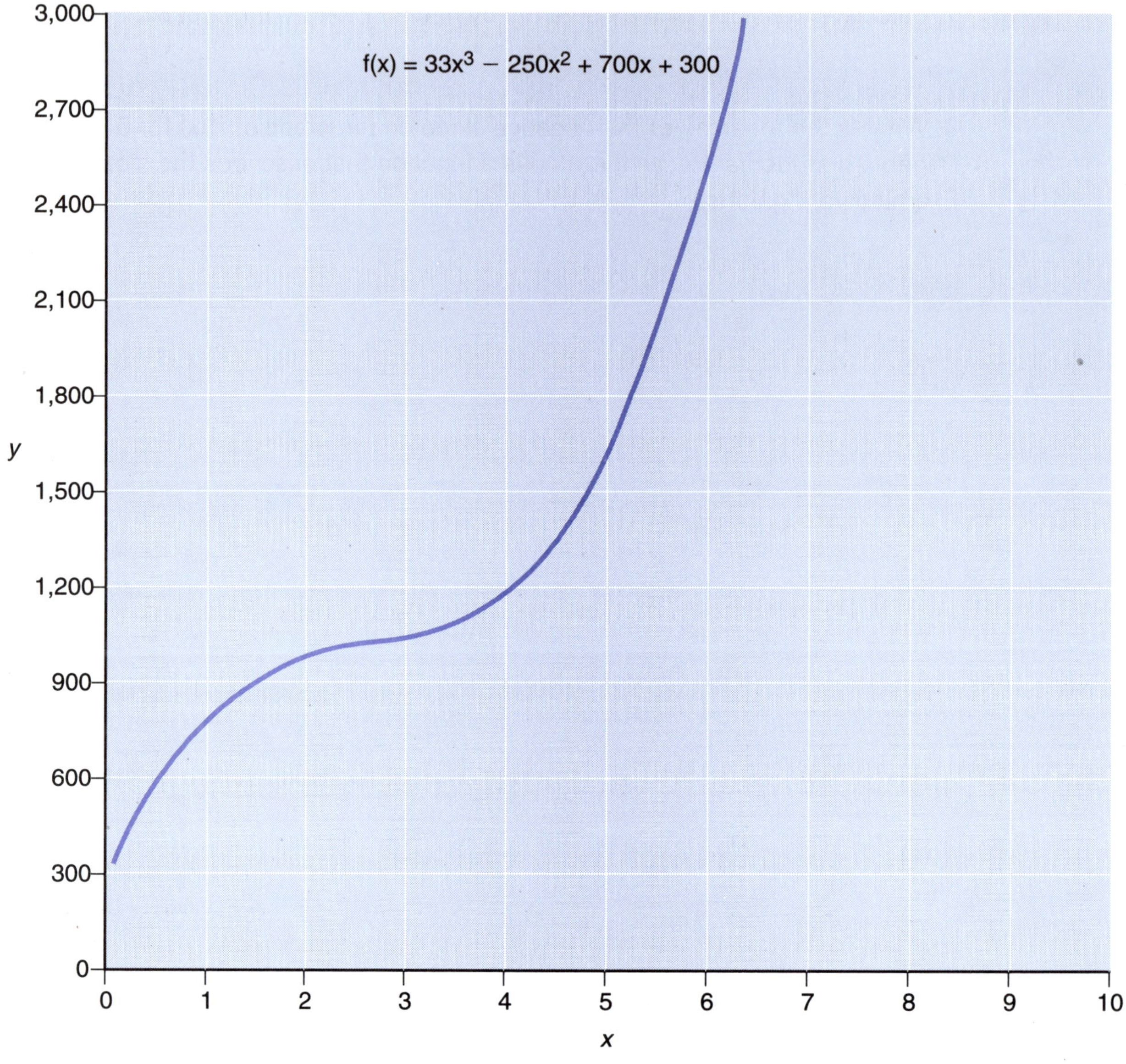
f(x) = 33x3 – 250x2 + 700x + 300
3,000
2,700
2,400
2,100
1,800
y
1,500
1,200
900
600
300
0
0 1 2 3 4 5 6 7 8 9 10
x

VISUAL 8.3

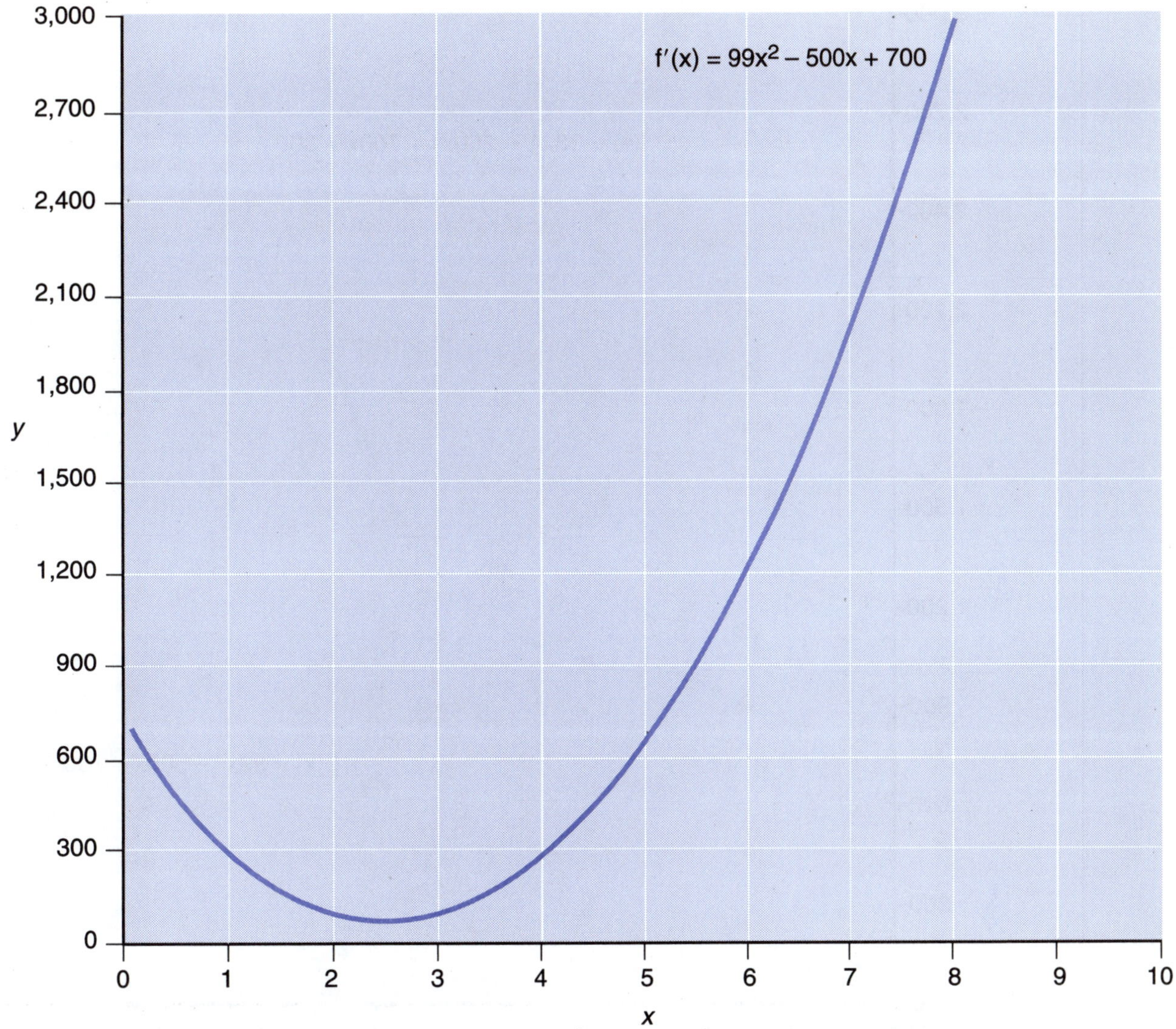

$f'(x) = 99x^2 - 500x + 700$
3,000
2,700
2,400
2,100
1,800
1,500
1,200
900
600
300
0
y
0
1
2
3
4
5
6
7
8
9
10
x

VISUAL 8.4

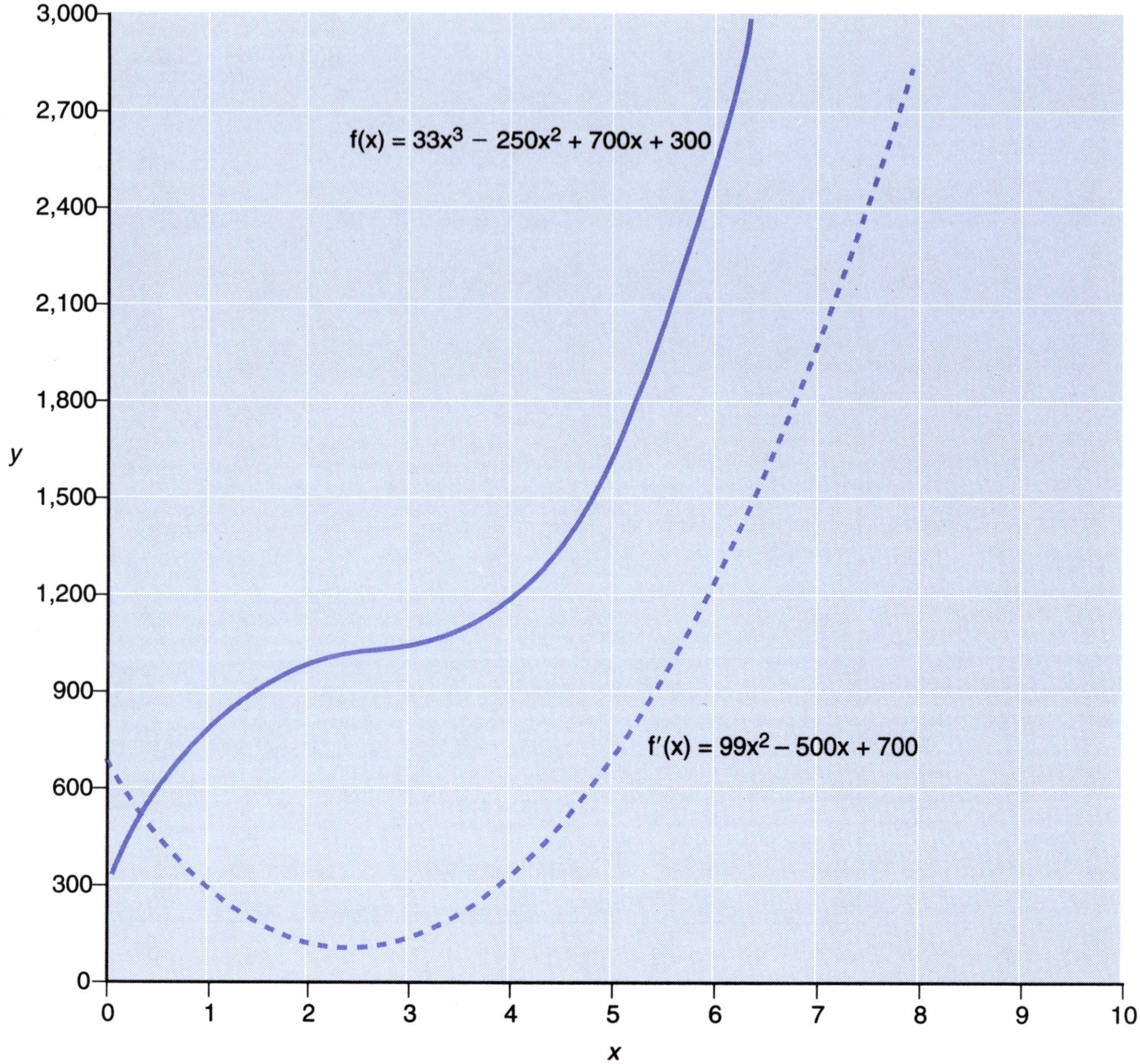
3,000
2,700
2,400
2,100
1,800
1,500
1,200
900
600
300
0
y
0
1
2
3
4
5
6
7
8
9
10
x
f(x) = 33x3 – 250x2 + 700x + 300
f′(x) = 99x2 – 500x + 700

VISUAL 8.5 ▲ The Climb Up Cost Mountain

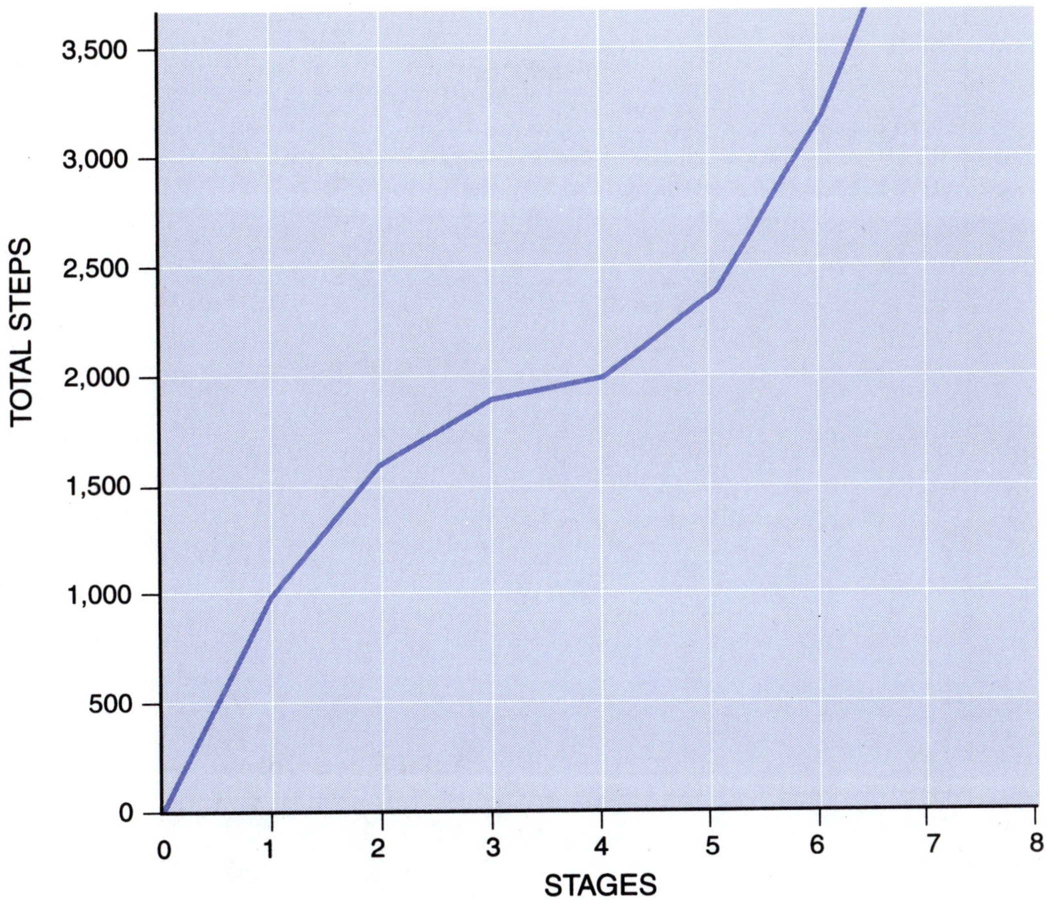

VISUAL 8.6

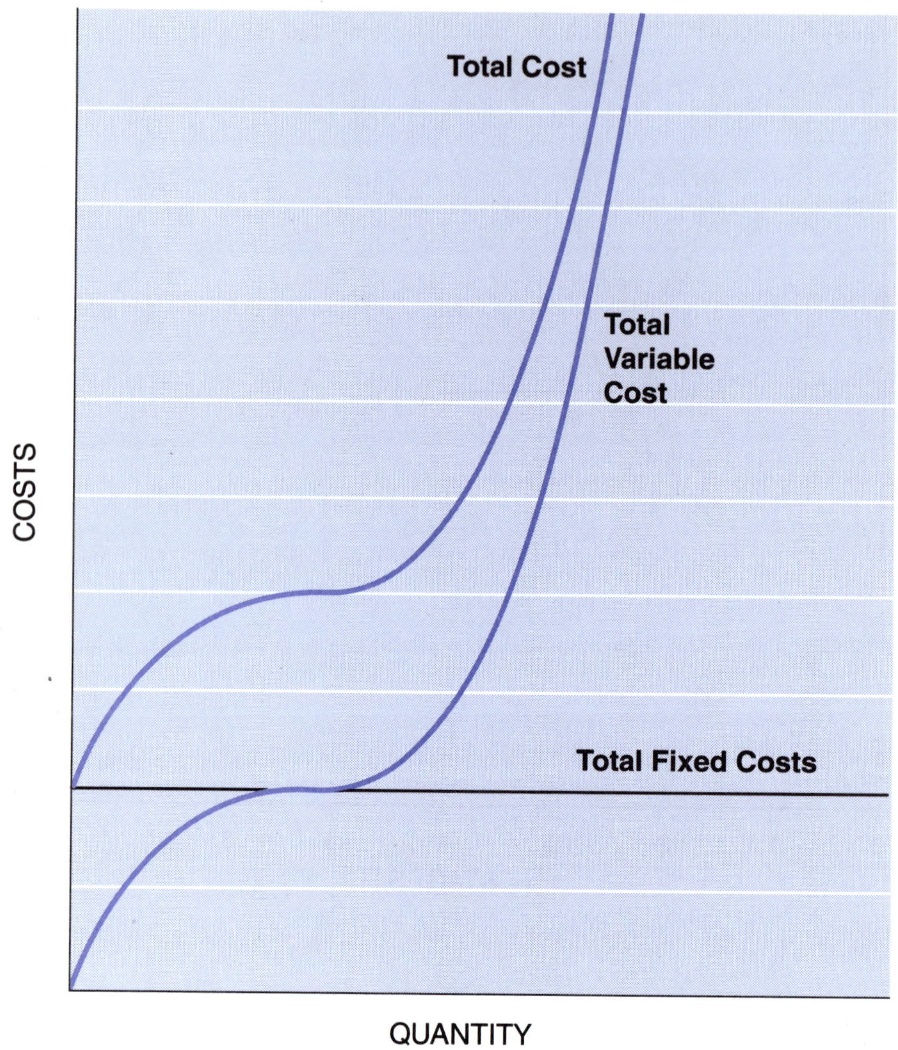
Total Cost
Total
Variable
Cost
Total Fixed Costs
COSTS
QUANTITY

VISUAL 8.7 ▲ Table Showing Total and Marginal Costs at Different Production Levels

Quantity of Bikes Made	Total Cost	Marginal Cost
0 bikes	$100.00	
1 bikes	$291.50	$191.50
2 bikes	$468.00	$176.50
3 bikes	$632.50	$164.50
4 bikes	$788.00	$155.50
5 bikes	$937.50	$149.50
6 bikes	$1084.00	$146.50
7 bikes	$1230.50	$146.50
8 bikes	$1380.00	$149.50
9 bikes	$1535.50	$155.50
10 bikes	$1700.00	$164.50

VISUAL 8.8 ▲ Marginal Cost

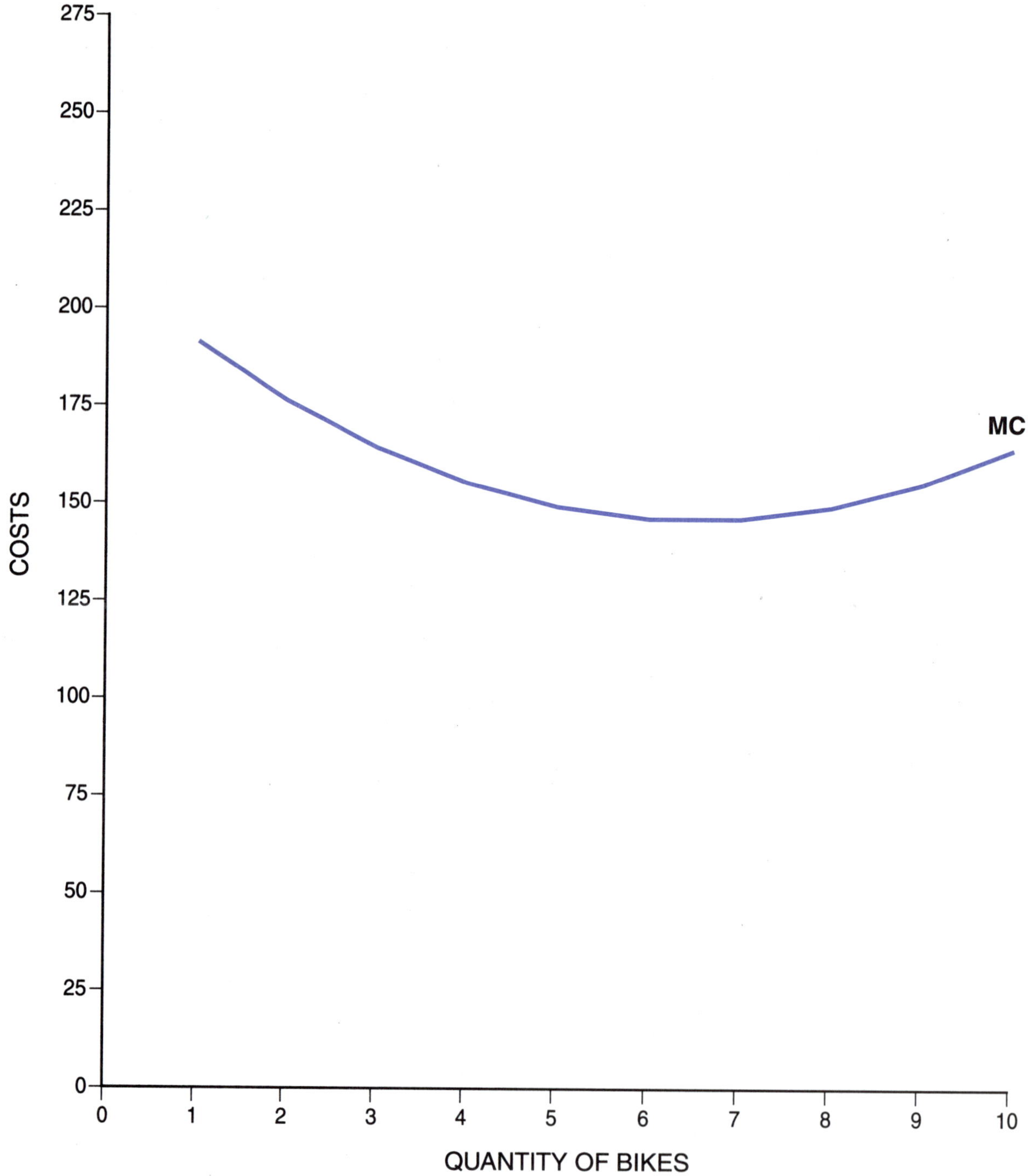

VISUAL 8.9 ▲ Growing the World's Food Supply in a Flowerpot

While it may be difficult to articulate, the law of diminishing marginal returns can be simply illustrated. The classic illustration involves agricultural output in a flowerpot.

Suppose you planted corn in a flowerpot. Here the fixed factor of production is the dirt that is used in the pot (economists refer to this as the productive resource called land). Suppose you were to add fertilizer to stimulate the production of corn in your flowerpot. When you add fertilizer, you observe that you produce more corn.

The first few units of fertilizer that are added may cause accelerating corn yields, but this cannot continue forever.

Why not?

If each additional unit of fertilizer contributed to a corn yield that was greater than the previous unit, you could produce the world's supply of corn in your flowerpot. You would just have to keep adding fertilizer. This, of course, is impossible because the soil will become somewhat sour after a certain amount of fertilizer has been applied. The acidity increases as more and more fertilizer is applied. Thus, the marginal return from each additional input starts to diminish.

The law of diminishing returns when applied to costs simply means that

marginal costs must eventually rise.

VISUAL 8.10 ▲ First Derivative of Total Cost Function

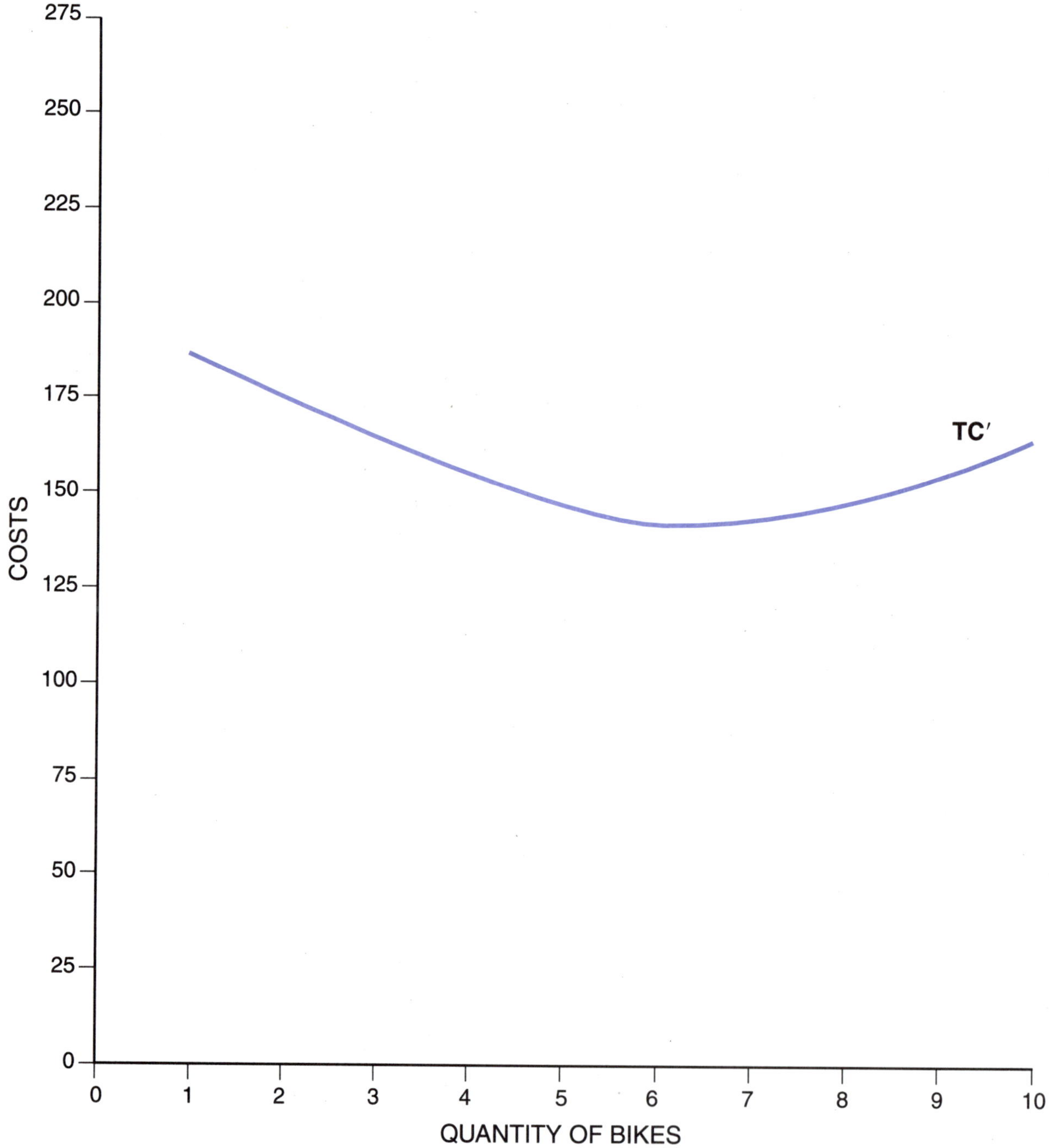

VISUAL 8.11 ▲ Completed Table for Activity 8.4

Quantity Q	Total Cost in Dollars	Marginal Cost in Dollars
0	625	—
1	813	188
2	989	176
3	1159	170
4	1329	170
5	1505	176

ACTIVITY 8.1 ▲ The Adventures of Anna and Milton

Anna and Milton are looking for a pot of gold at the top of Cost Mountain. Maynard told them that there is a pot of gold there. They are a little skeptical, but they realize that gold is valuable, so they are willing to commit a few days to this adventure. They hope to finish their journey in seven stages, one stage per day.

Use the following story and the enclosed graph paper to plot the points representing the path they take up the mountain. Note that the total number of steps taken is measured on the vertical axis and the number of miles traveled is measured on the horizontal axis. What path do they take? Do they find the pot of gold? Use the following entries from their trip diary to plot total steps taken and total miles covered on your graph paper.

Stage 1: A tough stage—we traveled one mile up steep terrain, taking 1000 small steps.

Stage 2: A little easier than the previous day, we still traveled one mile up fairly steep terrain. This time it took us only 600 steps. That's 1600 steps for both miles.

Stage 3: It feels like we are getting closer to the gold; we traveled one mile in only 300 steps today.

Stage 4: What a great day, only 100 steps to cover one mile. The terrain here was almost perfectly flat, allowing us to take a nearly perfect stride. We are sure that we are near the top of this mountain. We stopped at a scenic overlook to inspect the terrain we had covered over the three previous days. This scenic overlook had an interesting name. It was called Inflection Point. We think tomorrow will be the day that we find the pot of gold that Maynard told us about. We have now taken a total of 2000 steps in four days.

Stage 5: What a disappointment! It took us 400 steps to cover one mile today. The terrain started getting steeper. We hope this isn't a sign of things to come.

Stage 6: It is getting worse. We traveled one mile in 800 steps today over fairly steep terrain. This isn't looking good. We plan to give it one more day. We will have to turn back if things don't improve tomorrow.

Stage 7: We are forced to turn back. The mountain is the steepest we have seen, and there appears to be no end in sight. We used 1200 steps to travel one mile today. We have gone 4400 steps in seven days and have seen no indication that we are even close to the top of Cost Mountain. Maynard is going to have some explaining to do. We always were suspicious of him.

The Climb Up Cost Mountain

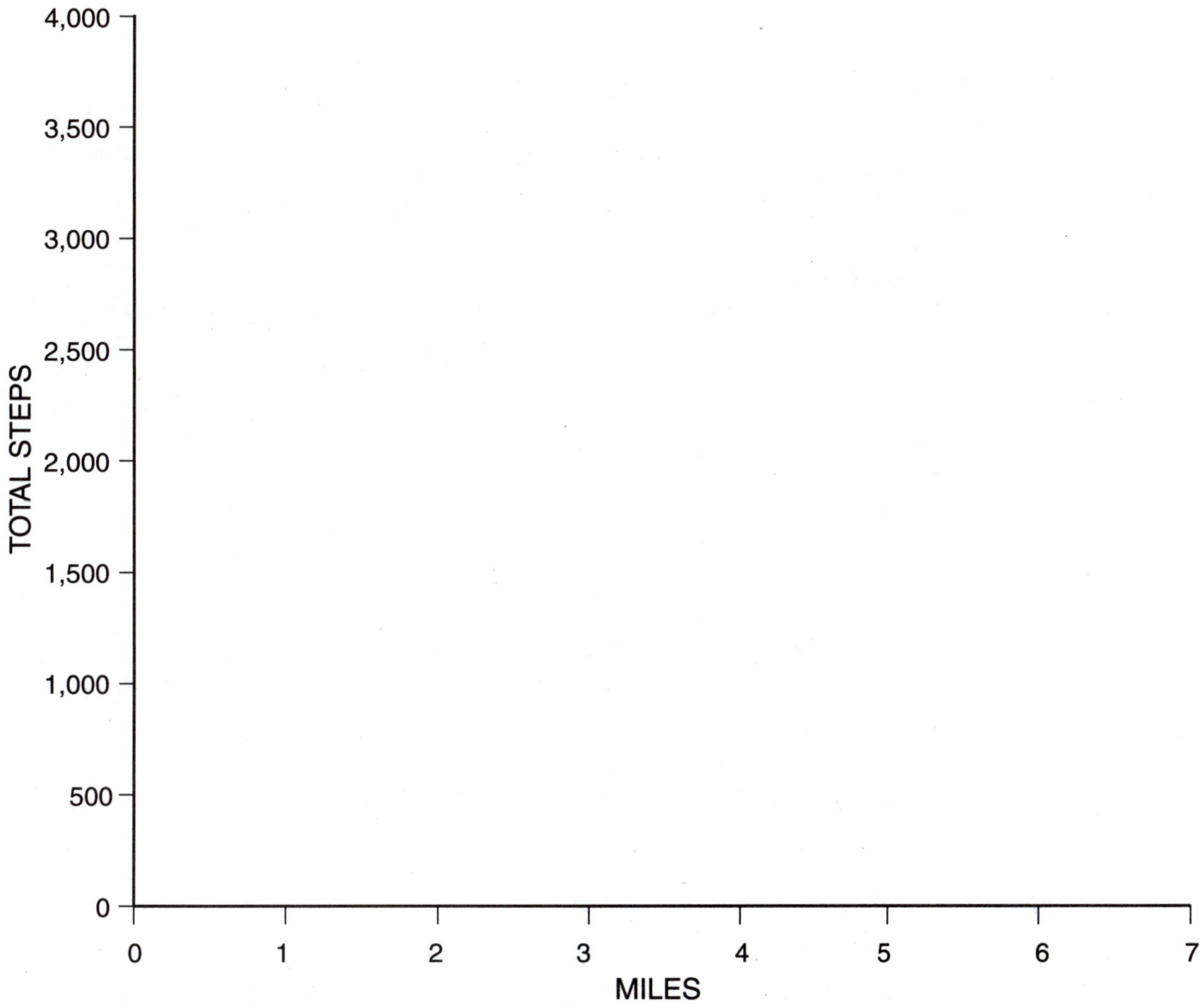

1. Look at the graph of this function. Is it linear?

2. What does it look like?

3. At what stage of the climb did the curvature of the graph change?

4. Did Anna and Milton find the pot of gold?

ACTIVITY 8.2 ▲ A Cubic Total Cost Function

Suppose that the cost function of Dave's Custom Made Mountain Bikes is as follows:

$$\text{Total Cost} = \tfrac{1}{2}Q^3 - 9Q^2 + 200Q + 100$$

This is the total cost that Dave, the proprietor of Dave's Custom Made Mountain Bikes, faces when building mountain bikes for his customers. Let total cost (TC) be the variable dependent upon Q, which is the quantity of bikes produced by Dave's Custom Made Mountain Bikes. Q is the independent variable.

1. Without graphing this function, what is the value of the vertical intercept?

2. Can you think of the economic meaning of this vertical intercept?

3. Calculate the **total cost** at each of the following levels of output.

Quantity of Bikes Made	Total Cost	Marginal Cost
0 bikes		
1 bikes		$191.50
2 bikes		
3 bikes		
4 bikes		
5 bikes		
6 bikes		
7 bikes		
8 bikes		
9 bikes		
10 bikes		

4. What happens to total costs as output increases? Is this what could be expected to occur in the real world?

5. Complete the **marginal cost** column of the table. Calculate the *marginal cost* of producing bikes by computing the difference between the total cost for x + 1 bikes and the total cost of x bikes as x increases from 1 to 10. The marginal cost is the change in total cost that arises from producing each additional unit. The marginal cost of the first unit is calculated for you.

6. What happens to the marginal cost of producing mountain bikes as production moves from 0 to 10 bikes?

7. Graph marginal costs on the coordinate axes below. What is the shape of this curve?

Marginal Costs

The curve looks like this because of the **law of diminishing marginal returns**, which states that as long as some productive factors are fixed, it must eventually get more and more costly to produce additional units of a product. That is, marginal costs must eventually increase.

ACTIVITY 8.3 ▲ The Calculus of the Cubic Cost Function

The relationships explored in Activities 8.1 and 8.2 can be examined by using calculus. The cost function for Dave's Custom Made Mountain Bikes is:

$$\text{Total Cost} = \tfrac{1}{2}Q^3 - 9Q^2 + 200Q + 100$$

1. Solve for the first derivative of this total cost function with respect to Q.

2. Explain the mathematical meaning of this first derivative.

3. What is the economic interpretation of this first derivative?

4. Substitute values of Q into the first derivative and plot the resulting curve on the graph paper provided below. Compare this to the graph that was plotted in Activity 8.2. How do they compare?

Graph of First Derivative of the Total Cost Function

 Mathematics and Economics: Connections for Life

An inflection point occurs at the point at which the curvature of the total cost function changes. This arises when total costs switch from rising at a decreasing rate to rising at an increasing rate. This point can be found by determining the second derivative of total cost with respect to Q, setting the function equal to 0, and solving for Q.

5. Calculate where the inflection point occurs in the total cost curve above.

6. What economic concept applies to this point?

7. What happens to the sign of the second derivative when an inflection point is experienced?

8. Summarize what you have learned by explaining what the first and second derivatives of the total cost function represent.

ACTIVITY 8.4

1. Given the total cost curve $TC = Q^3 - 9Q^2 + 196Q + 625$, calculate Total Cost and Marginal Cost for $0 \leq Q \leq 5$ at one-unit intervals.

Quantity Q	Total Cost in Dollars	Marginal Cost in Dollars
0		
1		
2		
3		
4		
5		

2. Explain marginal cost and find at what value Q marginal costs begin to rise, indicating diminishing marginal returns.

3. What are the fixed costs indicated in this function?

4. In the running of a business, what are some items that might be fixed costs?

Calculus Students:

5. Calculate the first and second derivatives for the total cost function given above.

6. Using calculus, find the point at which diminishing marginal returns begin to set in (where marginal costs begin to rise). Explain your work.

Lesson 9

Profit Mathematics

Mathematics Focus:

Calculus

Mathematics Prerequisites:

Prior to using this lesson, students should be able to:

- Solve quadratic equations
- Evaluate polynomials using synthetic substitution
- Calculate, plot, and interpret the first and second derivatives of a cubic equation using signs and critical values

Lesson Objectives:

To apply prerequisite mathematics concepts and business profit maximization strategies to:

- Explain that total profit is the difference between total revenue and total cost
- Explain that profit is maximized when the difference between total revenue and costs is at its greatest amount
- Explain that total revenue equals the price of a product times the quantity that is sold
- Explain the concepts of marginal revenue and marginal cost
- Explain that firms will produce at the point at which marginal revenue equals marginal cost
- Explain that marginal revenue is the first derivative of the total revenue function and that marginal cost is the first derivative of the total cost function
- Explain that a point of profit maximization is confirmed by a negative second derivative of the total profit function

Overview of Mathematics and Economics:

Most businesses in a market economy try to maximize profits. Economic profits are the difference between **total revenue** (the value of total sales for the business) and **total cost** (how much it costs the business to produce its goods or services). When total revenue exceeds total cost, then firms have earned a profit. **Breakeven** is said to occur when total revenue and total cost are equal. An economic loss arises when total cost is greater than total revenue.

In a market economy, entrepreneurs who are able to produce goods at a total cost that is less than the total revenue from sales are rewarded with a profit. In order to understand profit maximization, marginal cost and marginal revenue must be understood. **Marginal revenue** is the addition to total revenue that the firm receives for selling an additional unit of its product. **Marginal cost** is the addition to total costs that result from producing an additional unit of output. As long as marginal revenue (MR) is greater than marginal cost (MC), the business should produce and sell the good. When MR > MC, the firm is increasing total profit by producing additional units. Because of **diminishing marginal returns**, a firm's marginal costs ultimately increase. This means that, sooner or later, marginal cost will exceed marginal revenue. The business must produce only those units for which MR ≥ MC. To make a maximum profit a business should produce only up to the point where MR = MC.

Marginal revenue = (Δ total revenue) / (Δ output (Q)). This can be thought of as the first derivative (slope) of the total revenue function, where the change in Q approaches zero. Therefore

$$\text{Marginal Revenue} = d(\text{Total Revenue}) / d(\text{Quantity})$$

Likewise,

$$\text{Marginal Cost} = d(\text{Total Cost})/d(\text{Quantity})$$

As was seen in Lesson 8, the total cost function is often best represented by a cubic function. The profit-maximizing decision rule for the business is to produce so that the first derivative of its total revenue function (MR) equals the first derivative of its total cost function (MC). This procedure corresponds to the firm differentiating its total profit function with respect to quantity produced, and setting this first derivative equal to a critical value of zero. This is the point at which the profit function reaches its relative maximum. This can be verified by examining the second derivative of the total profit function. If the second derivative is negative, the curve is concave down and a relative maximum point exists.

Mathematics and Economics Terms:

- Concave down
- Diminishing marginal returns
- First derivative
- Marginal cost
- Marginal revenue
- Profit
- Relative maximum
- Second derivative
- Synthetic substitution
- Total costs
- Total revenue

Materials:

- Overhead transparencies of Visuals 9.1 through 9.10
- One copy of Activities 9.1–9.4 for each student
- Ruler
- Calculator
- Graphing calculator (optional)

Estimated Time:

80–100 minutes

Procedures:

1. Warm-Up: Show Visual 9.1 and have the students complete it.

The answers are:

1. $f'(x) = -6x^2 + 6x + 36$
2. The critical values occur when $f'(x) = 0$ so that $x = 3$ and $x = -2$.
3. Answers in the cells are:

Interval	$(-\infty,-2)$	$(-2,3)$	$(3, -\infty)$
Test point in interval	any pt. i.e. −3	any pt. i.e. 0	any pt. i. e. 4
Sign of $f'(x)$ in interval	negative	positive	negative

4. The value $x = 3$ is associated with a maximum because $f'(x)$ changes from + to – at this point (that is, it goes from a positive slope to a negative slope, therefore confirming that it is a relative maximum point).
5. $f''(x) = -12x + 6$ so that $f''(3) = -30$. Thus, graph of $f(x)$ is concave down indicating a relative maximum at this point.
6. Use a graphing calculator to verify your graph and sketch it on the overhead for students to see. See Visual 9.2. Students may evaluate the function at integral values in the domain using synthetic substitution.

2. Ask the students what is a major goal of running a business, especially when it is your sole source of income? Be sure to lead them to the idea of maximizing profit.

Write on the board or overhead :

In a business
Total profit (TP) = total revenue (TR) – total cost (TC).

3. Ask the students, "What must a business person do to maximize total profits?" As shown by the formula, there are two major factors which affect profits—revenues and costs. Business owners and managers try to produce the level of output where the difference between total revenue and total cost is at its greatest.

4. Distribute a copy of Activity 9.1 to each student. Indicate to the students that this is the first of four activity sheets which will demonstrate how a number of important economic concepts are interrelated.

Before having the students complete the activity, you may wish to remind them that graph 1 (the demand curve) illustrates the inverse relationship between the price of an item and the quantity people are willing and able to buy, holding everything else constant. The demand curve is obtained by plotting price and quantity demanded from columns 1 and 2 in Activity 9.1. You will also need to discuss with the class the difference between total revenue and marginal revenue. Total revenue (TR) is the total amount generated from sales. It is determined by multiplying price times quantity. Marginal revenue (MR) is defined as the addition to total revenue that results from selling an additional unit of output. For example, as shown in the example on Activity 9.1, the marginal revenue from the first unit sold is $24, because the addition to total revenue from selling an additional (in this case, the first) unit of output is $24 ($24 – 0). Likewise, the marginal revenue of the second unit of output is $22 ($46 – $24).

Have the students complete the total revenue and marginal revenue columns in Activity 9.1 and answer the questions at the end of the activity. Make sure the students save the completed Activity 9.1 for a later activity.

Answers:

1. **Price:** The amount (number of dollars) required to buy an item.
Quantity Demanded: The number of items consumers are willing and able to buy at a particular price.
Total Revenue: The value of total sales.
Marginal Revenue: The addition to total revenue that results from selling an additional unit of output.
2. Show Visual 9.3 which is a completed total revenue and marginal revenue schedule.
3. At point P = $13, Q = 12, and P= $12, Q = 13.
4. No. As will be seen later in this lesson, the point at which firms should produce in order to maximize profits also depends on costs.
5. They are decreasing throughout the entire range of output, and actually turn negative beyond the point at which total revenues are maximized.
6. See Visual 9.4 for the plot of the MR Curve. A mathematical description is that it is a linear function with a negative slope. The horizontal intercept is at Q = 13 where the function becomes negative.
7. See Visual 9.5 which shows the demand curve and the marginal revenue curve.

8. The marginal revenue curve lies below the demand curve for all values of Q > 1. This result occurs because most firms charge the same price to each one of their customers. This means that when a firm lowers its price for one customer, it lowers its price for all customers. When a firm lowers its price, it actually loses some of the revenue that it would have otherwise captured from its existing customers. That is, when a firm lowers its price from $18 to $16 per unit, it not only gains more customers, it also loses some of the revenue that it would have otherwise received from existing customers. The firm receives a lower price for units sold to these customers. This has the tendency of offsetting (at least partially) the gain in revenues that arises from attracting more customers.
9. The price (which is measured along the demand curve) is greater than marginal revenue for all values of Q > 1.

5. Distribute Activity 9.2 to students. Explain the difference between total costs (TC) and Marginal Costs (MC). **Total cost** is the amount that it costs businesses to produce all of their goods in a given time period. **Marginal cost** is the addition to total costs that results from producing an additional unit of output. Have the students complete all of the questions in Activity 9.2.

■ **COMMENT** The concepts of total cost and marginal cost should be familiar to your students if they have completed Lesson 8. In graphing the total cost curve, the cubic properties of this curve don't stand out because the range of output is so small. The total cost curve is, however, a visibly nonlinear function. Note that the MC curve in this activity is upward sloping (that this MC curve does not have a downward sloping portion is particular to this example—most MC functions are parabolas). Also note that MC is always positive since each additional unit produced always comes at an additional cost. Have the students keep their completed Activity 9.2.

◆ **Answers:**

Questions 1 and 3: Show Visual 9.6.
Questions 2 and 4: Show Visual 9.7.

6. Distribute Activity 9.3 to each student. Tell the students that they are going to use information from the first two activities to complete this exercise. They will be using units of output ranging from 0 through 6 in their tables to graph Total Cost and Total Revenue on Graph 4 and Marginal Revenue and Marginal Cost on graph 5.

■ **COMMENT** Graph 4 combines total revenue and total cost curves from Activities 9.1 and 9.2. Students are asked to examine only the first six units of Q. Note that the total revenue function is parabolic. This is apparent if you plot all points from the total revenue table. You may wish to have the students do this as an extension activity.

■ **COMMENT** Graph 5 looks at the relationship between MR and MC. Economic theory informs us that firms will maximize profits (or minimize losses) when they produce at the point at which MR = MC. When MR > MC, each additional unit produced increases profits. This can be seen by visually inspecting the optimal points of production from Graphs 4 and 5. The optimal level of output is the same in each graph.

◆ **Answers to Questions in Activity 9.3:**

1. See Visual 9.8.
2. It would be a parabola, reaching a peak between Q = 12 and Q = 13, and TR =156. It would intersect the horizontal axis at Q = 0 and Q = 25.
3. See Visual 9.8.
4. Total profits are positive over most of the range of Q. They are negative for Q > 5.
5. Profits are maximized at approximately Q = 3.5. The vertical distance between TR and TC is greatest at this point. If students report only whole numbers for units produced, this means that they will probably identify either Q = 3 or Q = 4 as the point where profits are maximized.
6. The slopes appear to be equal.
7. It is the change in total revenue divided by the change in quantity which we have previously called marginal revenue.
8. The slope of the total cost function is the formula for marginal cost. It is found by dividing the change in total cost by the change in quantity.
9. See Visual 9.9.
10. The point of profit maximization is the point where the vertical difference between TR and TC is greatest. At this point MR (marginal revenue) and MC (marginal cost) are equal.

7. Distribute a copy of Activity 9.4 to each student as a homework exercise. Ask the students to complete it, using calculus as directed to compute the point of profit maximization found in activities 9.1 through 9.3.

■ **COMMENT** This activity illustrates that there are different ways to calculate the point at which profits are maximized (and using calculus is a much less time-consuming and more precise way to achieve this result). Before the students are asked to complete this activity, be sure to instruct them on the following ways to determine the point at which profits are maximized:

Total Profit (TP) = Total Revenue (TR) – Total Cost (TC).

To find the quantity of output (Q) that the firm should produce to achieve maximum profits, find the zeros of the first derivative of TP where Q >0 (note that firms cannot produce an amount at which Q < 0). Then check for a negative second derivative result at that value of Q. A negative second derivative at that point will ensure a maximum point in the TP function. Students were not given a total revenue equation in Activity 9.1. Since the relationship between P and Q is $P = 25 - Q$, total revenue must be $TR = PQ = 25Q - Q^2$. This equation can be inferred, however, from the information given in the table in Activity 9.1. If you think your students can determine this on their own, then let them construct the appropriate equation $TR = 25Q - Q^2$. If you don't think that your students are capable of determining this equation, have them look at question #2 in Activity 9.4 where the equations are provided. Have the students do the activity; then go over it with them.

Answers:

1. $TR = a(Q-0)(Q-25)$
$46 = a(2-0)(2-25)$
$46 = -46a$
$-1 = a$, therefore the equation is $TR = -Q^2 + 25Q$
Concavity is established since TR at $Q = 2$, for example, is > TR at $Q = 0$ or $Q = 25$. Also, the coefficient of the quadratic term is negative.
2. $TP = -Q^2 + 25Q - (Q^3 - 2Q^2 + 2Q + 2)$
The equations for TR and TC are:
$TR = 25Q - Q^2$
$TC = Q^3 - 2Q^2 + 2Q + 2$
3. $TP = -Q^3 + Q^2 + 23Q - 2$
4. $TP' = -3Q^2 + 2Q + 23$
5. $Q = 3.12$ (the only positive solution)
6. This is close to our approximation of 3.5. (Note that calculus yields more precise results since, implicitly, the change in Q is allowed to approach 0.)
7. $TP'' = -6Q + 2$
If $Q = 3.12$, then $TP'' = -16.72$ which implies a relative maximum value at $Q = 3.12$ for TP.
8. $MR = TR' = -2Q + 25$ $MC = TC' = 3Q^2 - 4Q + 2$
Setting them equal we get $-2Q + 25 = 3Q^2 - 4Q + 2$
Setting them to zero we get $-3Q^2 + 2Q + 23 = 0$ which is the formula we have in #4 above.

8. To reinforce the importance of correctly calculating the sign of the second derivative, see "Blunders in Economics and Mathematics" in Visual 9.10. This describes the design of the B-2 Stealth Bomber and allegations by an engineering professor that the designers of the aircraft missed a sign when they calculated the second derivative of the mathematical formula that was used to design the aircraft.

Extension Activities:

1. The calculation of the area of a rectangle can be used to measure the amount of total revenue at various points along the demand curve on Graph 1, Activity 9.1. Using the points on the demand curve from Activity 9.1, have the students geometrically calculate total revenue at points B (5,20), C (10,15), E (15,10), and F (20,5). Using point B as an example, draw a vertical line segment from Point B to the horizontal axis, intersecting it at (5,0). Also draw a horizontal line segment from Point B to the vertical axis, intersecting it at (0,20). The area of the rectangle represents the amount of total revenue received by selling 5 items at a price of $20. Similarly calculate the corresponding revenue for the rectangles at points C, E, and F. Ask the students to visually inspect the area of each of the rectangles. How does the area of rectangle "B" compare to that of rectangle "F"?

◆ Answer: They are of equal size.

How does the area of rectangle "C" compare to that of rectangle "E"?

◆ Answer: They are of equal size.

How does the area of rectangle "B" compare to that of rectangle "C"?

◆ Answer: C is larger.

2. Given the total revenue function, $TR = 280Q - 3Q^2$ and the total cost function, $TC = Q^3 - 12Q^2 + 80Q + 180$, derive the profit maximizing level of output.

◆ Answer: ($TP = 280Q - 3Q^2 - \{Q^3 - 12Q^2 + 80Q + 180) = -Q^3 + 9Q^2 + 200Q - 180$; taking the first derivative of TP with respect to Q yields, $dTP/dQ = -3Q^2 + 18Q + 200$. Note that this equals 0 when $Q = 11.7$).

Show that this is a maximum point.

◆ Answer: The second derivative of TP with respect to Q is, $d^2TP/dQ^2 = -6Q + 18$. At a value of $Q = 11.7$, $d^2TP/dQ^2 = -52.2 < 0$. This therefore meets the condition for a relative maximum point. Profits are maximized when the firm produces 12 units of output.

3. Derive the equations for marginal revenue and marginal cost from #2 above.

◆ Answer: ($MR = dTR/dQ = 280 - 6Q$; $MC = dTC/dQ = 3Q^2 - 24Q + 80$). Confirm that you obtain an equivalent answer for profit-maximizing output by setting MR = MC.

4. Graph and examine the total profit function from Activity 9.4 on a graphing calculator. What does it look like?

Answer: Note that $TP = -Q^3 + Q^2 + 23Q - 2$, so this is a cubic function with vertical intercept equal to –2. It reaches a minimum at Q = –2.45 and TP = –67.06. This was previously eliminated from consideration as a viable maximum point because the second derivative is positive—and it reaches a maximum at Q = 3.12 and TP = 60.02. It declines thereafter.

VISUAL 9.1 ▲ Warm-Up

Given $f(x) = -2x^3 + 3x^2 + 36x - 14$

1. Find the first derivative of f(x).

2. Find all critical values of f(x).

3. Test the sign of f′(x) in each interval created by the critical values. Use the table below.

Interval			
Test point in interval			
Sign of f′(x) in interval			

4. Which critical value is associated with a relative maximum point? Explain your answer.

5. Verify your conclusion to the preceding question by finding f″ (x). Explain your answer.

6. Sketch f(x) on the graph for the domain $-5 < x < 5$ and the range $-75 \leq y \leq 75$. Plot the vertical scale in 25-unit increments and the horizontal scale in one-unit increments. Use all four quadrants.

VISUAL 9.2 ▲ Graph for Warm-Up Activity

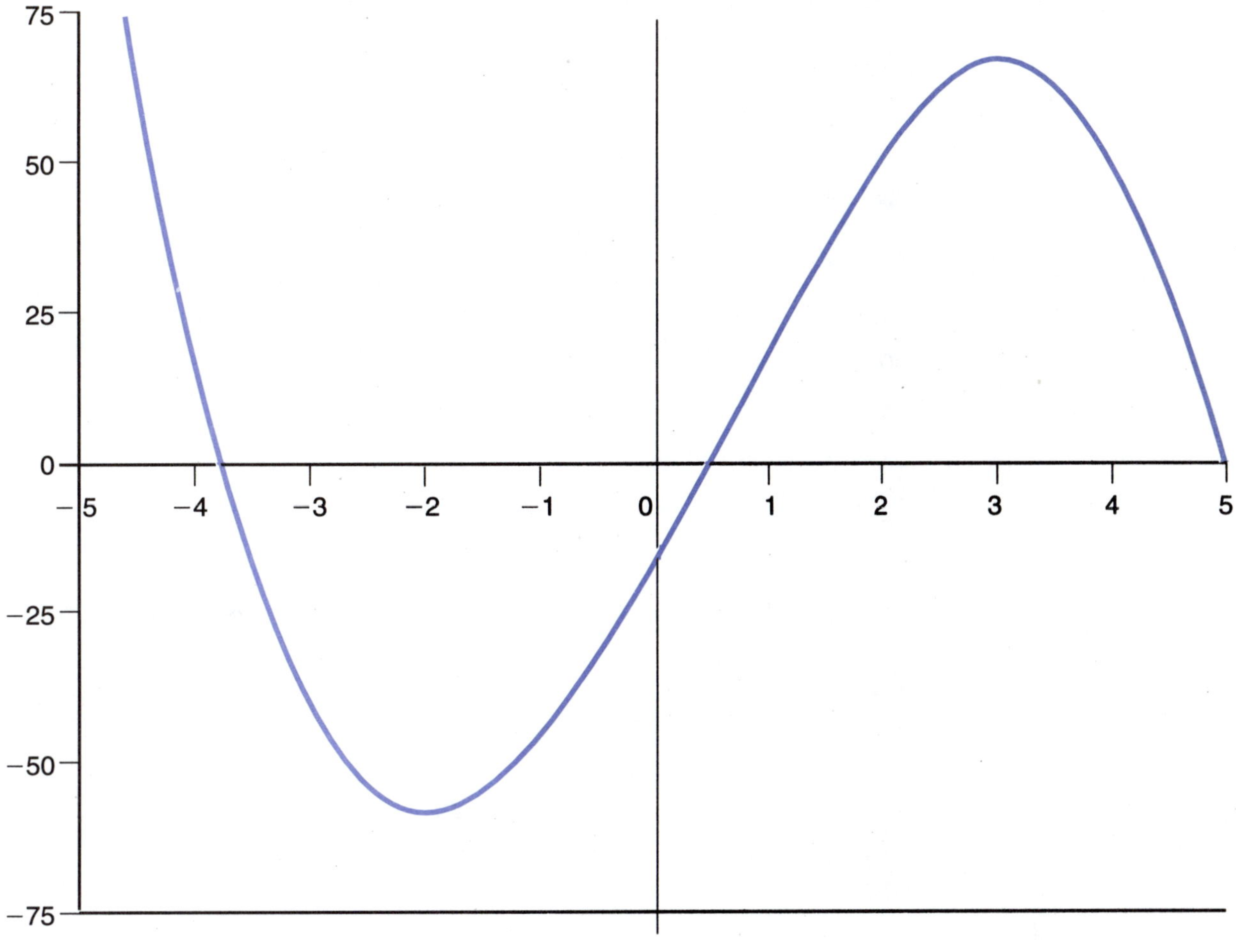

VISUAL 9.3 ▲ Calculating Total Revenue and Marginal Revenue

Price in $ (P)	Quantity Demanded (Q)	(Price)(Quantity) = Total Revenue (TR)	ΔTotal Revenue/Δ Quantity = Marginal Revenue (MR)
25	0	0	
24	1	24	24
23	2	46	22
22	3	66	20
21	4	84	18
20	5	100	16
19	6	114	14
18	7	126	12
17	8	136	10
16	9	144	8
15	10	150	6
14	11	154	4
13	12	156	2
12	13	156	0
11	14	154	–2
10	15	150	–4
9	16	144	–6
8	17	136	–8
7	18	126	–10
6	19	114	–12
5	20	100	–14
4	21	84	–16
3	22	66	–18
2	23	46	–20
1	24	24	–22
0	25	0	–24

VISUAL 9.4 ▲ Marginal Revenue Curve

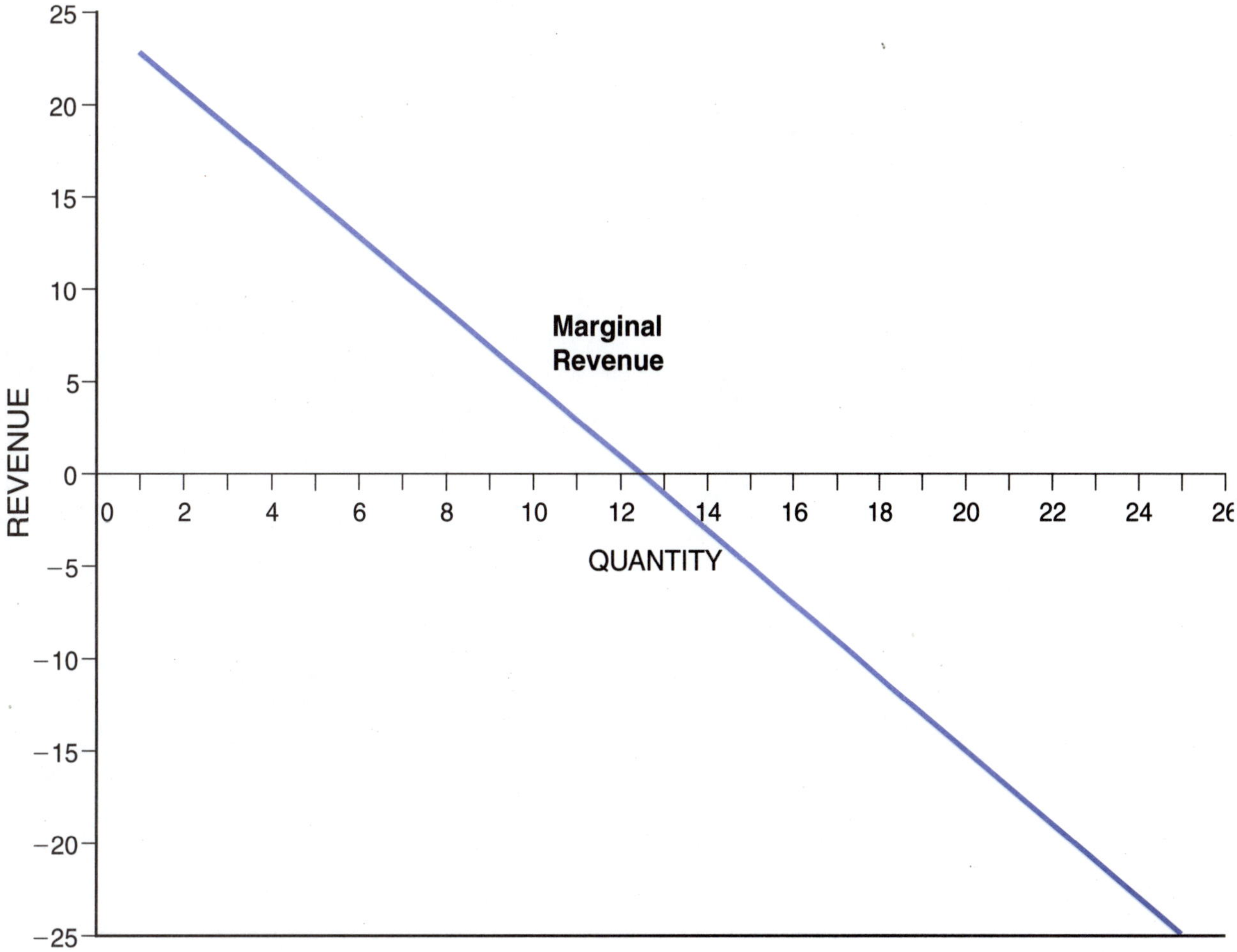

VISUAL 9.5 ▲ Marginal Revenue Curve with Demand Curve

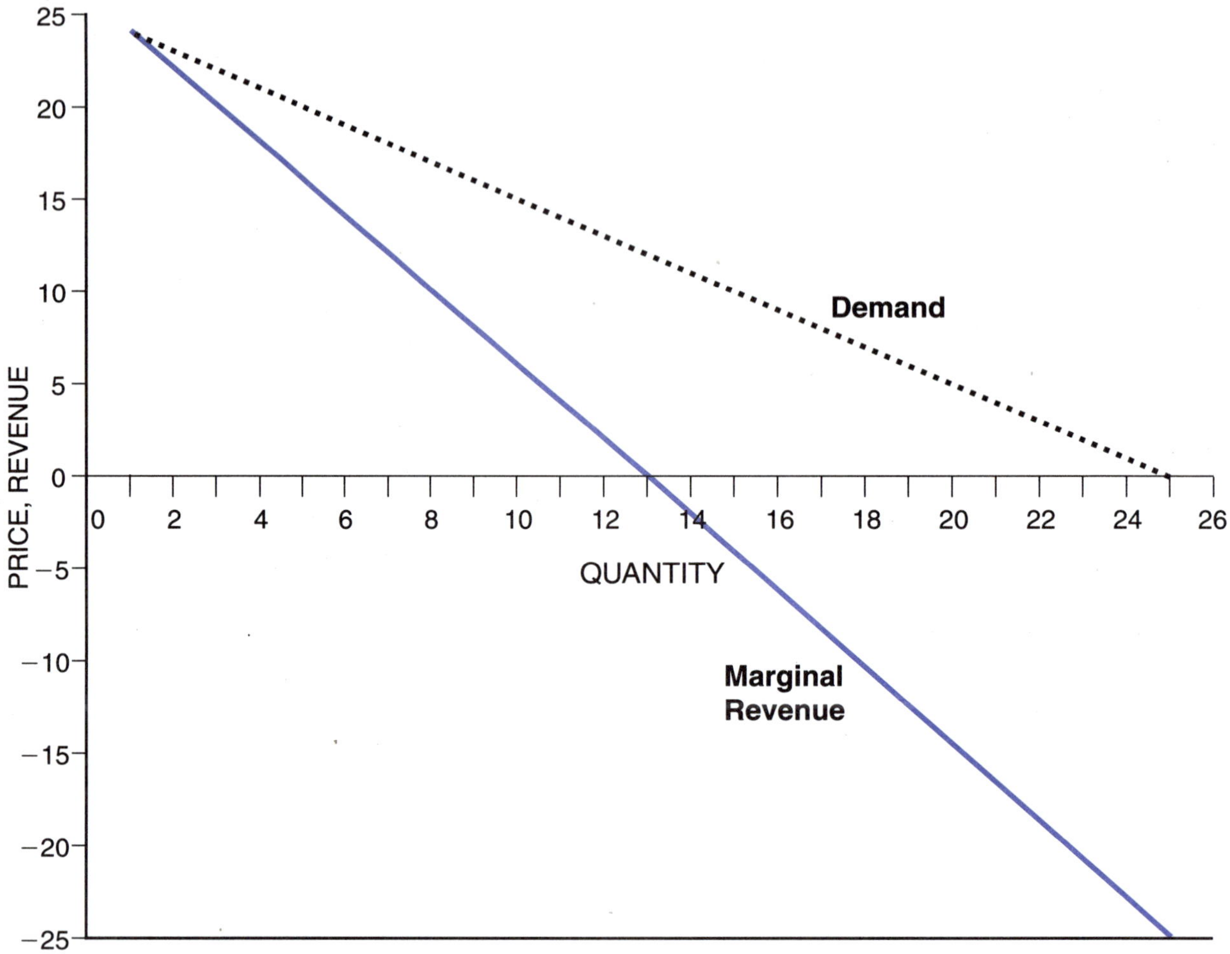

VISUAL 9.6 ▲ Calculating Total Cost and Marginal Cost

You are given the following total cost function:

$$\text{Total Cost} = Q^3 - 2Q^2 + 2Q + 2$$

Output (Q)	Total Cost (TC)	Marginal Cost (MC)
0	$2	
1	$3	$1
2	$6	$3
3	$17	$11
4	$42	$25
5	$87	$45
6	$158	$71

VISUAL 9.7 ▲ Total Cost and Marginal Cost Curves

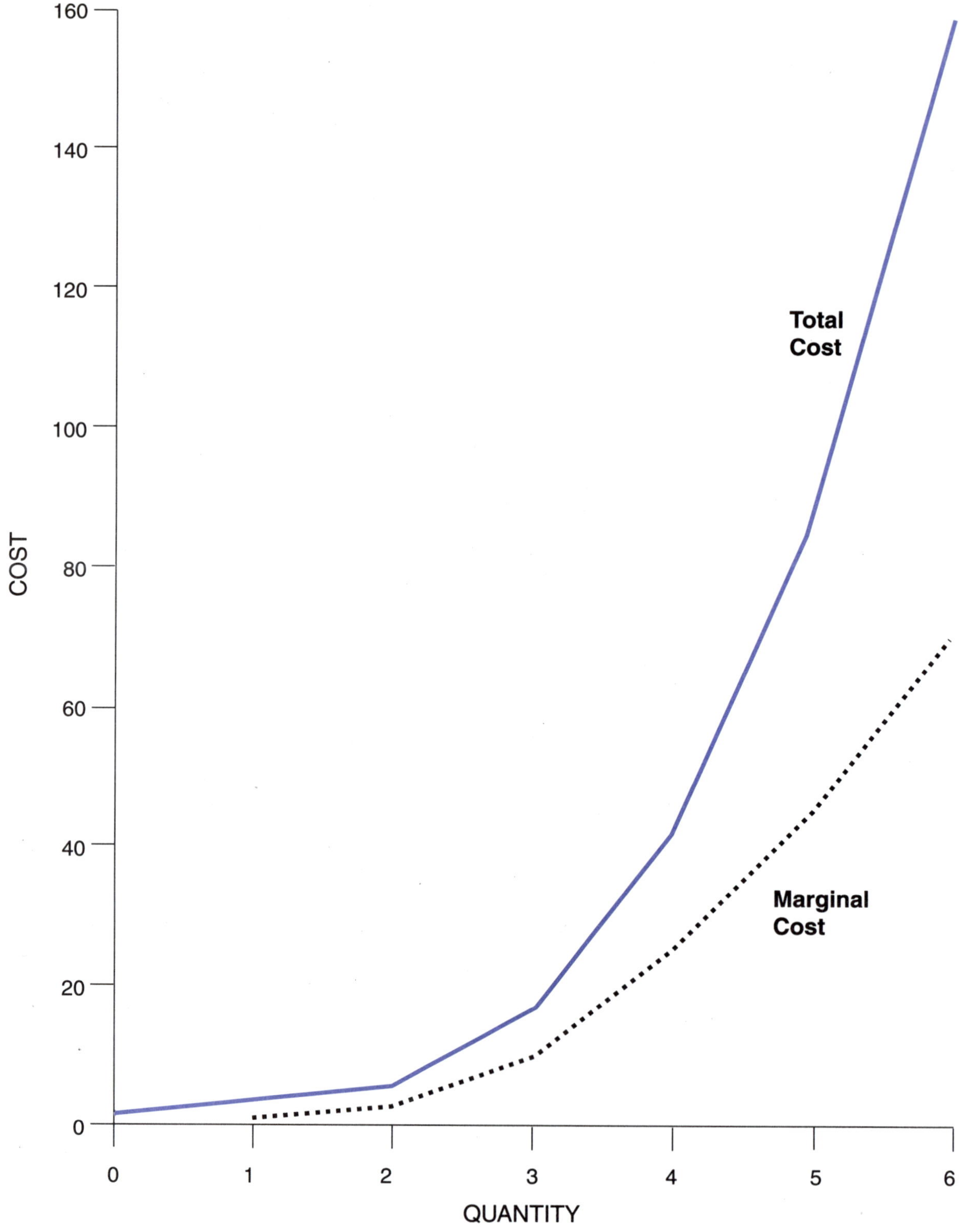

VISUAL 9.8 ▲ Total Cost and Total Revenue Curves

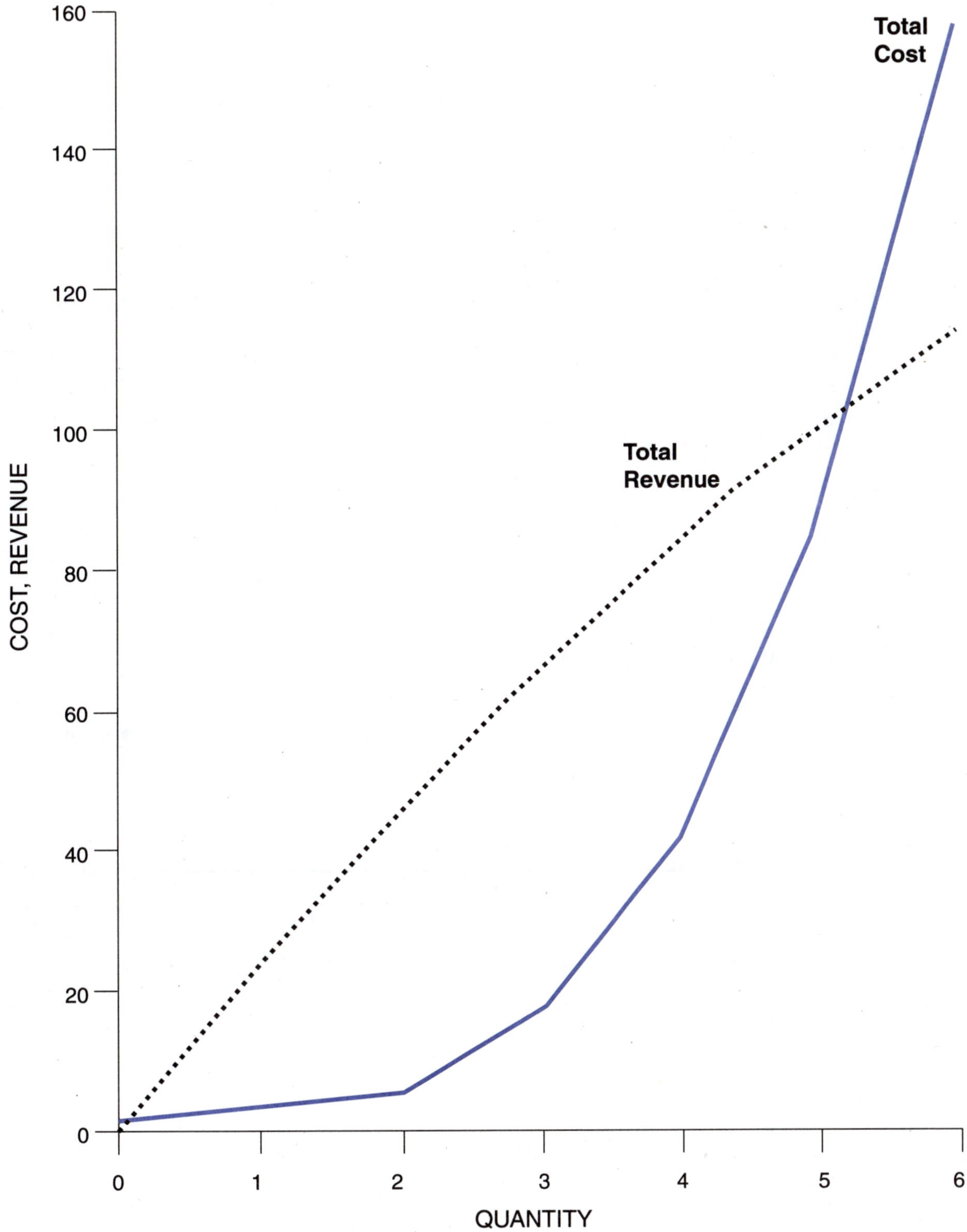

VISUAL 9.9 ▲ Marginal Cost and Marginal Revenue Curves

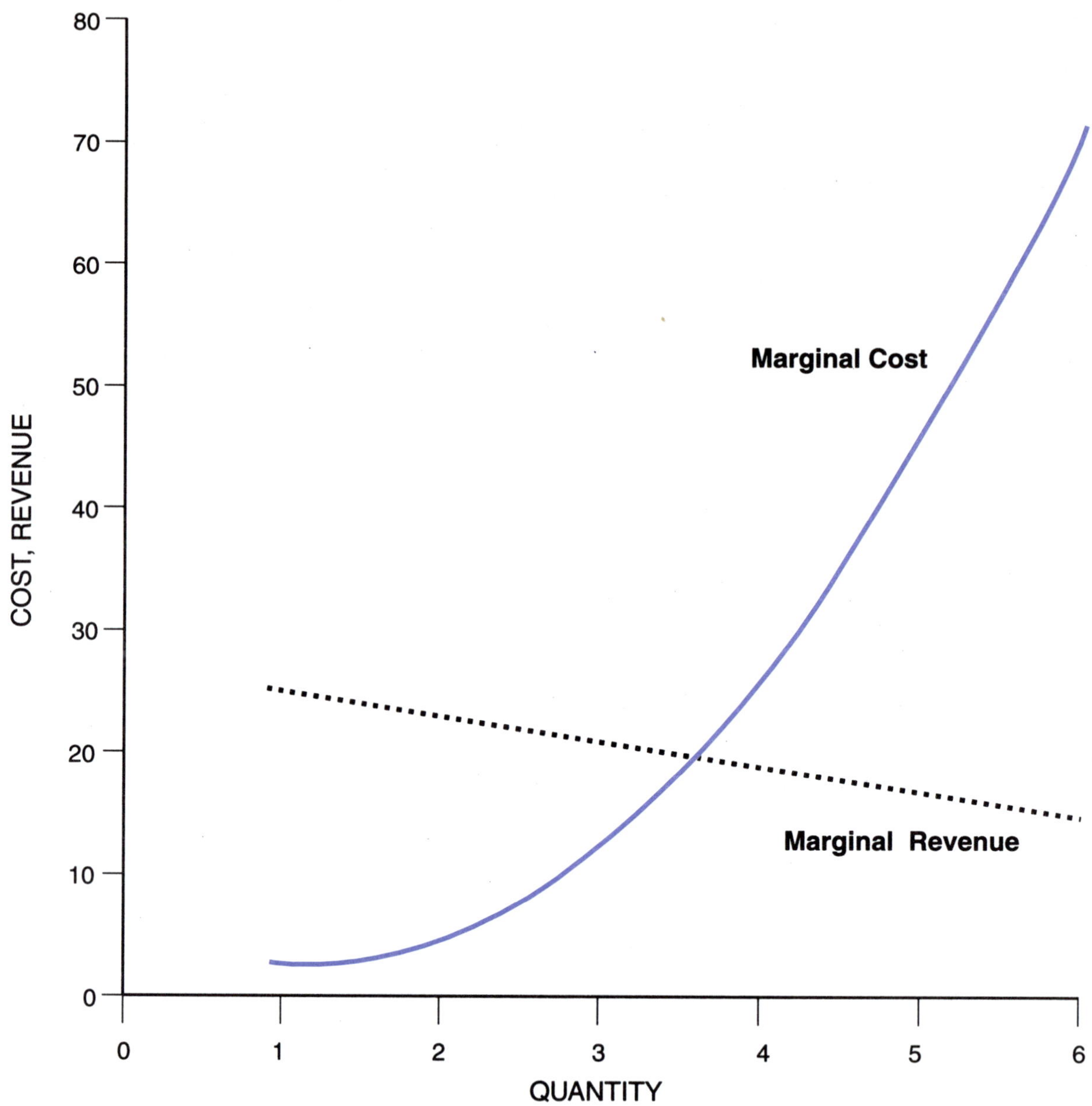

VISUAL 9.10 ▲ Blunders in Economics and Mathematics The Design of the B-2 Stealth Bomber

According to an article published in *Science* magazine,* an engineering professor alleges that the B-2 Stealth Bomber, with its volume disproportionately placed on the wing of the aircraft to achieve its "flying wing" design, is the worst possible configuration for the aircraft. This is because the study that was used to design the B-2 bomber relied upon early research in which a minimum point was mistaken for a maximum point. This occurred, it is alleged, because the original designers of "flying wing" aircraft failed to calculate the second derivative of the mathematical formula ultimately used in the design of the B-2 bomber. Instead of maximizing the range of the Stealth bomber, the designers thus configured an aircraft in such a way as to *minimize* its range. Think of this the next time you see a photo of the B-2 Stealth Bomber. Its peculiar design may well belie one of the great mathematical blunders of all time—mistaking a minimum point for a maximum point!

---

* See Wayne Biddle, "Skeleton Alleged in the Stealth Bomber's Closet." *Science*, May 12, 1989, p. 650.

ACTIVITY 9.1 ▲ Calculating Total Revenue and Marginal Revenue

Name ______________________________ Date ____________ Period ______

The table below corresponds to the demand curve which has been drawn in graph 1. Read and answer each of the questions which follow the table.

Price in $ (P)	Quantity Demanded (Q)	(Price)(Quantity) = Total Revenue (TR)	ΔTotal Revenue/ΔQuantity = Marginal Revenue (MR)
25	0	0	
24	1	24	24
23	2	46	22
22	3	66	20
21	4		
20	5		
19	6		
18	7		
17	8		
16	9		
15	10		
14	11		
13	12		
12	13		
11	14		
10	15		
9	16		
8	17		
7	18		
6	19		
5	20		
4	21		
3	22		
2	23		
1	24		
0	25		

ACTIVITY 9.1 (continued)

1. After looking at the table, explain the meaning of each column.

2. Complete the columns—you will note that the first couple of answers have already been entered for you.

3. Looking at your completed table, where is total revenue (TR) maximized?

4. Does this mean that total profits are maximized at the point where revenues are maximized?

5. Looking at the table, what do you notice about the pattern of results for your MR calculations?

6. Using graph 2 below, plot the MR curve. Describe it mathematically.

7. Copy the demand curve from Graph 1 to Graph 2. Use the table to find the appropriate values to enter.

8. Look at the graph that you have just developed. Where is the marginal revenue curve compared to the demand curve?

9. What is the relationship between the demand and marginal revenue curves?

Graph 1: Demand Curve

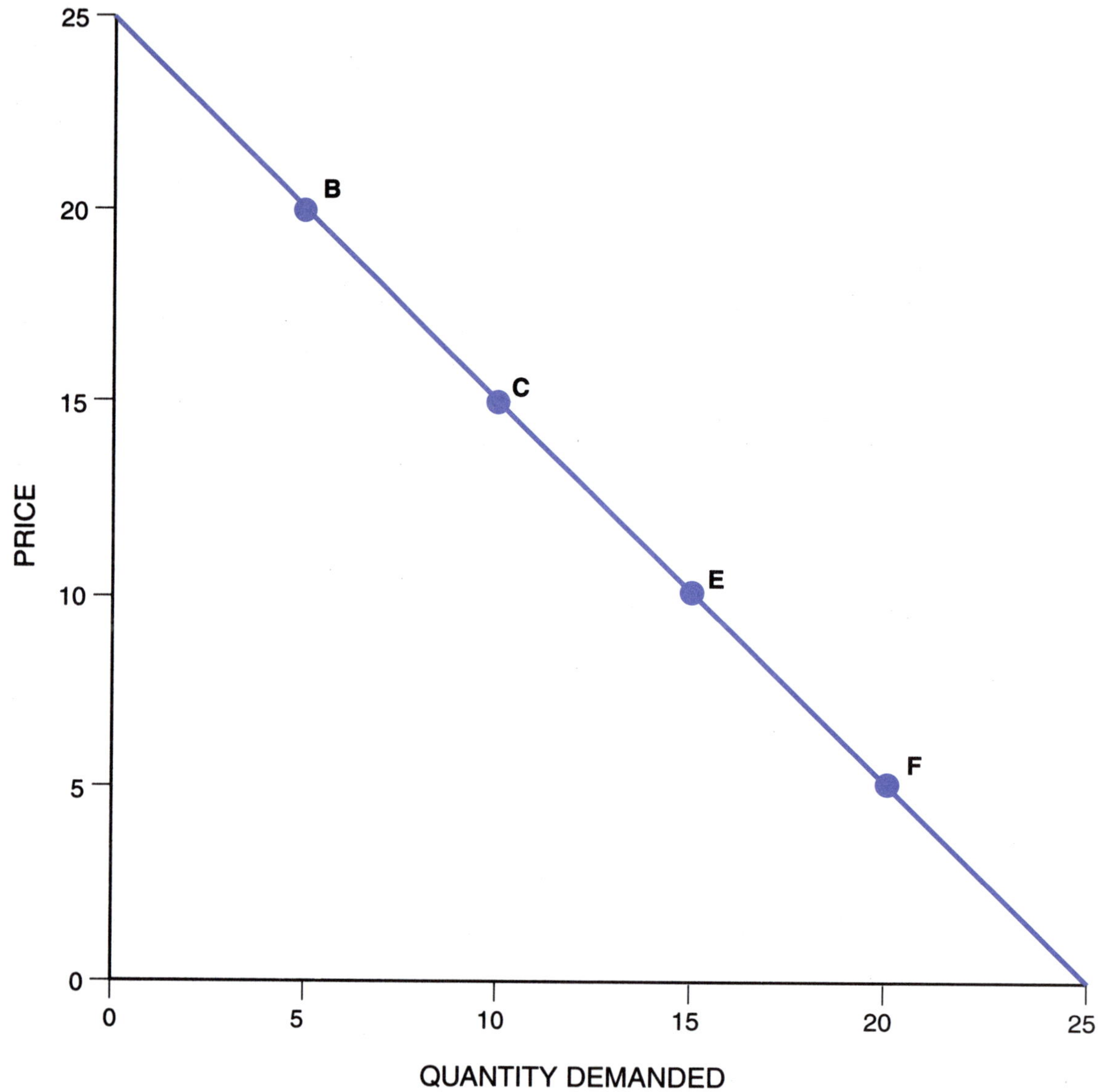

Graph 2: Marginal Revenue with Demand

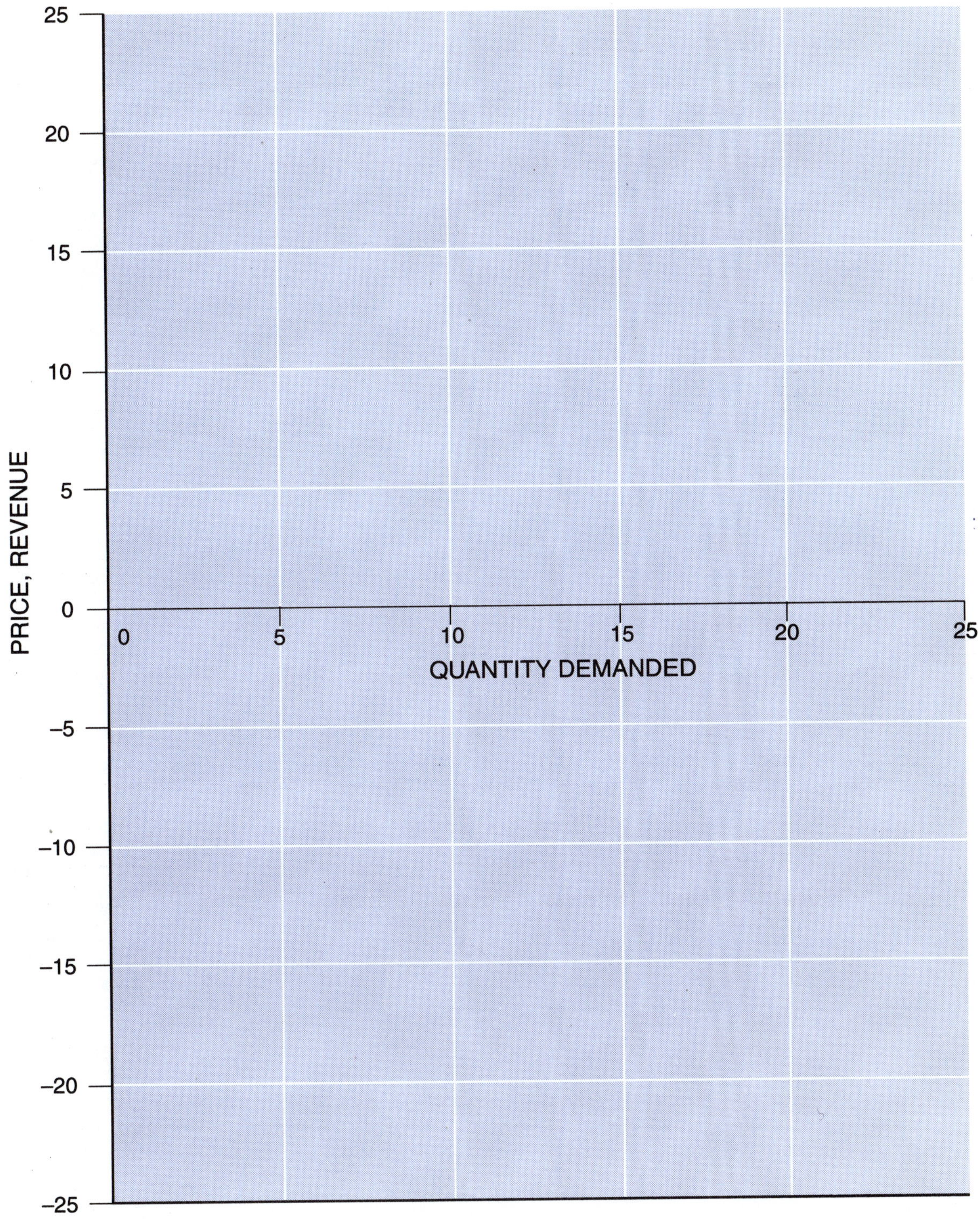

ACTIVITY 9.2 ▲ Calculating Total Cost and Marginal Cost

Name ______________________________ Date __________ Period _____

You are given the following total cost function:

$$\text{Total Cost} = Q^3 - 2Q^2 + 2Q + 2$$

1. Complete the Total Cost column by evaluating the above function at integral values 1 through 6.

Output (Q)	Total Cost (TC)	Marginal Cost (MC)
0	$2	
1		$1
2		$3
3		
4		
5		
6		

2. Plot the total cost curve on graph 3.

3. Marginal cost (MC) is measured by looking at the change in total cost that arises from producing each additional unit of output. Finish the table on marginal costs. The first two points are provided.

4. Plot the Marginal Cost curve on graph 3 also.

ACTIVITY 9.2 (continued)

Graph 3: Total Costs and Marginal Costs

Label the horizontal axis with values 0 to 6 and the vertical axis with values 0 to 100 in intervals of 10. The horizontal axis represents quantity, and the vertical axis represents both total cost and marginal cost.

ACTIVITY 9.3 ▲ Putting It All Together: Calculating Total Profit

Name ______________________________ Date ____________ Period ______

1. Use the table from Activity 9.1 to plot the relationship between quantity demanded (Q) and total revenue (TR) in graph 4. Place Q on the horizontal axis and Cost and Revenue on the vertical axis. Confine yourself to plotting the first 6 units of Q. Use vertical intervals of 10 and horizontal intervals of 1.

2. What would this function look like if you were to graph all points of TR and Q?

____

3. Use the table in Activity 9.2 to plot the relationship between quantity (Q) and a total cost (TC) on graph 4.

____

4. Recall that total profit (TP) equals total revenue − total cost. Are total profits positive or negative over most of the range of Q in graph 4?

____

5. Use a ruler to measure the distance between TR and TC at each level of output on the graph. At what quantity is total profit maximized?

____

6. Visually inspect the total revenue and total cost curves in graph 4. What seems to be the relationship between the slopes of the two curves at the point at which profits are maximized?

____

7. Using words, what is the slope of the total revenue function? How else have we previously referred to this slope?

____

8. Using words, what is the slope of the TC function? How else have we previously referred to this slope?

____

9. Use the tables in Activities 9.1 and 9.2 to plot on graph 5 the marginal revenue and marginal cost curves for the first six units of output. Place Q on the horizontal axis and Cost and Revenue on the vertical axis. Use vertical intervals of 10 and horizontal intervals of 1.

10. Use a ruler to draw a vertical dashed line extending through the intersection of MR and MC, up to graph 4. Use your ruler to determine if the vertical difference between the TR and TC curves is greater at this point than it is at the neighboring whole number values of Q. What is the relationship between MR and MC at the point of profit maximization?

Graph 4: Total Cost and Total Revenue

Graph 5: Marginal Cost and Marginal Revenue

ACTIVITY 9.4 ▲ The Calculus of Profit Maximization

Name ____ Date _____________ Period ______

The point at which profits are maximized in Activity 9.3 can also be determined using calculus. Total profits equal total revenues – total costs. That is:

$$TP = TR - TC$$

1. Using information from Activities 9.1 and 9.2, determine the equation for TR, total revenue. Use the horizontal intercept points (0,0) and (25,0) as well as a third point like (2,46) to establish concavity. Ask your teacher to help you with this equation if you are having difficulty with it.

2. Insert the equations for TR and TC into the total profit function above.

You should have the following equations for TR and TC:
$TR = 25Q - Q^2$
$TC = Q^3 - 2Q^2 + 2Q + 2$

3. Write the total profit equation.

4. Calculate the first derivative of the total profit equation.

5. A point of extrema (a maximum or minimum point) occurs where the first derivative of a function is set equal to 0. This is the point at which the rate of change of the function is 0. Use the quadratic formula or a graphing calculator to determine the point(s) at which profits are maximized.

6. Compare this point to that which was found in Activity 9.3 above.

7. Find the second derivative of the total profit function. In order to confirm that the point you have identified is indeed a maximum point, it is necessary to show that the second derivative of the profit function at this point is negative. A negative sign ensures that the slope of the TP function is falling as we approach the extreme point and the original graph is concave down. If the second derivative was positive, the slope would be increasing as we approach the

extreme point and the original curve would be concave up. This would identify this point as a relative minimum.

8. Check your work: Activity 9.3 noted that a different way of calculating the point at which profits are maximized is to set MR equal to MC. See if this yields the same prediction for profit-maximizing Q that was obtained above. (Hint: MR is the first derivative of the TR function and MC is the first derivative of the TC curve).

Lesson 10

Powerball Economics

Mathematics Focus:

Algebra II, Pre-calculus, Data Analysis/Probability

Mathematics Prerequisites:

Prior to using this lesson, students should be able to:

- Compute basic probabilities
- Calculate combinations
- Calculate probabilities of situations involving an exact number of successes

Lesson Objectives:

To apply prerequisite mathematics concepts and processes to consumer decision-making processes to:

- Explain the economic definition of a fair game
- Explain the calculation of the expected return from an uncertain event with a discrete number of choices
- Calculate the probability of winning a lottery
- Explain that a lottery and other games of chance typically have the characteristic that the cost of the game exceeds its expected return

Overview of Mathematics and Economics:

In games of chance, such as a lottery, economists refer to a *fair game* as one in which the expected return from the game equals the amount that one must pay to play the game. If a lottery costs one dollar to play and the expected return from the play is one dollar, then it is a fair game. Most games of chance, such as state lotteries and casino games, are not fair in the sense that the payouts to winners are less than that which is taken in by the organizers of the contest. Most people prefer less risk to more risk. This helps to explain our willingness to pay for car, home, health, and other forms of insurance. We are willing to pay to be protected against the possibility that a low probability event (such as a fire, accident, or catastrophic illness) will occur. In competitive markets, insurance policies are likely to be fair in the sense that premiums equal the expected payout for the insured event. Thus people are willing to pay to insure against uncertainty, but they also appear to be willing to pay small amounts for the possibility (at extremely low probabilities) of winning very large sums of money. This is the principle upon which many state lottery games are based. This lesson looks at the economics of one such game, Powerball.

State lottery authorities make public the probabilities of winning various prizes of their games as well as the overall chance of winning any prize. These are mathematical probabilities. However, the lottery player should not be interested in simple probabilities. Instead, economic theory suggests that the player should be concerned about the expected return for each $1 wagered. To calculate the expected return of such games, the lottery player must sum up the product of each dollar prize and its probability for each winning event. This is something that lottery officials rarely do. When you take a closer look at the expected return of these lotteries, it is clear that lottery tickets are rarely a good purchase. That people continue to play such games seems to indicate that they receive direct satisfaction from playing the games and/or are willing to risk small amounts for large potential (though very low probability) payouts.

Mathematics and Economics Terms:

- Combinations
- Expected return
- Fair game
- Probability

Materials:

- Calculator
- Two bags of numbers as described in the lesson procedures section
- Overhead transparencies of Visuals 10.1, 10.2, and 10.3
- A copy of Visuals 10.1, 10.2, and 10.3 and Activities 10.1, 10.2, and 10.3 for each student
- Playing cards (optional)

Estimated Time:

80–100 minutes

Procedures

1. Warm-Up Activity: Hand out Visual 10.1 to each student. Show Visual 10.1 and have the students complete their copies in pairs. Discuss the answers with the class.

The answers follow:

1. $^4/_{52}$ or $^1/_{13}$
2. $^{26}/_{52}$ or $^1/_2$
3. $^4/_{52} + {}^{26}/_{52} - {}^2/_{52} = {}^{28}/_{52}$ or $^7/_{13}$ $\quad ^1/_{1.86}$
4. ${}_5C_1 \cdot {}^4/_{52} \cdot {}^{48}/_{52} \cdot {}^{48}/_{52} \cdot {}^{48}/_{52} \cdot {}^{48}/_{52} = {}^{414720}/_{1485172}$ $\quad ^1/_{3.58}$

5. ${}_5C_2 \cdot \frac{4}{52} \cdot \frac{4}{52} \cdot \frac{48}{52} \cdot \frac{48}{52} \cdot \frac{48}{52} = \frac{276480}{5940688}$ $\quad \frac{1}{21.49}$
6. ${}_5C_4 \cdot \frac{4}{52} \cdot \frac{3}{51} \cdot \frac{2}{50} \cdot \frac{1}{49} \cdot \frac{48}{48}$ or $({}_4C_4 \cdot {}_{48}C_1) / ({}_{52}C_5) = \frac{1}{54145}$
7. ${}_5C_4 \cdot \frac{2}{52} \cdot \frac{4}{51} \cdot \frac{3}{50} \cdot \frac{2}{49} \cdot \frac{1}{48}$ or $({}_2C_1 \cdot {}_4C_4 \cdot {}_{46}C_0) / ({}_{52}C_5) = \frac{1}{1299480}$
8. ${}_5C_1 \cdot {}_4C_3 \cdot \frac{2}{52} \cdot \frac{4}{51} \cdot \frac{3}{50} \cdot \frac{2}{49} \cdot \frac{46}{48}$ or $({}_2C_1 \cdot {}_4C_3 \cdot {}_{46}C_1) / ({}_{52}C_5) = \frac{1}{7062.40}$

2. Tell the students that they are going to examine Powerball to see if it is a fair game, one in which the expected return from the game equals the amount that one must pay to play the game. Ask how many students know the Powerball rules. Put Visual 10.2 on the overhead and explain the rules to students as follows:

a) Powerball is a lottery game offered by 22 U.S. states.
b) This twice-weekly contest involves drawing five white ping pong balls that have been numbered from 1 through 49 from one hopper (without replacement) as well as one red ping pong ball (the Powerball) from a different hopper that contains balls numbered from 1 through 42.
c) For $1 per play, Powerball players select (or have a "quick pick" random number generator select) five numbers from 1–49 (corresponding to the white balls) plus a Powerball number (from 1–42). Since the Powerball comes from a different hopper, the Powerball can be the same as one of the other numbers that has been selected.
d) Prizes are paid out in nine categories.

3. Pass out Visuals 10.2 and 10.3. Tell the students that economists believe that state lotteries, such as Powerball, are rarely fair games. Only rarely does the expected return from the game equal or exceed its cost (which is how a fair game is defined). Looked at this way, games such as Powerball are bad purchases. If a person expects to earn a positive return on his/her money, a $1 per week Powerball player is much better off putting the money in a savings account because doing so yields positive net returns over time. The same cannot be said of the net expected returns from repeated Powerball plays.

4. Put students into pairs and ask them to determine how to calculate the probability of winning the $3.00 prize, which is correctly given as 1 in 73.7, yet there are only 42 balls in the Powerball hopper. How can this probability be 1 in 73.7 instead of 1 in 42?

■ **COMMENT** The probability of having the Powerball, but no correct white balls is 1 in 73.7 (as opposed to 1 in 42) and is calculated by computing the joint probability that the Powerball is chosen along with the probability that no white balls selected by the player are chosen. This probability is found by multiplying the probability of picking the one Powerball, $({}_1C_1\,{}_{41}C_0)/{}_{42}C_1$, by the probability of not picking a white ball, ${}_{44}C_5/{}_{49}C_5$. Also, in the case in which combination form is not used, the same probability can be found by calculating the following product: $\frac{1}{42} \cdot \frac{44}{49}$

· $^{43}/_{48}$ · $^{42}/_{47}$ · $^{41}/_{46}$ · $^{40}/_{45}$. Work through this with the students. It is also the first question on Activity 10.3, where they have an opportunity to try it again for homework.

5. Tell the students that they will be playing Powerball in their class to see how fair this game is. Distribute a copy of Activity 10.1 to each student.

▪ **COMMENT** In preparation for this activity, cut out numbered slips of paper to replicate the Powerball drawing. That is, place numbers 1–49 in a white paper sack (representing the white balls) and numbers 1–42 (put these numbers on different colored paper than those in the white sack) in a red paper sack (representing the Powerball). Feel free to use ping-pong balls and real hoppers if you wish. Make sure the students understand that when they draw their daily numbers, they are to draw five white numbers without replacement. When they are finished with their drawing, they are to put the numbers back in the appropriate sack.

6. Tell the students that they will pick numbers each day, and each day you will pick the winning numbers in front of the class. They can then calculate their net gains or losses for the day. Students are to keep track of their net receipts from the simulated Powerball play each day for the entire school week. At the end of the week, each student will tabulate what his or her net earnings have been and report those earnings in class.

▪ **COMMENT** You will use these reports to calculate the (hypothetical) amount of money that the entire class won or lost for the week. It is possible, although unlikely, that the class as a whole will make money. If this happens, you can still use this exercise to discuss why this was an unlikely outcome and how the distribution of income was affected. Most students will have fewer hypothetical dollars than they started with. They are clearly worse off. One or two lucky students who have been fortunate enough to hit an unlikely payout are the ones who are better off. While the entire class may have more money, it is not clear that the entire class is better off. In fact, the median class member has no doubt lost money over the week. Note that if you want to complete this activity in one class period, simply have each student draw five sets of numbers during class. This will require that you submit the winning numbers for each round. Some students may want to select their own "special" numbers and use them more than once.

7. When you have finished and have calculated the classroom net losses, ask your students for alternative uses for the dollars that were lost (they could have had a pizza party, donated it to charity, saved it in the bank for prom night, etc.).

▪ **COMMENT** You may wish to note that in the real world, lottery officials argue that the net proceeds of the lottery help fund government programs such as education, parks, roads, and the environment. While this is true, paying for such programs through lottery earnings is not likely to be the most efficient means to finance state government. You can confirm this by stating that you are planning to use the net proceeds (since you represent the state lottery) for some purpose (such as buying new playground equipment, repaving the school parking lot, buying new books for the public library, etc.) which, while sounding good, is clearly not the first choice of every member of the class. In this sense, the lottery represents an inefficient "tax" on the classroom.

8. Distribute Activity 10.2 to each student. Tell the students that when they finish the activity, the class will discuss the answers. You may wish to place students in groups if you think they would benefit from each other's help in completing this activity. Also make sure that the students write down the formulas for their calculations.

■ **COMMENT** The students will be calculating how large the jackpot must be in order to make this a fair game. Note that it costs one dollar to play the game. Economists refer to a fair game as one in which the expected return of the game equals its cost. That is, if Powerball is a fair game, then the player should expect an average payout of $1 from each play. Students will see that it is extremely uncommon for the expected return to equal or exceed the cost of the game. Indeed the jackpot has to have a cash value of $63,424,178.95 in order for the expected return to equal the cost of one play. Over the period 1997–July 22, 2000, there were 48 Powerball grand prize winners, but only three of these winning tickets had a cash value in excess of $63,424,178.95. Note that these calculations essentially ignore the fact that there is an increased likelihood of multiple winners when the jackpot grows large. It is also assumed that the prize is paid in cash (as opposed to annuity. See Lesson 11 for more on cash versus annuity). Finally, the effect of taxes on take-home winnings has not been considered in this example. In short, it is not hard to show that Powerball is a bad purchase.

9. The second part of this activity asks students to calculate what the fair price is for one play of Powerball when the jackpot is worth $25 million. Students will discover that, when the jackpot is this size (which is not uncommon for the Powerball jackpot), the true expected return on this game is significantly less than the $1 spent to play the game. For those classrooms in a Powerball state, use the current projected *cash value* for the bi-weekly drawing to determine the fair price. (Do not use the annuity value—see lesson 11 for the mathematical distinction between cash and annuity.)

Answers to Activity 10.2 questions follow:

1. Calculation of the probability of winning the jackpot:

P(player selects the 1st white ball number) = 5 chances out of 49 balls or $5/49$;
P(player selects 2nd white ball number) = 4 chances out of the remaining 48 balls or $4/48$;
P(player selects 3rd white ball number) = $3/47$;
P(player selects 4th white ball number) = $2/46$;
P(player selects 5th white ball number) = $1/45$;
P(player selects Powerball number) = $1/42$.

Thus, the player's total probability of having her 5 white balls and Powerball selected is:

P(Jackpot) = $(5/49) \cdot (4/48) \cdot (3/47) \cdot (2/46) \cdot (1/45) \cdot (1/42) = 120/9{,}610{,}695{,}360 =$ 0.000000012, which is a probability of 1 in 80,089,128!!!).

2. Calculate what would have to be paid for each ticket in a $25,000,000 lottery if it were a fair game.

Expected Return = $3\,(1/73.7) + 4\,(1/118) + 7\,(1/604.7) + 7\,(1/206.5) + 100\,(1/8466.1) + 100\,(1/8879.1) + 5000\,(1/364041.5) + 100000\,(1/1{,}953{,}393.4) + 25{,}000{,}000\,(1/80{,}089{,}128) = \$.52$

3. Calculate how large the jackpot must be in order for Powerball to be a fair game at a price of $1.

$\$1 = [\{(1/73.7) \cdot \$3\} + \{(1/118) \cdot \$4\} + \{(1/604.7) \cdot \$7\} +$
$\{(1/206.5) \cdot \$7\} + \{(1/8466.1) \cdot \$100\} + \{(1/8879.1) \cdot \$100\} +$
$\{(1/364{,}041.5) \cdot \$5000\} + \{(1/1{,}953{,}393.4) \cdot \$100{,}000\}] +$
$\{(1/80{,}089{,}128) \cdot \text{JACKPOT}\}$

where JACKPOT is the dollar value of the grand prize.

$\$1 = [\$0.208080041] + \{(1/80{,}089{,}128) \cdot \text{JACKPOT}\}$
$\$0.791919959 = \{(1/80{,}089{,}128) \cdot \text{JACKPOT}\}$
$\$63{,}424{,}178.6 = \text{JACKPOT}$)

10. Distribute Activity 10.3 to each student as a homework assignment or pairs project for the next day in class. Ask students to use formulas for combinations to calculate the probability of each of the prizes in the Powerball game. Below you will find how to calculate the first two of these prizes without using combinations. This may be reserved as an exercise for your students.

The answers follow:

Calculations for prize probability:

Player Match	Probability
1 Powerball	1 in 73.7

This probability is found by multiplying the probability of picking the one Powerball $({}_{1}C_{1}\ {}_{41}C_{0})/{}_{42}C_{1}$ by the probability of not picking a white ball ${}_{44}C_{5}\ /\ {}_{49}C_{5}$

Also, in the case in which combination form is not used, the same probability can be found by calculating the following product:
$1/42 \cdot 44/49 \cdot 43/48 \cdot 42/47 \cdot 41/46 \cdot 40/45$

1 Powerball and 1 White 1 in 118

Since the white ball can occur in any of the 5 positions this can be calculated by the sum of the ball occurring in each of the 5 positions:

white	non	non	non	non	power	(which translates to)
$5/49$	$\cdot\ 44/48$	$\cdot\ 43/47$	$\cdot\ 42/46$	$\cdot\ 41/45$	$\cdot\ 1/42$	$= 387860/228826080$

PLUS

non	white	non	non	non	power	
$44/49$	$\cdot\ 5/48$	$\cdot\ 43/47$	$\cdot\ 42/46$	$\cdot\ 41/45$	$\cdot\ 1/42$	$= 387860/228826080$

PLUS

non	non	white	non	non	power	
$44/49$	$\cdot\ 43/48$	$\cdot\ 5/47$	$\cdot\ 42/46$	$\cdot\ 41/45$	$\cdot\ 1/42$	$= 387860/228826080$

PLUS

non	non	non	white	non	power	
$44/49$	$\cdot\ 43/48$	$\cdot\ 42/47$	$\cdot\ 5/46$	$\cdot\ 41/45$	$\cdot\ 1/42$	$= 387860/228826080$

PLUS

non	non	non	non	white	power	
$44/49$	$\cdot\ 43/48$	$\cdot\ 42/47$	$\cdot\ 41/46$	$\cdot\ 5/45$	$\cdot\ 1/42$	$= 387860/228826080$

TOTAL $(5 \cdot 387860)\ /\ 228826080 \approx 1/118$

This can be calculated more simply by using combination notation as follows:

$$[({}_{5}C_{1} \cdot {}_{44}C_{4})\ /\ {}_{49}C_{5}] \cdot [({}_{41}C_{0} \cdot {}_{1}C_{1})\ /\ {}_{42}C_{1}]$$

Similarly, the other probabilities can be calculated in combination form as follows:

2 white 1 power = $[({}_5C_2 \cdot {}_{44}C_3) / {}_{49}C_5] \cdot [({}_{41}C_0 \cdot {}_1C_1) / {}_{42}C_1]$ = 9460 / 5720652

3 white = $[({}_5C_3 \cdot {}_{44}C_2) / {}_{49}C_5] \cdot [({}_{41}C_1 \cdot {}_1C_0) / {}_{42}C_1]$ = 387860 / 80089128

3 white 1 power = $[({}_5C_3 \cdot {}_{44}C_2) / {}_{49}C_5] \cdot [({}_{41}C_0 \cdot {}_1C_1) / {}_{42}C_1]$ = 9460 / 80089128

4 white = $[({}_5C_4 \cdot {}_{44}C_1) / {}_{49}C_5] \cdot [({}_{41}C_1 \cdot {}_1C_0) / {}_{42}C_1]$ = 9020 / 80089128

4 white 1 power = $[({}_5C_4 \cdot {}_{44}C_1) / {}_{49}C_5] \cdot [({}_{41}C_0 \cdot {}_1C_1) / {}_{42}C_1]$ = 220 / 80089128

5 white = $[({}_5C_5 \cdot {}_{44}C_0) / {}_{49}C_5] \cdot [({}_{41}C_1] \cdot [{}_1C_0) / {}_{42}C_1]$ = 41 / 80089128

JACKPOT (5 white 1 power) = $[({}_5C_5 \cdot {}_{44}C_0) / {}_{49}C_5] \cdot [({}_{41}C_0 \cdot {}_1C_1) / {}_{42}C_1]$ = 1 / 80089128

Extension Activities

1. Suppose that lottery officials decide to increase the likelihood that the jackpot is won by reducing the number of balls in the Powerball hopper to 30. What does this do to the probability of winning the Powerball jackpot?
Answer: Increases it to 1 in 57,206,520

2. As a result of a survey commissioned by lottery officials, it is decided to increase the average size of the Powerball jackpot by increasing the number of white balls in the hopper to 54. Officials decide to leave the number of balls in the Powerball hopper unchanged at 42. What does this do to the probability of winning the Powerball jackpot?
Answer: Decreases it to 1 in 132,825,420

3. Replicate Activity 10.2 using a different state lottery. For example, the Florida lottery involves selecting 6 balls out of a total of 53. Have the students calculate the probability of winning the jackpot in this game, the size that the jackpot needs to be in order to make this a fair game, and what the cost of a play would have to be in order to make it a fair game for a current, projected jackpot total. Details on the Florida lottery can be found at http://www.flalottery.com/games/lotto/l6howto.htm. Details about other lotteries can be found at http://www.uslotteries.com/links2.asp. This activity will help reinforce that state lotteries are universally a poor purchase.

VISUAL 10.1 ▲ Warm-Up

Find the probabilities for the following situations using a standard deck of 52 cards. Show your work.
Remember: Probability of an event = (Successes)/(Total Number of Possibilities)

1. Selecting an ace.

2. Selecting a red card.

3. Selecting an ace or a red card.

4. Selecting exactly one ace when five cards are drawn with replacement.

5. Selecting exactly two aces when five cards are drawn with replacement.

6. Selecting exactly four aces when five cards are drawn without replacement.

7. Selecting exactly one red king and four aces when five cards are drawn without replacement.

8. Selecting exactly one red king and three aces when five cards are drawn one at a time without replacement.

VISUAL 10.2 ▲ How to Play Powerball

Pick five balls without replacement

Pick one red ball

____ 1 ____ 2 ____ 3 ____ 4 ____ 5

____ 1

Pay $1 for each chance to pick the winning numbers

VISUAL 10.3 ▲ Powerball Prizes

Correct Powerball	Correct White Balls	Prize	Probability
Yes	0	$3.00	1 In 73.7
Yes	1	$4.00	________
Yes	2	$7.00	________
No	3	$7.00	________
Yes	3	$100.00	________
No	4	$100.00	________
Yes	4	$5,000.00	________
No	5	$100,000.00	________
Yes	5	JACKPOT!!!	________

Now that you know how Powerball is played, can you calculate the probability of winning $3 by picking only the powerball correctly? Compare your answer with the calculated result above.

ACTIVITY 10.1 ▲ Classroom Powerball

Name ______________________________ Date __________ Period _____

Your assignment is to draw five numbers from the white paper bag and one number from the red paper bag (the Powerball) each day for one school week (or five days). Your teacher will pass this bag around during class. Record the numbers that you have drawn each day and compare them to the winning numbers drawn by your teacher and posted for that day. On any given day, if you did not match any of the combinations, enter a net loss of $1 (represented by –$1) in the space next to your entry for that day. Also record any winnings in this space, but remember that it costs you one fictitious dollar to play each day. This needs to be subtracted from the fictitious winnings for any given day. For example, if you matched the Powerball, the prize would be $3, but your net gain is only $2 for that day.

At the end of five days, calculate your net gain or net loss.

Official Winning Numbers

	Numbers on White Balls					Powerball Number	Net Gain or Loss
Day 1							
Day 2							
Day 3							
Day 4							
Day 5							
						Total	

Classroom powerball payouts (all monies are fictitious)

Player Match	Prize Level
1 Powerball	$3
1 Powerball, 1 White Ball	$4
1 Powerball, 2 White Balls	$7
3 White Balls	$7
1 Powerball, 3 White Balls	$100
4 White Balls	$100
1 Powerball, 4 White Balls	$5000
5 White Balls	$100,000
1 Powerball, 5 White Balls	JACKPOT

ACTIVITY 10.2 ▲ The Probability of Winning, the Expected Return on $1 Spent, and the Fair Price for a Ticket

Name ______________________________ Date ____________ Period ______

1. Can you calculate the probability of the jackpot? The probability of selecting all five white balls and one Powerball is given below. See if your calculation can achieve the same result.

2. The expected return on $1 spent on Powerball is determined by calculating the sum of the products of the probability for each prize and the associated prize level.

The formula is:

Expected Return on $1 spent on Powerball =

$$\sum_{i=1}^{9} (\text{Prizelevel})_i \ (\text{Probability})_i$$

where i is the number of the prize level and its corresponding probability for each of the nine Powerball prizes.

Suppose the Powerball jackpot is currently worth $25 million. Assuming that you are the only winner (if there is more than one winner, the jackpot is split), calculate what the expected return is when one dollar is spent on the game. Show your work.

Player Match	**Prize Level**	**Approximate Probability on $1 Purchase**
1 Powerball	$3	1 in 73.7
1 Powerball and 1 White Ball	$4	1 in 118
1 Powerball and 2 White Balls	$7	1 in 604.7
3 White Balls	$7	1 in 206.5
1 Powerball and 3 White Balls	$100	1 in 8466.1
4 White Balls	$100	1 in 8,879.1
1 Powerball and 4 White Balls	$5,000	1 in 364,041.5
5 White Balls	$100,000	1 in 953,393.4
1 Powerball and 5 White Balls	JACKPOT	1 in 80,089,128

3. Calculate how large the jackpot must be in order for Powerball to be a fair game. That is, calculate how large the jackpot must be to make the expected return from one play equal its cost, one dollar. [Hint: set expected return of $1 equal to the sum of probabilities times payouts for each category. This leaves one equation and one unknown, the JACKPOT. Solve for the JACKPOT and you will have the cash amount needed in the JACKPOT in order to make Powerball a fair game.]

ACTIVITY 10.3 ▲ Calculating Powerball Probabilities

Name ______________________________ Date __________ Period _____

The probability of winning each prize was reported in Activity 10.2. You were also asked to calculate the correct probability of winning the jackpot in that activity. Now use the information below to calculate the correct stated probabilities of each of the other outcomes. You may use a calculator, but you must also state the formula that is used in your calculation. If you are familiar with the use of combinations, write out the formulas in combination form.

Player Match	Approximate Probability of Winning
1 Powerball	1 in 73.7
1 Powerball and 1 White Ball	1 in 118
1 Powerball and 2 White Balls	1 in 604.7
3 White Balls	1 in 206.5
1 Powerball and 3 White Balls	1 in 8466.1
4 White Balls	1 in 8,879.1
1 Powerball and 4 White Balls	1 in 364,041.5
5 White Balls	1 in 1,953,393.4
1 Powerball and 5 White Balls	1 in 80,089,128

Event	Calculation	Result
1 Powerball		
1 Powerball and 1 White Ball		
1 Powerball and 2 White Balls		
3 White Balls		
1 Powerball and 3 White Balls		
4 White Balls		
1 Powerball and 4 White Balls		
5 White Balls		
1 Powerball and 5 White Balls		

Lesson 11 Cash or Annuity?

Mathematics Focus:

Algebra II, Precalculus, Data Analysis/Probability

Mathematics Prerequisites:

Prior to using this lesson, students should be able to:

- Calculate simple interest
- Calculate annual compound interest
- Calculate interest compounded a finite number of times annually
- Calculate continuous interest

Lesson Objectives:

To apply prerequisite mathematics concepts and processes to consumer decision-making processes to:

- Explain that a dollar received today is worth more than a dollar received one year from today
- Explain the difference between the payments options of cash and annuity
- Explain interest compounding and its effect on the future value of money saved/invested for a period of time

Overview of Mathematics and Economics:

Jackpot winners of state lotteries may have the choice of receiving their winnings in the form of cash or an *annuity.* An annuity is a financial instrument that provides income at regular intervals over a specified time period. For example, New York's Lotto and California's SuperLotto offer an annuity with an annual payment for 26 years, and the multi-state Powerball lottery has a 25-year annuity option. Not many people will be lucky enough to win a lottery grand prize, but a great number of us will have a cash versus annuity option for receiving retirement distributions. These choices also exist for a number of other financial options, such as bonds and insurance accumulations. It is therefore important that students understand the economics of alternative payment options.

A fundamental principle of economics is that a dollar received today is worth more than a dollar received in one year's time. Economists use *present value* analysis to make comparisons between the value of payments received at different intervals. This lesson instructs students on the mathematics of financial payments options that they will encounter in their lifetime. Among other things, students are asked to complete an activity in which they analyze the accumulations that will arise from making a commitment to saving a small amount of their weekly earnings. This involves calculating the future value of a stream of periodic payments.

Mathematics and Economics Terms:

- Annuity
- Compound interest
- Future value
- Interest
- Present value
- Principal

Materials:

- Calculator
- One copy of Visuals 11.1, 11.2, and 11.3 as well as Activities 11.1, 11.2, and 11.3 for each student
- Overhead transparencies of Visuals 11.1, 11.2, and 11.3

Estimated Time:

80 minutes

Procedures:

1. Warm-Up Activity: Distribute a copy of Visual 11.1 to each student and show a copy on the overhead. If you have not previously covered the calculation of compound interest in your class, the first four formulas will allow you to do so. If this has already been covered, ask students to identify the formulas associated with the particular form of compounding that is illustrated.

1) Total = $P(1 + nr)$

Answer: This is the total value of an investment, P, after n years at interest rate r (when r is expressed as a decimal) when the interest is not compounded.

2) Total = $P\,(1 + \frac{r}{k})^{nk}$

Answer: This is the total value of an investment, P, after n years at interest rate r (when r is expressed as a decimal) when the interest is compounded k times annually. The value of nk is the total number of compoundings during the duration of the investment.

3) Total = $P\,(1 + \frac{r}{1})^{n}$

Answer: This is the total value of an investment, P, after n years at interest rate r (when r is expressed as a decimal) when the interest is compounded once annually.

4) Total = $P\,e^{rt}$

Answer: This is the total value of an investment, P, after t years at interest rate r (when r is expressed as a decimal) when the interest is compounded continuously.

5) Total = $P\,(1 + r/1)^n = 4000(1+.07)^{10}$ = \$7868.61

6) Total = $P(1 + r/k)^{nk} = 4000\,(1+.07/4)^{40}$ = \$8006.39

7) Total = $P\,e^{rt} = 4000e^{.07(10)}$ = \$8055.01

8) Total = $P(1 + nr) = 4000(1+ 10(.07))$ = \$6800

2. Distribute a copy of Visual 11.2 to each student and project a copy on the overhead projector. Tell the students the following: As long as interest, the amount that a borrower pays a lender for the use of funds, can be earned, a dollar received today is more valuable than a dollar received a year from today. Have the students complete Visual 11.2 either individually or in groups.

The answers to the questions are listed below:

1. This item is descriptive only; no answer is needed here.
2. Original principal = (future value)/(1 + interest rate)
3. \$.926
4. Present value of the future dollar is \$.926
5. \$0.91

After going over the answers, ask how much the students would be willing to pay today for a certain amount of money received one year from today. Of course, the answer depends on what the interest rate is over the period. Other things equal, the higher the interest rate, the less they will be willing to pay today for the future dollar.

3. Explain to the students that an annuity is a sum of money payable yearly or at regular intervals. Often this choice is an alternative to a single cash payment now. Explain lottery option payments to students. Tell them that when states publicize the amount in the jackpot for an upcoming lottery drawing, they are almost always highlighting the annuity value of the grand prize. This is the total amount of payments that a winner can expect to receive over the next 25 or 26 years, not the amount of cash that the winner can expect to receive immediately. The cash equivalent of the annuity value is substantially less than the total reported jackpot amount. In fact, state lottery authorities typically suggest that the cash payout is about one-half of the publicized jackpot.

■ COMMENT: For purposes of this lesson, we are disregarding the taxes that must be paid on lottery winnings. To be sure, taxes reduce the amount of take home winnings, but since we are focusing on the mathematics of the cash versus annuity option, taxes are not included in the calculation.

4. Distribute a copy of Activity 11.1. Tell the students that the table in this activity is adapted from a table that California lottery authorities produced in June 2000. This table reports the payment amounts over the years for the winner of a hypothetical $7 million jackpot of the Super Lotto game. The 26 payments sum up to $7 million. Lottery authorities indicate that the cash equivalent option of this annuity would be about $3.4 million. Ask students to use information given in this table in order to determine whether the authorities are correct. This involves calculating the present value of future annuity payments. At the time that this table was produced, the interest rate was approximately 6 percent (so that r = 0.06 in the present value calculation). Tell the students that this is the rate to be used.

Allow the students to work in groups to complete the table. You may want the students to round the present value to the nearest whole dollar. Then sum up the 26 present value calculations. You may wish to note that a present value calculation is not needed for the first payment (payment number 0), because this payment is received immediately. Students should be able to verify by their totals that the cash option of $3.4 million is essentially equivalent to the future $7 million value. The answers appear in the table below.

■ COMMENT: This is an excellent time to remind the students that they will confront this option repeatedly in their adult lives. This analysis is used when deciding on the type of pension you choose, how you choose to use funds from an insurance distribution, what type of bond you purchase, and even whether or not to pre-pay a home mortgage. This exercise is about present value analysis. It just turns out that the most visible example of this important concept is the state lottery.

Payment Number	Annual Payment	Present Value
0	$175,000.00	$175,000.00
1	$189,000.00	$178,301.89
2	$196,000.00	$174,439.30
3	$203,000.00	$170,442.71
4	$210,000.00	$166,339.67
5	$217,000.00	$162,155.02
6	$224,000.00	$157,911.16
7	$231,000.00	$153,628.19
8	$238,000.00	$149,324.14
9	$245,000.00	$145,015.12
10	$252,000.00	$140,715.48
11	$259,000.00	$136,437.97
12	$266,000.00	$132,193.85
13	$273,000.00	$127,993.05
14	$280,000.00	$123,844.27
15	$287,000.00	$119,755.07
16	$294,000.00	$115,732.01
17	$301,000.00	$111,780.69
18	$308,000.00	$107,905.89
19	$315,000.00	$104,111.60
20	$322,000.00	$100,401.12
21	$329,000.00	$96,777.13
22	$336,000.00	$93,241.71
23	$343,000.00	$89,796.46
24	$350,000.00	$86,442.49
25	$357,000.00	$83,180.51
	TOTAL	$3,402,866.53

5. Tell the students that another calculation they will find useful in their lifetime is related to the future value of the money they have saved. Give each student a copy of Visual 11.3. This is a seemingly complicated formula that is used to calculate the future value of savings when the same amount, an annuity, has been saved over equal intervals during a pre-specified time period. This formula also requires knowledge of the interest rate over the investment period. While interest rates will certainly vary over time, this is still a useful approach to calculating the future value of savings. Note that the formula is written in the form of an annual rate of interest and an annual investment interval. If investments are made more frequently, then adjustments need to be made to the formula. Activity 11.2 deals with future value.

6. Distribute a copy of Activity 11.2 to each student. Suggest to the students that a one-pack-per-day smoker is likely to spend $25 per week on cigarettes. Ask the students to imagine that instead of spending this money on cigarettes or something of equivalent cost, they saved $25 per week for 30 years at a rate of 6 percent interest. What will the entire savings be worth at the end of 30 years? Students are asked to determine the future value of this annuity after 30 years.

◆ The answer is $109,290.

■ **COMMENT**: This activity looks at the calculation of the future value of $25 saved each week for 30 years. It draws on the importance of interest compounding. The $25 weekly amount was intentionally chosen to illustrate the financial cost of smoking one pack of cigarettes per day for 30 years. This illustration does not take into account the fact that health insurance is more costly for smokers or that smokers have shorter life expectancies.

If you want to show students how this number is calculated, note that the formula they are using is the sum of a finite geometric series consisting of the following payments: $FV = \$25(1.001154)^{n-1} + \$25(1.001154)^{n-2} + \ldots + \$25(1.001154)^3 + \$25(1.001154)^2 + \$25(1.001154) + \$25$. This series has 1560 terms and sums to $109,290. Extension exercise 3 shows how this geometric series can be reduced to the formula on Visual 11.3.

8. Distribute a copy of Activity 11.3 to be completed for homework.

◆ **The answers are:**

1. .9524
2. .8333
3. .1486
4. .3769
5. $20,020

Extension Activities:

1. Some state lottery sites on the Internet address the cash vs. annuity question. One such site (corresponding to the Lotto game in New York) can be found at www.nylottery.org/cashvsannuity.htm. Have your students find the payments schedule table and compute the cash value of the annuity in the same way that they completed Activity 11.1. All of the information except the interest rate is given. The most realistic interest rate for you to use is probably the rate on 30-year U.S. Treasury Bonds. See the *Wall Street Journal* for a current 30-year bond rate.

2. Suppose a friend of yours buys a lottery ticket each day when he goes to the convenience store to buy coffee. Also suppose that he has been doing this for 20 years. The lottery ticket costs \$1 and the expected return on each ticket purchased is \$0.40. Assuming that your friend goes to the store five times each week, what is his expected loss each week?

Answer: \$3. He expects to win 5 · (\$0.40) = \$2 each week, but the weekly cost of playing is \$5.

Over a 20- year period, what would your friend accumulate if he had saved his net loss each week in an account that earned 6 percent interest?

Answer: $FV = \$3\{\frac{(1.001154)^{1040} - 1}{.001154}\} = \$6027$

3. Using the formula for the sum of a finite geometric series, $S_n = a_1 \frac{1 - r^n}{1 - r}$, develop the Future Value formula as given in Activity 11.2

from the series FV = \$25(1.001154)$^{n-1}$ + \$25(1.001154)$^{n-2}$ +. . .+ \$25(1.001154)^3 + \$25(1.001154)^2 + \$25(1.001154) + \$25. This series has 1560 terms and sums to \$109,290.

Answer: In the formula $S_n = a_1 \frac{1 - r^n}{1 - r}$, a_1 is the constant factor removed from all the terms. The future value formula calls this PMT. The letter r denotes the ratio of one term to the term following it. That ratio is $\frac{1.001154^{n-1}}{1.001154^{n-2}} = 1.001154^{n-1-n+2} = 1.001154.$

If we let $S_n = \sum_{k=0}^{n-1} 25(1.001154)^k = 25 + 25(1.001154) + 25(1.001154)^2 +$

$25(1.001154)^3 + \ldots + 25(1.001154)^k$ and

$rS_n = 1.001154 \sum_{k=0}^{n-1} 25(1.001154)^k = 25(1.001154) + 25(1.001154)^2 +$

$25(1.001154)^3 + 25(1.001154)^4 + \ldots + 25(1.001154)^{k+1}$

then $S_n - rS_n = 25 - 25(1.001154)^n$

and $(1 - r)S_n = 25[(1 - 1.001154^n)]$

and $$S_n = \frac{25(1 - 1.001154^n)}{1 - 1.001154} = 25\left[\frac{1 - 1.001154^n}{-.001154}\right]$$

$$= 25\left[\frac{1.001154^n - 1}{.001154}\right] = PMT\left[\frac{(1 + r)^n - 1}{r}\right]$$

VISUAL 11.1 ▲ Warm-Up

For Questions 1 – 4 indicate whether the formula is associated with continuous compounding, annual compounding, no compounding, or multiple intra-year compounding, and explain the purpose of the formula.

1. Total = $P(1 + nr)$

2. Total = $P\,(1 + r/k)^{nk}$

3. Total = $P\,(1 + r/1)^{n}$

4. Total = $P\,e^{rt}$

Match and solve each interest calculation problem, with the corresponding formula in 1-4.

5. Suppose $4000 is invested at 7 percent interest and the investment is compounded annually. Find the investment value after 10 years.

6. Suppose $4000 is invested at 7 percent interest and the investment is compounded quarterly. Find the investment value after 10 years.

7. Suppose $4000 is invested at 7 percent interest and the investment is compounded continuously. Find the investment value after 10 years.

8. Suppose $4000 is invested in an account with 7 percent interest for 10 years, but the interest is not compounded. Find the value of the investment after 10 years.

VISUAL 11.2 ▲ The Time Value of Money: Computing Present Value

A dollar received today is more valuable than a dollar received one year from today.

1. The formula for the future value of an original principal after one year with an interest rate, r, is

$$\text{Future value} = \text{original principal } (1 + r)$$

2. Solve this equation for original principal.

3. What would the original principal be if the interest rate was 8 percent and you wanted to end up with a dollar one year from now?

4. The question above is the same as "How much would you be willing to pay today for the future payment of $1 received one year from today?"

Let the original principal be referred to as present value.
Present Value of payment received one year from today = $\dfrac{\text{Future Value}}{(1 + r)^1}$

In symbols: $PV = \dfrac{FV}{(1 + r)^1}$

where FV is the future value and r is the interest rate expressed in decimal form.

5. Calculate the Present Value of the future payment of $1, one year from today when the interest rate r = 10%.

A general Present Value calculation for payment n years from today:

$$PV = \frac{FV}{(1 + r)^n}$$

VISUAL 11.3 ▲ The Future Value of an Annuity

PMT represents Constant Annual Payment

r represents interest rate for each payment interval in decimal form

n represents the number of payment intervals in the future for which the computation is being made

$$\text{Future value} = \text{PMT}\ \frac{\{(1 + r)^n - 1\}}{r}$$

This formula can be used to calculate the future value of payments you make to an account for any future purpose.

ACTIVITY 11.1 ▲ The Lottery Jackpot: Cash or Annuity?

Lottery officials report that the size of the lottery jackpot for an upcoming drawing is $7 million. But then they report that this is the annuity value of the jackpot. If you actually want cash, you will *only* get $3.4 million (and that is before taxes). **Are the grand prizewinners being cheated if they take the cash option?** Fortunately, your mathematics and economics background allows you to answer this question. You know that if the present value of the future annuity payments sum up to $3.4 million, then the cash option is equivalent to the annuity. Your job is to determine whether or not the $3.4 million is the correct amount for the cash option.

In your analysis, assume that the interest rate, r, equals 6 percent. To complete this exercise, you must determine the present value of each annual payment. Use the future value formula in Visual 11.2 and solve for present value. When you are done with this, total your present value calculations. (Note that the first two calculations are already done for you.)

1. What is the total of the 26 present value amounts?

2. Is the lottery officials' cash option equivalent to the annuity amount?

In your calculations, round off the present value calculation to a whole dollar amount. Use your calculator to help you complete this activity.

ACTIVITY 11.1 (continued)

Payment Number	Annual Payment	Present Value
0	$175,000.00	$175,000.00
1	$189,000.00	$178,301.89
2	$196,000.00	
3	$203,000.00	
4	$210,000.00	
5	$217,000.00	
6	$224,000.00	
7	$231,000.00	
8	$238,000.00	
9	$245,000.00	
10	$252,000.00	
11	$259,000.00	
12	$266,000.00	
13	$273,000.00	
14	$280,000.00	
15	$287,000.00	
16	$294,000.00	
17	$301,000.00	
18	$308,000.00	
19	$315,000.00	
20	$322,000.00	
21	$329,000.00	
22	$336,000.00	
23	$343,000.00	
24	$350,000.00	
25	$357,000.00	
	TOTAL	

ACTIVITY 11.2 ▲ The $100,000 Habit

Students often hear about the undesirability of smoking, but do you ever wonder about the long-run cost of buying cigarettes? Your teacher has already discussed how the future value of an annuity is calculated. Essentially this involves calculating how much an annual investment of equal amounts sums to over a pre-specified time period. This exercise asks you to apply this formula to weekly savings over a 30-year period. This savings amount, a modest $25 per week, roughly corresponds to the amount that would be spent each week by a one-pack-per-day smoker. How much does the cost of one-pack-per-day add up to after 30 years?

The formula for the future value of an annuity needs to be modified because we are now considering a time interval that is shorter than one year. Because $25 is to be saved each week, the interest rate must be adjusted to be a weekly rate of interest. The number of periods must also be adjusted to be the total number of weeks over 30 years. The appropriate formula for calculating the future value of an annuity when weekly contributions are made is:

$$\text{FV} = \text{Weekly Payment} \cdot \frac{\{(1 + \text{weekly interest rate})^{n} - 1\}}{\text{weekly interest rate}}$$

where n is the total number of weeks over the time period examined.

Suppose the interest rate is 6 percent expressed on an annual basis. This means that the weekly rate of interest is 0.06/52 = 0.001154. The total number of weeks over the 30 year period is n = 30 · 52 = 1560.

Suppose you save $25 per week for 30 years at 6 percent per year. What will be the future value of this annuity after 30 years?

The title of this activity is **The $100,000 Habit**. Do you agree?

ACTIVITY 11.3

1. Calculate the present value of $1 received 1 year from today when the interest rate is 5 percent.

2. Calculate the present value of $1 received 1 year from today assuming a 20 percent rate of interest.

3. What is the present value of a dollar received 20 years from now if the interest rate is 10 percent?

4. What is the present value of a dollar received 20 years from now if the interest rate is 5 percent?

5. What is the future value of $20 deposited every week from 3rd grade through 12th grade if the interest rate is 12 percent annually but compounded weekly?

Lesson 12

Autonomics

Mathematics Focus:

Pre-Algebra

Mathematics Prerequisites:

Prior to this lesson, students should be able to:

- Use numbers and operations to interpret numerical examples that are appropriate in personal finance mathematical applications
- Calculate percentage changes
- Calculate proportions and ratios
- Calculate average values

Lesson Objectives:

To apply prerequisite mathematics concepts and processes to owning and operating an automobile to

- Explain the total cost of owning an automobile
- Explain the difference between implicit costs and explicit costs
- Explain the difference between economic costs and accounting costs
- Explain the difference between variable costs and fixed costs
- Calculate the difference in the total cost of various modes of transportation
- Explain that the opportunity cost of a choosing to spend time on an activity may involve income that you could have earned otherwise

Overview of Mathematics and Economics:

This lesson develops the idea of opportunity cost by examining the costs of owning and operating an automobile. *Opportunity cost* is the value of the next best alternative when a choice is made.

When people consider their choices, they should analyze the implicit and explicit costs of their choice. *Explicit costs* are the observable costs where cash outlays actually occur. *Implicit costs* are implied costs, such as the value of time and interest earnings given up. The explicit costs of maintaining an automobile include gas, replacement tires, registration, inspection, license, and insurance. Implicit costs can include personal time spent maintaining a vehicle and the interest earnings that are given up when a cash payment is made for an automobile. The sum of these explicit and implicit costs equals the total opportunity costs of owning and operating an automobile. Rational economic decisions are those for which the expected benefits of a choice are at least as large as the opportunity costs associated with the choice. Implicit costs are easy to ignore, but they, along with explicit costs, must be considered when making an economic decision.

Although depreciation can appear as an explicit cost on an accounting statement, economists typically think of it as an implicit cost because the value of the automobile declines with wear and tear through the passage of time. Even if they choose not to sell their automobiles, owners who drive their own vehicles experience an opportunity cost (what they give up) associated with depreciation as the resale value of their vehicles decline. Note that depreciation is not considered in this lesson because its calculation is beyond the scope of what is typically found in a pre-algebra course.

The costs of owning and operating a vehicle are either variable or fixed. *Variable costs*, such as tires, maintenance, fuel, and parking, change depending upon how much the automobile is used. However, *fixed costs* are the same regardless of how many miles are driven. These include registration, inspection, license, insurance, and loan interest.

Mathematics and Economics Terms:

- Average
- Down payment
- Explicit cost
- Fixed cost
- Implicit cost
- Opportunity cost
- Percent change
- Variable cost

Materials:

- One copy of Activities 12.1, 12.2, and 12.3 and Data Sheet 12.1 for each student
- Overhead transparencies of Visuals 12.1 and 12.2, 12.3

Estimated Time:

80 minutes

Procedures:

1. Warm-Up Activity: Have students do the warm-up which is on Visual 12.1.

The answers are as follows

1. 50%; .50
2. 33⅓%; .333
3. 25%; .25
4. 20%; .20

5. 16⅔%; .1667
6. 12.5%; .125
7. 10%; .10
8. 5%; .05
9. 4%; .04
10. 70
11. 71.34
12. 10%
13. 12.5%
14. 60
15. 3261.54
16. $180
17. 17.24%

2. Ask the students to brainstorm about all of the costs associated with owning and operating a car. Record student responses on the overhead or board. Be sure that students consider the costs they personally incur as well as the costs that their parents cover.

3. Distribute a copy of Activity 12.1 to each student. Ask the students to estimate the total monthly expense associated with owning and operating an automobile. Have the students record their estimates as the first item on the activity.

Distribute Data Sheet 12.1 to each student. This sheet includes information about various used cars. Assign each student or group of students a car. Each student should assume for this activity that "the perfect used vehicle" is the one that has been assigned. As noted on the data sheet, other costs of operating the car are given. These data will be needed as the students work their way through the activity.

An assumption in this lesson is that the car has no residual value after four years due to the age of the automobile. This assumption allows students to use the monthly car payment as the cost of owning the car instead of calculating depreciation. Depreciation is that part of the value of the automobile which is estimated to be used each year.

Students should complete this activity either individually or in groups. Answers to the questions are based upon the type of car purchased. Answers for all questions are given in Visual 12.2 A–C.

Spend some time discussing the implicit costs of owning a car addressed in this activity. Ask the students why they may not have considered implicit costs. Students should share their decision—in a written or an oral report—as to whether it is a good idea to buy the car.

4. Remind the class that Activity 12.1 focused on the distinction between explicit and implicit costs. Activity 12.2 looks at fixed versus variable costs. Define fixed and variable costs and give examples of each. Have the students complete Activity 12.2 individually or in groups, using the data that they developed in Activity 12.1.

■ **COMMENT**: Students tend to think more readily of variable costs (because these are the costs that they have to pay with some frequency) while ignoring fixed costs (such as insurance, registration, etc.). One monthly fixed cost that students are not likely to ignore is the car payment! This activity will help students understand that fixed costs—those that are unavoidable in the short run—are very significant. Should the students encounter difficulties in affording the car, it will be very difficult for them to cut back on variable costs as a way to make ends meet. Note that some students may question the extent to which some of the categories should be considered variable costs. For example, some maintenance costs may occur as the car ages (whether or not is used). It may also be noted that insurance rates may be lower when fewer miles are driven (so that insurance may not be entirely a fixed cost). If this happens in class, inform the students not to get too literal. The point of the exercise is that there are clearly costs that students are simply unable to avoid if they choose to own a car. These costs are the same whether students drive 1 mile or 100,000 miles.

◆ Answers to the questions are given in Visual 12.3 A–C.

5. In Activity 12.3, the students look at the critical importance of the implicit cost of time when deciding the most economical mode of long-distance travel. The activity might also help them consider the importance of the personal value of time in non-travel applications. This worksheet presents an example in which the explicit cost of traveling round trip between Los Angeles and New York City is the lowest for train travel. Despite this fact, the difference in the implicit time costs of travel using the three modes of transportation leads to the conclusion that travel by airplane is the best choice for most people. Distribute Activity 12.3 to each student and have students complete the activity individually or as groups.

◆ **Answers to the questions include:**

1. Air travel: $499
   Train Travel: $406
   Automobile Travel: $2,335.62
   Note that $.345 per mile for automobile travel is not strictly an explicit cost (because it includes imputed depreciation, maintenance, etc.). For simplicity, it is assumed that this entire amount is an explicit cost. This assumption does not alter the fundamental conclusions of the lesson.
2. Train travel has the lowest explicit cost.
3. No, most people would not automatically choose the mode of transportation on the basis of the cheapest explicit cost. Most people value the time they spend traveling between cities. The value of time is an implicit cost. In this situation, most people would choose to travel by plane. Those who have an extremely low value of their time

or have a fondness for train travel will be more apt to choose train travel.

4. $25 per hour is how much Jerry earns.
5. The implicit costs for each mode of transportation based on Jerrry's hourly earnings are:
   Air Travel: $425
   Train Travel $3250
   Automobile Travel $2550
6. Total costs, explicit and implicit, are:
   Air Travel: $924
   Train Travel: $3656
   Automobile Travel: $4885.62
7. Planes are the least expensive. It is therefore not surprising that most people use air transportation to travel between the east and west coasts.
8. If they place little value on their time or if they have non-economic reasons, such as fear of flying and desire to see relatives and sights along the way. Some have fascination with a particular mode of travel, such as taking the train.

Extension Activities:

1. Have the students work in groups to research in detail the total cost of a particular car that has been chosen by the entire class. Information on both new and used car prices can be found at www.edmunds.com or at www.kbb.com. After finding information about car prices (and perhaps also depreciation), students can get current interest rates and find a monthly payments calculator at www.kiplinger.com. Gas, tire, routine maintenance, parking, and other such costs can be obtained locally. Registration and license information can be obtained at the state Department of Motor Vehicles; insurance quotes can be obtained from a local insurance agent, and so on. Make sure that students are as realistic as possible. Have them compare their results to their work in Activity 12.1. Given the typical hours worked and hourly wage received by students, how does before-tax and after-tax income compare to the monthly cost of the automobile?

2. Have the students analyze the total cost of a hypothetical (or real) class trip to a chosen site. Consider air, train, automobile, and bus travel. Airfares can be obtained from www.lowestfare.com; train fares can be found at www.amtrak.com; driving directions (including mileage) can be found at many Internet search sites such as www.mapquest.com; and a regional touring bus company can be reached for bus information. Note that it will likely turn out that a bus is the most economical choice because the costs are spread over a large number of people.

3. Ask your students to consider some of the social costs of driving that were not addressed in this lesson. These might include, for example, the costs of having to build and maintain roads and bridges, the air pollution from auto exhaust, the increased congestion that is experienced, and other external costs. Have the students research the magnitude of these other, non-private costs, in order to come up with a projection of the total costs of driving.

VISUAL 12.1 ▲ Warm-Up

Write the exact percent equivalents and decimal equivalents for these fractions to the nearest 100th:

1. $\frac{1}{2}$
2. $\frac{1}{3}$
3. $\frac{1}{4}$
4. $\frac{1}{5}$
5. $\frac{1}{6}$
6. $\frac{1}{8}$
7. $\frac{1}{10}$
8. $\frac{1}{20}$
9. $\frac{1}{25}$

Find the indicated number

10. 2% of 3500 =
11. 5.8% of 1230 =
12. 120 is _____% of 1200?
13. 25 is _____% of 200?
14. 30 is 50% of _____?
15. 212 is 6.5% of _____?

16. The price of a camera was just reduced by $9. This reduction was 5% of the original price. Find the original price.

17. A car bought for $5800 decreased in value by $1000 the first year. What was the percent of decrease in its value to the nearest 100th?

VISUAL 12.2 A Answer Key to Activity 12.1

Question #		#2	#3		#4	#5	#6	#7	#8	#10	#11	#12
Car #	Type	Price (Q1)	Sales tax	Fees	Final price	% diffrce	20% Down	Ins Cost	Savings Acct Bal	# mon pay	Amt finan	Mon Paym
1	89 Camaro	2750	192.50	275.00	3217.50	17	550	808	2642	48	2667.50	67.95
2	91 Firebird	5000	350.00	275.00	5625.00	13	1000	934	2066	48	4625.00	126.81
3	93 Mustang	4000	280.00	275.00	4555.00	14	800	1021	2179	48	3755.00	101.45
4	94 Taurus	4500	315.00	275.00	5090.00	13	900	753	2347	48	4190.00	114.13
5	92 T-bird	3000	210.00	275.00	3485.00	16	600	758	2642	48	2885.00	76.09
6	92 Metro	1450	101.50	275.00	1826.50	26	290	745	2965	48	1536.50	36.78
7	91 Accord	4250	297.50	275.00	4822.50	13	850	770	2380	48	3972.50	106.52
8	90 Camry	3700	259.00	275.00	4234.00	14	740	653	2607	48	3494.00	93.84

9. Answers will vary.
13. 10,950 miles
14,15,16. See chart above. (Visual 12.2 B)
17. Monthly maintenance = $41.67 which ≈ $42.00
18. Monthly Parking = $8.00
19. Monthly Improvements = 12.50 ($150/12)
20. Monthly Cost of Regis, lic 25.00 ($300/12)
21-22. See Visual 12.2 C

VISUAL 12.2 B

Question #		#13	#14		#15	#16				#17	#18	#19	#20	
Car #	Type	Ann miles	MPG	Avg $ gas	Ann cost gas	Mon cost gas	Year cost insurance	Mon cost insurance	Monthly payment	Monthly mainten	Monthly parking	Monthly access	Monthly regis, lic, insp	Total explicit
1	89 Camaro	10,950	23	$1.429	$680.33	$57.00	$808.00	$67.33	$67.95	$42.00	$8.00	$12.50	$25.00	$279.78
2	91 Firebird	10,950	22	$1.429	$711.25	$59.00	$934.00	$77.83	$126.81	$42.00	$8.00	$12.50	$25.00	$351.14
3	93 Mustang	10,950	26	$1.429	$601.83	$50.00	$1,021.00	$85.08	$101.45	$42.00	$8.00	$12.50	$25.00	$324.03
4	94 Taurus	10,950	24	$1.429	$651.98	$54.00	$753.00	$62.75	$114.13	$42.00	$8.00	$12.50	$25.00	$318.38
5	92 T-bird	10,950	20	$1.429	$782.38	$65.00	$758.00	$63.17	$76.09	$42.00	$8.00	$12.50	$25.00	$291.76
6	92 Metro	10,950	38	$1.429	$411.78	$34.00	$745.00	$62.08	$36.78	$42.00	$8.00	$12.50	$25.00	$220.36
7	91 Accord	10,950	26	$1.429	$601.83	$50.00	$770.00	$64.17	$106.52	$42.00	$8.00	$12.50	$25.00	$308.19
8	90 Camry	10,950	30	$1.429	$521.59	$43.00	$653.00	$54.42	$93.84	$42.00	$8.00	$12.50	$25.00	$278.76

Answers to Questions 23–27

23. Answers vary, but most people do not consider all the implicit and explicit costs of ownership.
24. $480.
25. Studying, socializing, playing sports/exercising, reading, TV, etc.
26. $480 × .12 = $57.60 $480 – 57.60 = $422.40
27. Answers vary.

VISUAL 12.2 C ▲ Implicit Costs of Automobile Ownership: Answer Key

21.

Car #	Type	Savings original	Savings spent	Savings remaining	Interest lost per year	Interest lost per month
1	89 Camaro	4000	1358	2642	$67.90	$6.00
2	91 Firebird	4000	1934	2066	$96.70	$8.00
3	93 Mustang	4000	1821	2179	$91.05	$8.00
4	94 Taurus	4000	1653	2347	$82.65	$7.00
5	92 T-bird	4000	1358	2642	$67.90	$6.00
6	92 Metro	4000	1035	2965	$51.75	$4.00
7	91 Accord	4000	1620	2380	$81.00	$7.00
8	90 Camry	4000	1393	2607	$69.65	$6.00

22. Total Economic (Opportunity) Costs

Car #	Type	Explicit	Implicit	Economic Cost
1	89 Camaro	279.78	$6.00	$285.78
2	91 Firebird	351.14	$8.00	$359.14
3	93 Mustang	324.03	$8.00	$332.03
4	94 Taurus	318.38	$7.00	$325.38
5	92 T-bird	291.76	$6.00	$297.76
6	92 Metro	220.36	$4.00	$224.36
7	91 Accord	308.19	$7.00	$315.19
8	90 Camry	278.76	$6.00	$284.76

VISUAL 12.3A ▲ Answers to Activity 12.2

1,2: Variable costs (gas, maintenance, parking, and accessories) are shown with totals.

Variable Cost Items *are italicized*	Car #1	Car #2	Car #3	Car #4	Car #5	Car #6	Car #7	Car #8
Gas	$57.00	$59.00	$50.00	$54.00	$65.00	$34.00	$50.00	$43.00
Auto Insurance								
Car Loan Paymt								
Maintenance	$42.00	$42.00	$42.00	$42.00	$42.00	$42.00	$42.00	$42.00
Parking Fees	$8.00	$8.00	$8.00	$8.00	$8.00	$8.00	$8.00	$8.00
Accessories	$12.50	$12.50	$12.50	$12.50	$12.50	$12.50	$12.50	$12.50
Regis, Lic, Inspec								
Implicit Costs								
Total Variable Costs	$119.50	$121.50	$112.50	$116.50	$127.50	$96.50	$112.50	$105.50

VISUAL 12.3 B ▲ Answers to Activity 12.2

3. Monthly fixed costs (insurance, loan payment, registration, license, inspection and implicit costs) are shown with totals.

Fixed Cost Items **are in bold**	Car #1	Car #2	Car #3	Car #4	Car #5	Car #6	Car #7	Car #8
Gas								
Auto Insurance	$67.33	$77.83	$85.08	$62.75	$63.17	$62.08	$64.17	$54.42
Car Loan Payment	67.95	126.81	101.45	114.13	76.09	36.78	106.52	93.84
Maintenance								
Parking Fees								
Accessories								
Regis, Lic, Inspect	25.00	25.00	25.00	25.00	25.00	25.00	25.00	25.00
Implicit Costs	6.00	8.00	8.00	7.00	6.00	4.00	7.00	6.00
Total Fixed Costs	**166.28**	**237.64**	**219.53**	**208.88**	**170.26**	**127.86**	**202.69**	**179.26**

VISUAL 12.3 C ▲ Answers to Activity 12.2

4. and 5. Percentage costs of total for variable and fixed expenses.

	#1	#2	#3	#4	#5	#6	#7	#8
Total Variable Costs	$119.50	$121.50	$112.50	$116.50	$127.50	$96.50	$112.50	$105.50
Total Economic Cost	285.78	359.14	332.03	325.38	297.76	224.36	315.19	284.76
% of Total cost	41.8%	33.8%	33.9%	35.8%	42.8%	43.0%	35.7%	37.0%
Total Fixed Costs	166.28	237.64	219.53	208.88	170.26	127.86	202.69	179.26
Total Economic Cost	285.78	359.14	332.03	325.38	297.76	224.36	315.19	284.76
% of Total Costs	58.2%	66.2%	66.1%	64.2%	57.2%	57.0%	64.3%	63.0%

6. Fixed costs constitute a higher percentage (in some cases almost 2/3) of the total cost, and cannot be reduced. Thus, the smaller percentage (variable costs) is the only one that can be reduced and there is much less of that to reduce. It therefore pays to get the lowest fixed costs possible at the time of purchase.

ACTIVITY 12.1 ▲ The Cost of Owning and Operating and Automobile

Record your estimate of the monthly cost of owning and operating an automobile: ________

Finding the Right Car

Now that you have a part-time job and your driver's license, you decide that you want to buy a car. You go shopping and find the perfect used vehicle.

1. Your perfect used vehicle: ______________________________

2. After negotiating with the sales person, you settle on a purchase price of ____________. (The purchase prices are supplied with the list of cars on data sheet 12.1)

Sales tax is applied to automobile purchases. Since the tax rate for your local area is 7 percent, you need to add a 7 percent sales tax to the purchase price of the vehicle.

3. Taxes on your car will be ______________.

Next, you find out that you must pay a $50 fee for transferring the title of the vehicle, a $25 document-processing fee, and the annual registration fee for this car of $200.

4. The final price of your car including taxes and fees is ___________.

5. Calculate and record the percent increase between the final price and the agreed upon purchase price: _____.

Financing Your Car: The Downpayment

Imagine that you have $4,000 in your savings account. You want to keep part of that money for your college fund. You decide to secure a bank loan and make a 20 percent down payment and finance the remainder through a loan. The loan officer at a bank informs you that the bank can lend you funds at a 10 percent interest rate if you make a 20 percent down payment on the vehicle's final price (the price found in answer 2 above).

6. The down payment for your car is ______________.

Insuring Your Car

The bank needs proof that the vehicle is insured before it can give you a loan on the car. Your local insurance agent asks you a number of questions: how old are you, how many years have you been driving, what is your gender, how do you plan to use the vehicle, how many miles do you plan to drive each day, what are the make and model of the vehicle, do you smoke, are you a good student, how much liability protection do you want, do you wish to insure the vehicle for collision damage, what size of insurance deductible do you want, etc?

7. When you have answered all of the agent's questions, she tells you that the annual cost of your insurance will be __________. (Obtain from Data Sheet 12.1)

The agent explains that insurance is expensive because you have no driving experience and are very young. Accident statistics indicate that drivers in your age category are more likely than those in any other age category to have an accident. She also tells you that if you were not a good student, your insurance costs would be even higher! Fortunately, she also tells you that you can expect the annual premium to go down for every year that you drive without an accident.

8. After paying for insurance and the down payment, you have __________ left in your savings account.

9. List some alternative uses for the money you spent on the down payment and insurance. How else could you have used the money?

10. The loan officer tells you that after four years the residual value of your car will be about zero. You decide that you don't want the term of the loan to be any longer than four years. For a four-year loan, you will have a total of ______ equal-sized monthly payments.

11. Since you made a down payment of 20 percent of the price of the vehicle, the amount you are borrowing is _________.

12. Taking into account the interest rate of 10 percent, the amount you are borrowing, and the term of the loan, the monthly payment will be _________. (Secure from Data Sheet 12.1)

Other Costs: Gas, Maintenance, Parking, and Accessories

To determine the amount of money you will spend on other costs, you must decide how many miles you expect to drive each year. Suppose you calculate that over the course of a year you will drive, on average, 30 miles each day.

13. Calculate the total number of miles you expect to drive in a year: _____________.

14. The gas mileage (the number of miles per gallon) that your car gets is __________. (Secure from Data Sheet 12.1)

15. If the average price for regular unleaded gas is expected to be $1.429 per gallon, then the annual cost of gasoline will be _____________.

16. The monthly cost of gasoline will be ______________ (rounded to the nearest dollar).

17. To keep the car running well, you will need to pay for oil changes, a periodic tune-up, replacement tires, and other required maintenance. This averages at least $500 per year. The monthly cost of this maintenance is _____________ (rounded to the nearest dollar).

18. The cost of a parking sticker at school and for the parking meters where you work is about $96 per year. What is the monthly cost for parking?

19. You are likely to want to make some improvements to your car, such as an improved sound system, deluxe seat covers, etc. Suppose that accessories for your car cost $150 per year. These accessories add a monthly expense of ________.

Registration, License, Inspection, etc.

20. You have managed to bundle this year's fees for registration, license, etc. into your auto loan, but each successive year you will have to pay approximately $300. These fees add a monthly expense of __________.

Use the information that you gathered above to complete this table of explicit costs. Explicit costs are the costs for which cash is actually used to make payment—costs for which a financial transaction actually takes place.

ACTIVITY 12.1: Table 1

The Average Monthly Cost of Owning And Operating an Automobile: Some Unpleasant Automotive Arithmetic?

Cost Item	Average Monthly Cost
Gas	
Auto Insurance	
Monthly Payment	
Maintenance (including oil changes, tires, tune-ups, scheduled and unscheduled maintenance, etc.)	
Parking	
Accessories	
Registration, License, Inspection, etc	
Total Explicit Costs (Monthly)	

Implicit Costs

21. With *implicit costs* no actual exchange of money takes place, but the individual is still giving up something as a result of making a choice. In this example, by purchasing a vehicle, you are giving up the interest your savings could have earned in your savings account. If you could be earning 5 percent interest on your savings account, then the monthly interest that you are giving up is ________ (round to the nearest dollar). This amount is the monthly implicit cost of using the money in your savings account to pay for your down payment and auto insurance.

Total Economic (Opportunity) Costs

22. The sum of the explicit and implicit costs of owning and operating your car is ___________. This amount represents the total opportunity cost of owning and operating the car. This amount is also often referred to as the "economic cost." It is different from an "accounting cost" in that it includes both implicit and explicit costs. Accounting cost generally looks at explicit costs only.

23. Compare the total economic cost of owning and operating a car above with the estimate you made at the beginning of this activity. Why are the two amounts different?

Are you surprised by how money is needed to pay for your car?

The Monthly Income Needed to Afford a Car

24. If you work 80 hours each month (about 20 hours per week) in a part-time, after-school job, earning $6 per hour, your monthly earnings will be ________.

ACTIVITY 12.1 (continued)

25. List some activities you could be doing instead of working.

26. The earnings you calculated above are called *pre-tax earnings*. The government withholds money for Social Security, Medicare, state and federal income taxes, etc. If the money the government withholds is about 12 percent of your earnings, you will have approximately _________ to spend each month. This amount is your *after-tax earnings*.

27. Compare the explicit and implicit costs of owning and operating your car and your earnings after taxes from your part-time job. Think about whether purchasing the car is a wise decision. What would be the best decision to make about purchasing a car?

ACTIVITY 12.2 ▲ The Fixed and Variable Costs of Owning and Operating a Car

Refer to Table 1 in Activity 12.1. One way of reducing the cost of owning and operating a car in the short-run is to cut back on the usage of your vehicle. Such a change will help reduce the *variable costs* of driving. Variable costs increase when you drive more miles. They decrease when you drive fewer miles.

Not all costs are variable. Some costs are fixed. *Fixed costs* refer to those costs that do not change with the number of miles that you drive. These costs are unavoidable unless you decide you no longer wish to own a car.

As long as you have decided that you are going to have a car, the only way to actually reduce the cost of driving is to reduce the variable costs in Table 1.

1. Look at Table 1. What are the variable costs of owning and operating your own car?

2. What is the total monthly sum of these variable costs?

3. What is the total monthly sum of the fixed costs listed in Table 1 (assume the implicit cost is fixed)?

4. What percent of the total cost is represented by variable costs?

5. What percent of the total cost is represented by fixed cost?

6. How does this breakdown of costs show that it is difficult to control the total cost of owning and operating a car in the short run?

ACTIVITY 12.3 ▲ Planes, Trains, and Automobiles: The Economics of Long Distance Travel

What do you think is the least expensive way for people to travel across the United States (circle one)? (Airplane, Train, Automobile) Economics can help you decide what the best option is for long distance travel.

Suppose you live in Los Angeles and you want to see a Broadway show in midtown Manhattan in New York City. You research some costs and find the following (the following information is adapted from real information in September 2000):

Air Travel

Cost of round trip ticket from Los Angeles to New York airport:	$384
Round trip cab fare from New York airport to Broadway (with tip):	$90
Cost of parking car at Los Angeles airport for 2 days:	$25
Total time spent, round trip:	17 hours

Train Travel

Cost of round trip ticket from LA to NY Penn Station	$326
Round trip cab fare from NY Penn Station to Broadway (with tip)	$20
Round trip cab fare from LA train station (with tip)	$60
Total time spent, round trip	130 hours

Automobile Travel

Cost per mile	$.345*
Length of Trip--5596 miles	
Cost of lodging round trip: 4 nights at $75 per night	
Highway tolls, round trip	$75
Parking in NY	$30
Total time spent, round trip	102 hours

1. Calculate the explicit cost of each type of transportation. For simplicity, assume that the $.345 cost per mile is an explicit cost.
Air Travel __________
Train Travel __________
Automobile Travel _________

2. Which type of travel has the lowest explicit costs?

3. Do you think most people would choose the type of transportation with the lowest explicit cost to travel to Manhattan in this situation? Explain why or why not.

4. If Jerry earns $1000 per week for working 40 hours, then how much does Jerry earn per hour?

5. Use Jerry's hourly wage to calculate the implicit cost of each type of travel for Jerry. That is, what is the cost of the time that Jerry would spend traveling?
Air Travel __________
Train Travel __________
Automobile Travel _________

6. What is the total cost (explicit and implicit) of each type of travel?
Air Travel __________
Train Travel __________
Automobile Travel _________

7. Which type of travel is the least expensive for Jerry?

8. Why might someone choose to travel between the cities by train or automobile?

DATA SHEET 12.1

Car Number	Type of Car	Sales Price	Annual Insurance Cost	Monthly Payment	Gas Mileage
1	'89 Chevrolet Camaro	$2750	$808	$67.95	23
2	'91 Pontiac Firebird	$5000	$934	$126.81	22
3	'93 Ford Mustang	$4000	$1021	$101.45	26
4	'94 Ford Taurus	$4500	$753	$114.13	24
5	'92 Ford Thunderbird	$3000	$758	$76.09	20
6	'92 Geo Metro	$1450	$745	$36.78	38
7	'91 Honda Accord	$4250	$770	$106.52	26
8	'90 Toyota Camry	$3700	$653	$93.84	30

Lesson 13

Tax Math

Mathematics Focus:

Pre-Algebra, Algebra I

Mathematics Prerequisites:

Prior to using this lesson, students should be able to:

- Possess a sense of numbers and operations
- Understand how to apply percentage calculations in the solving of problems
- Know how to calculate rates, percentages, and proportions
- Understand the basic properties of a step function

Lesson Objectives:

To apply prerequisite mathematics concepts and processes to the structure of U.S. taxes to:

- Explain the difference among progressive, proportional, and regressive taxes
- Explain that the federal income tax is progressive and the payroll tax is both proportional and regressive
- Explain the difference between average and marginal tax rates

Overview of Mathematics and Economics:

People pay a variety of taxes. Among the different types of taxes that we pay are the federal income tax and the payroll tax. How these taxes are applied has interesting economic implications. The income tax is a *progressive tax*. When a tax is progressive, the average rate of taxation is higher for higher-income earners than it is for lower-income earners. The payroll tax has two parts (Social Security and Medicare) and is primarily a *proportional tax*. For the most part, everyone pays the same tax rate on the payroll tax regardless of his/her level of income. However, since there is an earnings limit applied to one portion of the payroll tax, it is also a *regressive tax* over a range of earnings. That is, the average rate of taxation is higher for low-income earners than it is for high-income earners.

Economists find it useful to distinguish between *marginal* and *average* tax rates. The federal income tax is progressive because higher marginal tax rates are applied to higher levels of taxable income. Marginal tax rates refer to the different incremental rates of taxation that are applied over different ranges of income. In 2000, the federal government had five different marginal income tax rates. The average tax rate is measured as the entire tax liability divided by overall taxable income.

This lesson acquaints students with some of the economic properties of the taxes for which they will be responsible over their lifetimes. It also looks at some of the simple mathematics underlying tax calculations. Graphs and percentages are used to help connect mathematics to various tax concepts.

Mathematics and Economics Terms:

- Average tax rate
- Income tax
- Marginal tax rate
- Medicare
- Payroll tax
- Progressive tax
- Proportional tax
- Regressive tax
- Social Security
- Step function
- Taxable income

Materials:

- Straight edge
- Overhead transparencies of Visuals 13.1 and 13.2
- One copy of Activities 13.1 and 13.2 for each student
- Graphing calculator (optional)
- 1040 federal tax form, note that this form can be found on the Internet at ftp.fedworld.gov/pub/irs-pdf/f1040.pdf

Estimated Time:

80–100 Minutes

Procedures:

1. Warm-Up Activity: Have the students complete the warm-up found on Visual 13.1. Go over the answers with the class.

1. $12.99 + .84 = $13.83
2. Total for the books: $5.98 + $12.50 + $35.99 + $7.99 = $62.46
   Total with tax: $62.46 · 1.05 = $65.58
   Handling charge: $3.20 + 3 · $2 = $9.20
   Total charge = $65.58 + $9.20 = $74.78

2. Tell the students that in this lesson they will investigate the mathematics behind some of the taxes that they can expect to pay in their working lifetimes. The specific taxes they will investigate are the federal income tax and the payroll tax. This latter tax has two components: a tax to pay for Social Security (the program that provides retirement, disability, and survivor benefits) and another one to pay for Medicare (the program that provides hospital insurance for the elderly). Each of these taxes has interesting economic properties that can be explained by using simple algebra.

3. Before distributing Activity 13.1, indicate that this activity focuses on average, marginal, and progressive tax rates as they relate to income. Define each of these. *Average tax rate* is the amount of tax divided by taxable income. *Marginal tax rates* are the incremental rates of income taxation that apply to different ranges of taxable income. In the U.S., these marginal tax rates tend to increase as income increases. A progressive income tax is one in which the average tax rates increase as income increases, or conversely, average tax rates decrease as income decreases. Have the students work through Activity 13.1 individually or in groups.

The answers to the questions are:

1. Freddie: 15 percent
   Elissa 21.5 percent
   Velma 25.9 percent
2. Velma pays the largest share of her income in the form of income taxes. Freddie has the lowest average tax liability.
3. Elissa's taxable income is three times larger than Freddie's. Her tax liability is more than four times larger than Freddie's.
4. Velma's taxable income is twice as large as Elissa's and her tax liability is 2.4 times larger than Elissa's.
5. The average tax rate for the individuals increased as the taxable income increased. Since the average rate increased, the marginal rates must have increased for various increments of income to make the average rates higher for higher levels of income.
6. (\$51,000 – \$25,750) · (0.28) + 25,750 · (0.15) = 7070 + 3862.50 = \$10,932.50. Notice that it does not equal the \$10,940 given in the above table. This discrepancy occurs because the tax tables report the same tax liability for each level of income within a range of \$50. For example, the tax owed on \$51,050 is the same as the tax owed on \$51,000. The IRS calculates the tax liability within each \$50 range by calculating the tax for the middle income of the range. In this case, Elissa's tax liability could more accurately be calculated by using the middle of the range. Notice the answer when the middle of the range is used: (51,025 – \$25,750) · (0.28) + (25,750) · (0.15) = \$7077 +

$3862.50 = $10,939.50, which rounded upward to the nearest whole number is $10,940. Note that these income thresholds are adjusted upward each year, so you may need to alter the formula if you are using a more recent tax form.

7. The income tax is progressive in that the rates increase as the income level increases. When graphed, the relationship between the marginal tax rate and the level of taxable income is a step function. Show Visual 13.2 when they have completed this activity. Note that this visual applies to single taxpayers. Taxpayers with different filing status, such as married, filing jointly, face different income threshholds at which the different marginal tax rates are applied.

■ COMMENT: As the students are going through the activity, point out examples of average, marginal, and progressive tax rates. Have the students indicate how marginal tax rates affect average tax rates. Have them also indicate the relationship between marginal and progressive tax rates. Point out that the marginal tax rates are often hidden since they are buried in the tax table calculations. That is, the tax tables have different marginal rates in the federal tax code embedded within the tables themselves.

4. Students are also asked to graph the marginal tax rates for different levels of taxable income. The resulting graph shows that the marginal tax rate is an application of a step function. You may wish to take this opportunity to explain (or reiterate) some mathematical properties of a step function. Exercise #3 in the Extension Activities section extends this analysis to writing out a system of inequalities to represent the structure of the personal income tax.

5. Distribute Activity 13.2 and discuss the two types of payroll taxes: Medicare and Social Security. Remind the students that in the last activity we looked at the federal income tax, which is a progressive tax. There are other forms of taxation, which are regressive and proportional. Define these terms. A regressive tax is one that is just the opposite of a progressive tax; the percentage of income paid in taxes goes down as the income increases. A proportional tax occurs when the tax rate stays the same across all levels of income. Have the students do Activity 13.2 either individually or in groups.

◆ **The answers to the questions are:**

1. Jerry's total payroll tax is $1,147.50, which is 7.65 percent of his income.
2. Janice's average payroll tax is also 7.65 percent.
3. (.0765) · ($76,200) + (.0145) · ($100,000 − $76,200) = $6,174.40
   Jimmy's payroll tax is 6.17 percent of his income.
4. The Social Security portion of the payroll tax is proportional up to the

limit and then becomes regressive because people who make more than the limit do not pay any more Social Security taxes, thus making their average tax rate lower than those whose earnings are below the limit. The Medicare tax is a proportional tax since everyone pays the same percentage regardless of level of income. Putting the two taxes together, the payroll tax is proportional up to the Social Security earnings limit (in this case $76,200) and then becomes regressive.

... will total $7624.40 if he earns $200,000. The formula ... n be written as follows: For a year in which Bill's labor ... er than $76,200: Bill's payroll tax liability = ($76,200) · ... income – $76,200) · (0.0145).

... hich Bill's labor income is less than $76,200: Bill's pay- ... (0.0765) x Bill's income.

■ **COMMENTS**: A payroll tax is, for the most part, a proportional tax. However, once a person's annual labor earnings reach a certain limit, Social Security taxes are no longer deducted from the person's paycheck. At the point at which the earnings limit is reached, the Social Security portion of the payroll tax becomes a regressive tax (one in which workers with higher incomes pay a smaller share of their income in the form of taxes than do workers with lower incomes).

This threshold amount varies from one year to the next, so be aware that some of the information in this activity may become outdated. You can easily update this information by visiting the Social Security Web site at www.ssa.gov. The Medicare tax is proportional throughout the entire range of employee earnings. You may wish to tell the students that the payroll taxes that are paid by an employee are matched dollar for dollar by the employer. Even though the employers pay the tax, economists argue that it is employees, customers, and/or business owners who bear the burden of this matching contribution. A firm that pays 7.65 percent of an employee's earnings to Social Security and Medicare must be charging higher prices, paying workers less than they would otherwise, or providing a lesser amount of net profit to the firm's owners (the shareholders of corporations for example). Only the employee share of the payroll tax is outlined in Activity 13.2. Extension exercise #4 is a graphical extension of Activity 13.2.

Extension Activities:

1. Using the information on Velma's income in the table for Activity 13.1 and the marginal tax rate information reported in #7 of Activity 13.1, calculate Velma's tax liability.

(Velma's income tax liability is calculated as ($102,000 – $62,450) · (0.31) + ($62,450 – $25,750) · (0.28) + (25,750) · (0.15) = $26,399). What is Velma's marginal tax bracket? (31%).

2. If you live in a state or city with an income tax, design an activity similar to Activity 13.1, using your state or local tax information.

3. Use a system of inequalities to represent the personal income tax structure that is reported in #7 of Activity 13.1. Write out the formula for tax liabilities over each of the five intervals of the tax structure.

◆ For example, for taxable income such that $\$130,250 \geq x > \$62,450$, the tax liability formula can be written:
Tax liability = $(x - 62,450) \times (0.31) + (\$62,450 - \$25,750) \times (0.28) + (\$25,750) \times (0.15)$
The tax formulas are:
For taxable income $x > \$283,150$
Tax liability = $(x - \$283,150) \times (0.396) + (\$283,150 - \$130,250) \times (0.36) + (\$130,250 - \$62,450) \times (0.31) + (\$62,450 - \$25,750) \times (0.28) + (\$25,750) \times (0.15)$
For taxable income $\$283,150 \geq x > \$130,250$
Tax liability = $(x - 130,250) \times (0.36) + (\$130,250 - \$62,450) \times (0.31) + (\$62,450 - \$25,750) \times (0.28) + (\$25,750) \times (0.15)$
For taxable income $\$130,250 \geq x > \$62,450$
Tax liability = $(x - 62,450) \times (0.31) + (\$62,450 - \$25,750) \times (0.28) + (\$25,750) \times (0.15)$
For taxable income $\$62,450 \geq x > \$25,750$
Tax liability = $(x - \$25,750) \times (0.28) + (\$25,750) \times (0.15)$
For taxable income $\$25,750 \geq x$
Tax liability = $0.15x$

4. Have the students graph total payroll tax contributions on the vertical axis and labor income on the horizontal axis (let income range from 0 to \$200,000). What type of function results? *(It is a piecewise function.)* What happens to the slope of the function at income = \$76,200? *(It declines from 0.0765 to 0.0145.)* Ask the students to comment on this slope. What is the economic interpretation of the slope of this function? *(It is the total payroll tax rate up to \$76,200 and the Medicare tax rate thereafter.)*

VISUAL 13.1 ▲ Warm-Up

1. A new CD that Janice has wanted to buy for a long time is on sale for $12.99. The sales tax where Janice lives amounts to 6.5 percent. With tax included, how much will Janice have to pay for the CD?

2. Jeremy is buying four books from an on-line bookstore. The prices of the books are $5.98, $12.50, $35.99, and $7.99. Jeremy lives in a state where the bookstore must charge 5 percent sales tax. In addition, Jeremy will have to pay shipping and handling charges. The bookstore's handling charges are as follows: $3.20 for the first item; $2.00 each for the second through fourth items; and $1.00 each for any additional items. Note that the handling charge is not taxed. What is Jeremy's total bill for the four books?

VISUAL 13.2 ▲ The Structure of the Federal Income Tax

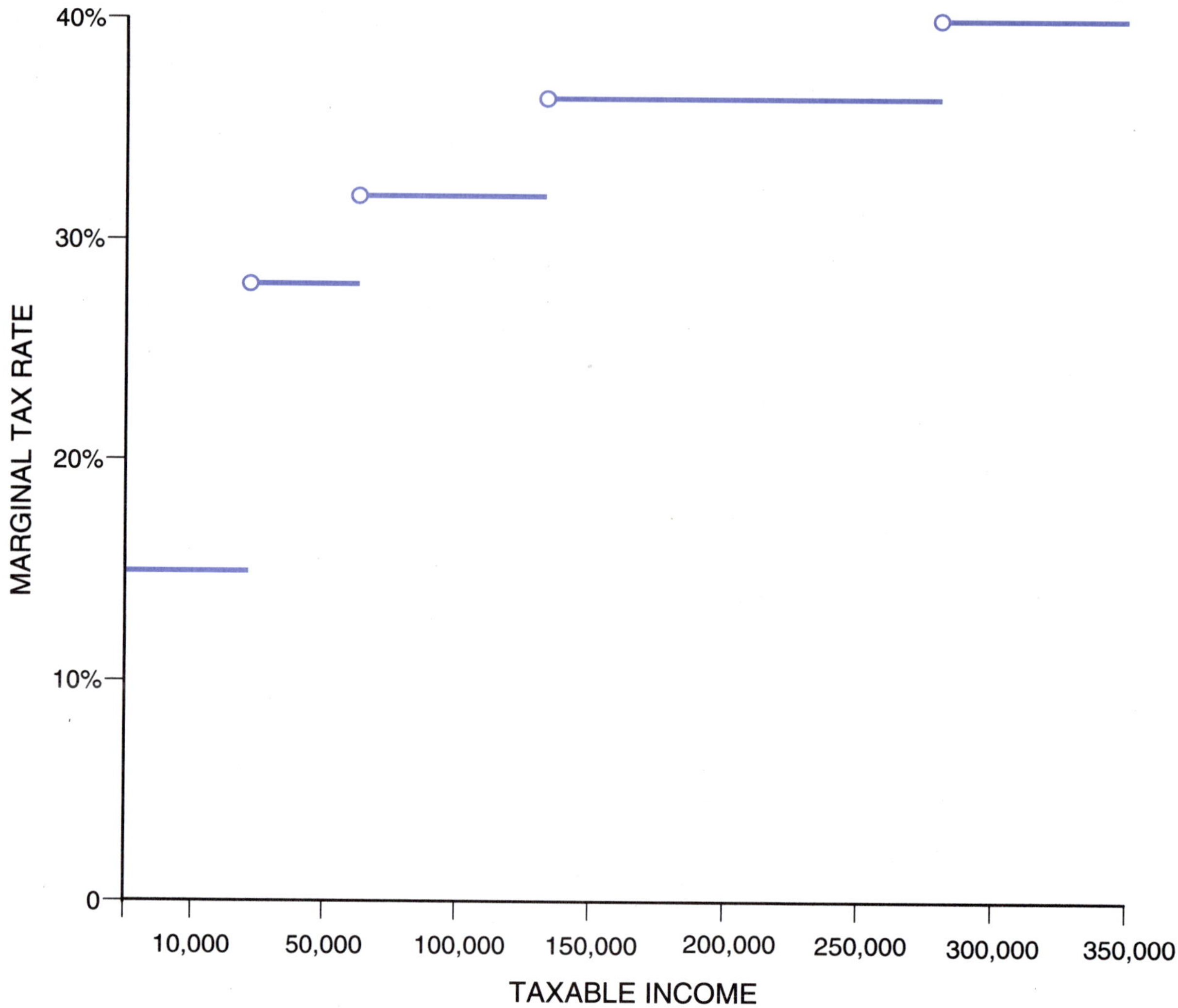

ACTIVITY 13.1 ▲ The Federal Income Tax: A Progressive Tax

How does the government determine how much income tax people should pay? The table below shows the total income tax paid by three hypothetical single taxpayers. These numbers are taken from the 1999 federal personal income tax form—the 1040 form. Taxable income is that income which is subject to taxation. It equals total income minus exemptions, deductions, and adjustments. Study the table below in answering the questions that follow.

	Taxable Income	Income Tax Paid	Tax Paid as a *Percent* of Taxable Income
Freddie	$17,000	$2,554	
Elissa	$51,000	$10,940	
Velma	$102,000	$26,399	

1. Calculate the total tax paid by each person as a percent of his/her taxable income; enter this percentage in the last column of the table. This percent is known as the *average tax rate.*

2. Which of the three individuals has the highest average tax liability? That is, who pays the largest share of taxable income in the form of income taxes? Who has the lowest average tax liability?

3. Elissa's taxable income is how many times larger than Freddie's? Elissa's tax liability is how many times larger than Freddie's?

4. How does Velma's taxable income compare to Elissa's? How does Velma's tax liability compare to Elissa's?

5. Our federal income tax is known as a progressive tax in that as the taxable income rises, the average tax rate increases. The average income tax rate is also lower for people with lower incomes. How does the above table indicate that we have a progressive income tax system?

6. Look at the instructions in a recent 1040 federal tax form or go to the Internet site of the Internal Revenue Service, which is www.irs.gov. Embedded within the IRS tax tables is an algebraic formula that is used to calculate tax liability. The IRS applies higher *marginal tax rates* to higher levels of income in the tax tables. A marginal tax rate is an incremental tax rate that applies only to income within certain ranges. For example, in 1999, the marginal tax rate for single taxpayers for the first $25,750 of income was 15 percent. Income between $25,750 and $62,450 was taxed at a marginal rate of 28 percent. Using this information, recalculate Elissa's tax liability and verify the amount reported in the table. Remember that the first $25,750 of Elissa's income is taxed at a different rate than the rate for the rest of her income.

ACTIVITY 13.1 (continued)

7. The 1999 income tax structure for single taxpayers was as follows:

Range of Taxable Income	Marginal Tax Rate
From $0 to $25,750	15%
From $25,750 to $62,450	28%
From $62,450 to $130,250	31%
From $130,250 to $283,150	36%
From $283,150	39.6%

The highest marginal tax rate is 39.6 percent. Why is our income tax structure considered a progressive tax?

Use graph paper to graph the relationship between the marginal tax rate and the level of taxable income. What type of function is this?

ACTIVITY 13.2 ▲ The Payroll Tax

Parts of the Payroll Tax

- Social Security Tax (includes contributions for retirement, survivor-benefits, and disability insurance)
  6.2 percent of annual labor income earned up to a maximum of $76,200
  0 percent for earnings in excess of $76,200
- Medicare Tax (hospital insurance for the elderly)
  1.45 percent of all earnings
- Total Payroll Tax for 2000
  7.65 percent of earnings up to $76,200, 1.45 percent thereafter

1. Using this information, calculate the amount of payroll tax that Jerry will pay if his total earnings for the year total $15,000. What is his average payroll tax liability, as a percent of his income?

2. Earnings for Janice during the year totalled $55,000. What is her average payroll tax liability as a percent of her income?

3. Jimmy earns $100,000 for the year. What is his average payroll tax liability as a percent of his income?

4. Is the Social Security part of the payroll tax a progressive, proportional, or regressive tax? What about the Medicare part of the payroll tax: progressive, proportional or regressive? Explain.

5. Bill is having a good earnings year and needs help in planning for his payroll tax contributions. Can you help him calculate what his total contribution will be if he earns $200,000 this year? Bill just found out his income is likely to be at least $250,000 this year. Perhaps, it is best if you just write out the formula for calculating the payroll tax liability so Bill can calculate his tax every year regardless of what he makes. What is (are) the formula(s)?

Lesson 14

The Mathematics of Savings

Mathematics Focus:

Algebra I, Algebra II, and Precalculus

Mathematics Prerequisites:

Prior to using this lesson, students should be able to:

- Use simple and compound interest formulas
- Evaluate functions containing the value "e" with the help of a calculator and direction
- Calculate percentages
- Evaluate expressions which contain exponents

Lesson Objectives:

To apply prerequisite mathematics concepts and processes to situations involving personal savings to

- Explain that, because of interest compounding, funds saved today by a 22 year old will accrue to sums that are multiples of the original investment upon reaching retirement age
- Explain the mathematics that underlies the mechanical calculations of such things as the future value of savings, the future value of an annuity, and compound growth of interest

Overview of Mathematics and Economics:

Because of interest compounding, establishing a commitment to personal savings early in one's professional career can yield large long-run benefits. This lesson looks at the mathematics that underlie the computations of the future value of savings. These computations are now commonly found at many on-line financial calculators. Students will see that relatively modest savings, when compounded over many years at rates of interest that appear to be historically achievable, can lead to the student being a multi-millionaire by the end of his or her working lifetime. The key is, of course, that students abstain from spending and commit to saving early on in their working life.

This lesson also looks at a simple mathematical rule (an application of a logarithmic function) for understanding the economics of compound growth of interest payments. The "rule of 72" is a useful tool that will help reinforce the notion of interest compounding. You may wish to note that, for simplicity, tax liabilities of future savings and the loss of purchasing power due to inflation, have been suppressed from the analysis of the future value of savings.

While this lesson has been created for the use of algebra instructors, business teachers may also find the activities useful for their students as well.

Mathematics and Economic Terms:

- Annuity
- Exponent
- Future value
- Interest compounding
- Interest rate
- Percent
- Present value
- Savings

Materials:

- One copy of Visuals 14.1, 14.2, and 14.3 and Activities 14.1, 14.2, and 14.3 for each student
- Scientific calculator
- Access to the internet (optional)

Estimated Time:

80–100 minutes

Procedures:

1. Warm-Up Activity: Distribute a copy of Visual 14.1 to each student. Ask students to complete this warm-up activity and discuss the answers in class.

Answers to Visual 14.1 follow.

1 (a).

Pennies	Day 1	Day 2	Day 3	Day 4	Day 5	Day 6	Day 7
Week 1	1	2	4	8	16	32	64
Week 2	128	256	512	1024	2048	4096	8192
Week 3	16384	32768	65536	131072	262144	524288	1048576

Total = 2097151 pennies = $20,971.51

1 (b). This is an unreasonable savings plan because you will not be able to acquire that many pennies each day.

1 (c). Answers should include saving a modest amount regularly, placing money in an interest accumulating situation, and not removing money from the account.

2. Give each student a copy of Visual 14.2. Inform students that these are the formulas they will use to complete Activities 14.1, 14.2, and 14.3. (Suggest that students save this page for future reference and discussion with their parents.) The future value of savings formula is that which is used by a calculator to compute the amount to which a given amount of savings invested today at an interest rate of "r" will accumulate in "n" years time. Another formula in Visual 14.2 is used to calculate the future value of an annuity after "n" years when a constant monthly payment is made and invested at a monthly interest rate of "r/12". The final formula in Visual 14.2 is used to determine the amount to which the value of an asset will accrue over time when interest continuously compounds. You may wish to note that these formulas are similar to those found in Lesson 11. While it isn't necessary for students to memorize these formulas, you may wish to inform students that these are the formulas that underlie the financial computations that are made mechanically by calculators and computers.

3. Distribute a copy of Activity 14.1 to each student. This activity looks at the incredible benefit of making a commitment to saving at an early age. In this exercise, students find that if they are able to invest $5000 at a 9 percent rate of interest at age 22 (this is the approximate age of the typical student in her first year of full-time work after graduating with a 4-year university degree), they can expect a sum of $241,636 when retiring at age 67.

1. $241,636
2. The "miracle" of compound growth. Interest is not only being earned on the original amount invested, it is also being earned on previous interest earnings. Note that this result, subject to the normal differences associated with rounding, is the same as that which is obtained from a financial calculator, such as "How much will my savings be worth?" at www.kiplinger.com.

4. Distribute a copy of Activity 14.2 to each student. This exercise asks students to imagine making a commitment to investing $300 each month in a retirement account for 45 years. This could involve, say, personal retirement contributions of $150 per month ($1800 a year) that are matched by an employer. If funds accumulate in this retirement account at an annual rate of 9 percent (this is roughly the long-term rate on stock investments), students can expect a sum of $2,221,464 at the end of 45 years. This is due to the "miracle" of compound growth. Explain that this occurs because interest accrues on itself by a remarkable amount over a long time series. Extension exercise number 2 addresses what happens to annuitized calculations when the investment period is shortened and the interest rate is lowered.

1. $2,221,464. This too can be calculated by using financial calculators such as those at www.kiplinger.com.
2. Answers will vary, but this will seem like a tremendous amount of money to most students.
3. $17,500 per year.
4. $1458 per month.
5. $1158 is left.
6. About $35 per week, or $5 per day.
7. This should seem quite realistic to many students. You may wish to note that it is common for many businesses to contribute to employee retirement funds.

5. Distribute a copy of Visual 14.3 to each student. The formulas in this visual look at the growth of $1 of savings at a hypothetical interest rate of 100 percent, assuming different frequencies of interest compounding. Discuss each formula, noting that a 100 percent rate of interest is represented in decimal form by 1, 100 percent compounded semiannually is represented by a semiannual interest rate of 50 percent (0.5 in decimal form), and so on.

When you have finished discussing these compounding formulas, inform students that an interesting case occurs when interest is allowed to compound continuously. In this situation, it can be shown that $1 invested at a rate of 100 percent for one year, accumulates to a value of $2.71828. Since this is the number for "e", it can be said that $1 that is continuously compounded at a rate of 100 percent for one year will accumulate to $e.

6. Ask students to review the formula for compound growth in Visual 14.2. This is a general formula that relates to interest compounding. An asset, A, that is invested at an interest rate, r, for a period of t years, will grow into a value of $\$Ae^{rt}$ by the end of those t years. As noted above, in the case of $1 initially invested at a rate of 100 percent for 1 year, with continuously compounding interest, the formula Ae^{rt} is equivalent to $\$1e^1 = \$e$. This formula is more general because it allows us to substitute in different interest rates, time periods, or initial asset values.

7. Distribute a copy of Activity 14.3 to each student. This activity uses the continuous growth formula from Visual 14.2. Students are asked to determine how long it will take $500 to double at alternative interest rates when interest is compounded continuously. If you have not covered natural logarithms (and log operations) in your class, you will need to help your students through the derivation of the "doubling" formula. Make sure they have a scientific calculator so that they can compute the value of ln 2. The "rule of 72" is a simple "back of the envelope" way to approximate how long it takes for money to double. Seventy-two divided by the prevailing interest rate gives you a rough approximation of how many years it takes an asset of initial value \$A to double to \$2A. Students see that the reason 72 is used is because it is close to the actual value for doubling of magnitudes (69.3—but who ever heard of the "rule of 69.3"?), and it is convenient, because 72 is divisible by several whole numbers.

1. About 0.693
2. 0.693/0.06 = 11.55 years.
3. Answers will vary.
4. 1, 3, 23, 69. Note that 23 and 69 are not ordinarily considered viable rates of interest on savings—although rates paid on credit cards can be 23%—so 69 is not a particularly useful number for simple calculations.
5. 1, 2, 3, 4, 6, 8, 9, 12, 18, 24, 36, 72.
6. 12 years. This is 0.45 years longer than the earlier calculation—not too bad.

Extension Activities:

1. Alter the example in Activity 14.1 to see what happens to the future value of savings when the initial amount is changed, when the time period is changed, and/or when the interest rate is different.

2. Alter Activity 14.2 so that the time period is 35 years (so that contributions begin at age 32) instead of 45 years. How does this change the accumulation? *(It falls to \$882,535)*. What about if the time period is 25 years? *(It falls further to \$336,337)*. What happens if the time period remains at 45 years, but the annual interest rate is 6 percent instead of 9 percent? This can be thought of as the difference between investing in the stock market and investing in intermediate- or long-term Treasury securities. (The accumulation falls to \$826,798). Note how sensitive the accumulations are to length of time and rate of interest.

3. Ask students to use the formula that was derived in Activity 14.3 to determine how much their current savings will be worth when they reach the normal retirement age of 67. Note that they can do this both by using the simplified "rule of 72" and the continuously compounded growth formula. Have them calculate this at the alternative interest rates of 3 percent, 6 percent, 9 percent, and 12 percent. They will no doubt be surprised at the difference in accumulations at alternative assumed rates of interest. For the compound growth formula, you may need to give them the hint that t = 67 − current age. For example, if they are 17, then t = 50. If they wish to be more precise, they can break this into decimals. For example, if they are 16 years, 6 months old, then t = 67 − 16.5 = 50.5. For the rule of 72 calculation, a simple approximation method will do.

VISUAL 14.1 ▲ Warm-Up

1. You have decided to start a savings account with pennies you accumulate during a 3 week period. Each day you save twice as many pennies as you saved the day before. After 21 days how may pennies will you have to start your savings account? Assume that you begin on Day 1 with 1 penny.

a. Keep your penny count in the following table:

Pennies	Day 1	Day 2	Day 3	Day 4	Day 5	Day 6	Day 7
WEEK 1							
WEEK 2							
WEEK 3							

Total = ___________ pennies = $___________

b. Is this a reasonable savings plan? Why or why not?

c. Describe what you believe to be characteristics of a reasonable savings plan.

VISUAL 14.2

The Future Value of Savings

The Future Value (FV) of savings "n" years from today, when PV (the present value of current savings) is deposited today at an annual interest rate of "r" is expressed as:

$$FV = PV \cdot (1 + r)^n$$

where r is in decimal form.

The Future Value of an Annuity

$$\text{Future Value} = \text{Constant Annual Payment} \cdot \frac{\{(1 + \text{interest rate})^n - 1\}}{\text{interest rate}}$$

$$FV = PMT \frac{\{(1+ r)^n - 1\}}{r}$$

Where FV is future value, PMT is the constant annual payment, r is the interest rate expressed in decimal form, and n is the number of years in the future for which the computation is being made.

To calculate the future value of an annuity when the constant payment is made monthly,

$$FV = \text{Monthly PMT} \frac{\{(1+ r/12)^{n \cdot 12} - 1\}}{r/12}$$

A Formula For Compound Growth

An asset, A, that is earning an interest rate, r, will appreciate to a value of Ae^{rt} at the end of t years if interest is allowed to compound continuously.

VISUAL 14.3 ▲ Interest Compounding

Assuming a 100% rate of interest (r = 1).

Annual Compounding:
Value of \$1 at end of 1 year = $\$1(1 + 1)^1 = \$2$

Semiannual Compounding:
Value of \$1 at end of 1 year = $\$1(1 + .5)(1 + .5) = \$1(1 + .5)^2 = \$2.25$

Quarterly Compounding:
Value of \$1 at end of 1 year = $\$1(1 + .25)^4 = \$2.44$

Monthly Compounding:
Value of \$1 at end of 1 year = $\$1(1 + .0833)^{12} = \$2.61$

ACTIVITY 14.1 ▲ Saving for your Future

Your teacher has given you the formula for the future value of savings. The future value, "n" years from today, of an amount that is saved at an interest rate equal to "r" today, can be found by substituting the amount that you have saved today for PV (present value) in the following formula:

$$FV = PV \cdot (1 + r)^n$$

where "r" is expressed in decimal form.

Suppose you have been able to save up $5000 at age 22. You are told by your friend, who was just hired as a financial consultant, that if you invest this money in the stock market, you can expect to receive an average annual return of 9% on these funds. The trick is, however, that you can't touch the money until you have reached retirement age, at age 67. That means this money will be invested for 45 years. You decide that, although you would certainly like to use the money for a new wardrobe and a trip to Tahiti, it is a good idea to make a commitment to saving early on in your professional career.

1. Assuming that this $5000 is invested for 45 years at 9% interest, what will be your accumulation at age 67?

2. How can you explain this?

ACTIVITY 14.2 ▲ Who Wants To Be a Millionaire?

Your teacher has given you the formula for calculating the future value of an annuity.

An annuity refers to a periodic payment or receipt of income that commonly finances retirement. One way to use an annuity formula is to calculate the future value of periodic savings. Suppose that you are able to save $300 a month beginning at age 22. Suppose further that these funds are invested at an annual rate of 9% for the next 45 years. The following formula, can be used to determine the amount to which these monthly retirement contributions will accumulate by the end of 45 years.

$$FV = \text{Monthly PMT}\,\frac{\{(1 + r/12)^{n \cdot 12} - 1\}}{r/12}$$

Substitute $300 for the monthly payment, .09 for r, and 45 for n (this makes the exponent in the numerator 45 · 12 = 540).

1. What is the future value of $300 saved and invested each month at an annual rate of 9% for 45 years?
2. Does it surprise you that you can be a millionaire by saving a relatively modest amount each month?

Do you think that saving $300 a month is a viable goal once you reach age 22? One way to think of this is to imagine that you go to college and earn $25,000 per year in your first job. Since these are pre-tax dollars, suppose that you only take home 70% of this amount.

3. Calculate your annual after-tax income given these assumptions.
4. Convert this annual after-tax income into a monthly income. What is your monthly take-home pay?
5. Suppose that you were to save $300 each month. How much income does that leave for your other monthly expenditures?
6. Instead of saving $300 per month by yourself, suppose you are able to reach this goal by contributing $150 yourself with an equal match from your employer. How much would you have to save each week, on average, to reach this goal?
7. Does this seem achievable?

Chances are that you answered "yes" to the preceding question. And note that it gets a lot easier over time, when your income expands. So, who wants to be a millionaire? You do—and this is how you do it!

ACTIVITY 14.3 ▲ The Rule of 72

The expression for compound interest growth that your teacher covered in class, Ae^{rt} can be used to determine how long it takes for your money to double. Suppose you have $500 in a savings account, earning a 6% rate of interest. About how long will it take for the value of this savings to increase to $1000?

To answer this question, use the formula for continuously compounding growth of interest. If you think about it, you are basically asking how many years, t, it will take for $A to become $2A at an interest rate of r. The answer to the question must then be a solution to the equation:

$$2A = Ae^{rt}$$

Dividing both sides by A, leaves us with

$$2 = e^{rt}$$

Solve this by taking the natural logarithm of both sides

$$\ln 2 = rt$$

and divide both sides by r to get:

$$\frac{\ln 2}{r} = t$$

1. Using your calculator, what is the size of ln 2?

2. Now calculate how long it will take for your $500 to double in size to $1000 at a continuously compounded interest rate of 6 percent.

3. How old will you be when this happens?

The problem with using this formula is you always need a calculator to determine the answer. Even if you simplified the ln 2 to be 69, it is still difficult to find a divisor (the interest rate) that goes into 69 with no remainder.

4. How many whole factors of 69 can you think of?

For simple calculations of interest accumulations, it is often more convenient to use the "rule of 72". This gives you a rough approximation of the number of years that it will take for your money to double and is much easier to compute than using the formula above. The "rule of 72" is the solution to:

$$\frac{72}{r} = t$$

ACTIVITY 14.3 (continued)

5. Can you see why this is an easier number to work with than 69? List the whole factors of 72.

These factors represent alternative interest rates that can be used as a divisor. The result comes out as a whole number and is much easier to work with if you don't have a calculator.

6. Use the "rule of 72" calculation to calculate how many years it will take for $500 to double at an interest rate of 6 percent. How does this compare to your earlier calculation?

So the next time someone is talking to you about the money they have in the bank, find out the interest rate they are receiving, and then impress them by calculating in your head how long it will take for their savings to double.

Lesson 15

The Mathematics of Credit Card Interest and Fixed Payments

Mathematics Focus:

Pre-Algebra, Algebra I, Algebra II

Mathematics Prerequisite:

Prior to using this lesson, students should be able to:

- Perform basic percent calculations
- Use formulas
- Perform calculations involving integral exponents
- Understand summation notation (Optional)

Lesson Objectives:

To apply prerequisite mathematics concepts and processes to situations involving credit card interest and fixed payment loans to:

- Explain the calculation of finance charges on credit cards
- Explain the mathematics that underlies the mechanical calculations of such things as the average daily credit card balance, the monthly finance charges on a credit card balance, and the calculation of a fixed payment on an installment loan
- Explain that a fixed payment on a monthly installment loan is calculated by setting the current value of the loan equal to its present value of future payments

Overview of Mathematics and Economics:

It is common for a high school student to receive multiple invitations to enroll for a credit card. In fact, an increasing number of high school students even carry credit cards. One goal of this lesson is to try to uncover some of the mathematics that underlies the calculation of numbers that are found on a monthly credit card statement. While these calculations are done using technology, it will likely help students understand the cost of maintaining balances on a credit card if they are to work out the numbers on their own. The first part of this lesson looks at the computation of the average daily balance on a credit card as well as monthly finance charges. It illustrates how hard it is to pay down a credit card balance when finance charges are carried from month to month and the minimum monthly payment is made. It also illustrates how paying down a credit card balance becomes even more difficult when the card is used to obtain additional credit from one month to the next.

How is the monthly payment on an installment loan calculated? When a student visits a bank to borrow funds to purchase a used auto, the loan officer simply informs the student what the monthly payment will be. The same occurs for a fixed-rate mortgage loan as well as a student or debt consolidation loan. The common characteristic of each of these loans is that a fixed payment is made each month until the entire loan is paid off. The economic concept that underlies the mathematical calculation of a fixed payment has to do with present value analysis—the notion that one dollar received today is more valuable than a dollar received one year from today. In the last part of this lesson, students discover how the loan officer obtains the number that borrowers are given when the monthly installment on a fixed payment loan is calculated. The computation made by the student is (with rounding) equal to that which is found through using technology to arrive at a mechanical calculation.

Understanding where numbers (such as credit card finance charges and the computation of a monthly installment payment) come from can be very empowering for students. It will help them explain these relationships to others who don't understand the mathematics underlying complex financial calculations. It will also help keep them from having undesirable charges (such as optional payment insurance and mistaken card charges) added to loans and credit card balances. This makes students less vulnerable to unscrupulous finance officers and impersonal credit card companies. An ability to visualize the underlying mathematics and economics of financial calculations such as those demonstrated in this lesson will certainly serve students well in their personal and professional lives.

The mathematics used in this lesson ranges from simple computations of mathematical averages to more complex calculations of the sum of multiple degree polynomials. The first part of this lesson (on credit card economics) can be used in pre-algebra classes, while Algebra I or Algebra II may be required to complete Activity 15.2. Business teachers may also find this lesson to be useful for their more advanced students.

Mathematics and Economics Terms:

- Credit
- Future Value
- Installment Loan
- Interest Rates
- Mean (average)
- Percent
- Present Value

Materials:

- One copy of Visuals 15.1 and 15.2 and Activities 15.1 and 15.2 for each student
- Overhead transparencies of Visuals 15.1 and 15.2
- Calculator
- Access to the internet (optional but desirable)

Estimated Time:

80–120 minutes

Procedures:

1. Warm-Up Activity: Distribute a copy of Visual 15.1 to each student and show it on the overhead. Assist students in its completion.

Answers:

1. (a) 1225 (b) 3158.44
   (c) 39.0625 (d) –39.0625
   (e) ≈0.0977 (f) ≈27580.545
2. ≈1.0077
3. ≈0.0150
4. ≈0.10132
5. 9.825
6. 633.6

2. Distribute a copy of Activity 15.1 to each student. Work through this sheet with students. (Note: For all other activities in this publication, only the answers are given in the Procedures section. However for this activity, it would be very awkward to include only the answers and thus, at the end of the discussion you will find Activity 15.1 (Answers) beginning with *"A Fictitious Monthly Credit Card Statement"* with the answers in blue.)

This exercise ultimately looks at how the Monthly Finance Charge on a credit card is calculated. Explain to students that this is the cost of interest for those who do not pay off their credit card balances in full each month. Those who don't carry forward balances on their credit card need not worry about paying a Monthly Finance Charge. Prior to determining the size of each month's interest costs, it is necessary to determine the Average Daily Balance (ADB). Students are given an example in this activity of the way that the ADB is calculated. They are later asked to calculate the ADB on their own. Feel free to help students with this calculation, since it is important to accurately complete the rest of the exercise. Other important information in this example (which simulates a monthly credit card statement) includes the Minimum Payment, Annual Percentage Rate (APR), Monthly Rate (which is simply calculated by dividing the APR by

12), the New Balance, and the number of days in the statement period.

Inform students that each credit card company has its own policy about the Minimum Payment. This example uses 3% of the previous balance as the Minimum Payment. Note that this percentage can actually be as low as 2%. You may wish to comment on how willing credit card companies seem to be to allow borrowers to carry balances from one month to the next. This also may be a good time to note that the APR on credit card balances is among the highest in the entire financial marketplace. Chances are that if you are making interest payments on credit cards, the interest rates are very high. Finally, you may need to help students with the calculation of the New Balance. This is computed by adding the ending monthly balance and the Monthly Finance Charge. Be sure that students don't confuse the ADB with the ending monthly balance. You may also want to note that while some credit card companies have alternative means of calculating the Monthly Finance Charge, this is probably the most popular method. Credit card companies also typically treat purchases different from cash advances.

Activity 15.1 concludes with examples of the total interest cost of carrying forward credit card balances. Students should begin to see how difficult it is to pay off outstanding balances when minimum monthly payments are made. The example shows that it could take several years to pay off a $1500 credit card balance. You may ask students to consider how much interest would have been paid by the time the balance is paid off. Chances are it is something in the neighborhood of $1000. This should surely seem outrageous to your students. When high-interest credit card balances are carried forward, low-income debtors (such as your students) find themselves caught having to pay rising minimum monthly payments whenever the card is used to charge additional purchases during the statement period. Unfortunately, the interest payments continue to grow when this occurs. Interest payments take up a larger and larger share of the limited incomes of those who can least afford to use credit cards. The only way to reduce the minimum monthly payment is to stop charging purchases.

ACTIVITY 15.1 (Answers)
The Mathematics of Credit Card Interest: A Fictitious Monthly Credit Card Statement

Suppose you have had a credit card for the past few months and have an outstanding balance of $1000 at the start of this month. Your credit card company requires that you pay a minimum of 3 percent of your outstanding balance by the 21st day of each month. Since you have only a limited income, you make only the minimum payment each month. The statement period covers thirty days of card activity. The month's card activity is as follows:

Starting Balance	$1000
Gas purchase posted on the 6th day of the month	$20
Purchase of shoes posted on the 11th day of the month	$80
Minimum payment posted on the 21st day of the month	$30
CD purchases posted on the 26th day of the month	$30

Average Daily Balance	$1065
Annual Percentage Rate	21%
Monthly Rate	1.75%
Monthly Finance Charge	$18.64
New Balance	$1118.64
Statement Period	30 days

How is the Average Daily Balance calculated? It is the average credit card balance for each day, with payments subtracted and purchases added on the date that they are posted. The balance for each day during the statement period is summed up and divided by the total number of days in the statement period. The result is the Average Daily Balance (ADB). The ADB for this statement period is calculated as follows:

Balance for the first 5 days of the month	$1000
Balance for the next 5 days of the month ($1000 + $20)	$1020
Balance for the next 10 days of the month ($1020 + $80)	$1100
Balance for the next 5 days of the month ($1100 − $30 payment)	$1070
Balance for the final 5 days of the month ($1070 + $30)	$1100

ADB = [$1000 · (5 days) + $1020 · (5 days) + $1100 · (10 days) + $1070 · (5 days) + $1100 · (5 days)]/30 days

ADB = $1065

The Average Daily Balance is used to calculate the Monthly Finance Charge. Note that had you paid off your balance in full each month, you would not have a finance charge. But since you have carried a balance, you will face a finance charge. This charge is calculated by multiplying the ADB by the Monthly Rate (expressed in decimal form). Note that the Monthly Rate is the Annual Percentage Rate (APR) divided by 12. This expresses interest on a monthly basis.

Confirm that the Monthly Finance Charge calculation stated above is correct.
($1065 · 0.0175 = $18.64)

The Monthly Finance Charge is added to the monthly ending balance on the credit card statement to determine the New Balance for the next month.

Confirm that the New Balance calculation is correct.
($1100 + $18.64 = $1118.64)

Next Month's Credit Card Bill

Now that you know the mathematics of credit card interest, fill in the missing information on next month's credit card statement. Assume that the minimum payment of 3 percent of the starting balance is made (round this payment to the nearest whole number). You are given the following information:

Starting Balance $1118.64
Gas purchase posted on 6th day of the month $30.00
Concert ticket purchase posted on the 16th day of the month $80.00
Minimum payment on 21st day of the month
Answer: $1118.64 · [0.03] = $33.56 ≈ $34
Mall shopping spree posted on the 26th day of the month $300
Average Daily Balance
Answer: $1222.31.
Calculated as ({$1118.64 · [5] + $1148.64 · [10] + $1228.64 · [5] + $1194.64 · [5] + $1494.64 · [5]} / 30)
Annual Percentage Rate 21%
Monthly Rate
Answer: 21%/12 = 1.75% = 0.0175
Monthly Finance Charge
Answer: $1222.31 · 0.0175 = $21.39
New Balance
Answer: $1494.64 + $21.39 = $1516.03
Statement Period 30 days

1. How does the Monthly Finance Charge compare to the previous month?
Answer: It is higher.

2. Why?
Answer: Because the New Balance at the end of the month was higher than it was the previous month and also because only the minimum payment is made.

3. What percentage of the Minimum Payment goes toward the Monthly Finance Charge?
Answer: ($21.39/$34) · 100 = 62.9%.

4. How does this compare to the corresponding percentage calculation for the previous month?
Answer: It is higher. The corresponding percentage for the previous month was 62.1%

The Monthly Finance Charge and Minimum Payment in Future Months

Suppose that after your mall-shopping spree of the previous month, you decide to put your credit card away. You still have a limited income, so you are constrained to making the 3 percent minimum monthly payment (which is posted on the 21st day of the month).

5. What is the Minimum Payment for the current month (round to the nearest whole number)?
Answer: $1516.03 · 0.03 = $45.48 ≈ $45

6. What is the Average Daily Balance (assume a 30 day statement period)?
Answer: $1501.03—Calculated as ({$1516.03 · [20] + $1471.03 · [10]} / 30)

7. What is the Monthly Finance Charge?
Answer: $1501.03 · 0.0175 = $26.27

8. What is the New Balance?
Answer: $1516.03 − $45 = $1471.03 + $26.27 = $1497.30

9. What percentage of the Minimum Payment is accounted for by the Monthly Finance Charge?
Answer: $26.27/$45 · 100 = 58.4%.

10. How much of the Minimum Payment is available to pay off the credit card?
Answer: Even though the percentage of the Minimum Payment that is the Monthly Finance Charge is lower than it was in the previous month, it still means that only $18.73 is being used to pay off principal (the remaining balance).

11. At this rate, how long will it take to pay off the credit card?
Answer: Many years...at a rate of $18.73 net principal payment per month, it will take more than 6½ years {$1497.30/$18.73} = 79.9 months ≈ 6.7 years to pay off the balance which is not a good situation. Of course, this is not meant to be an exact calculation, but it should give students an idea about the long-term consequences of a credit card debt burden.

12. What is the average total monthly interest that you paid over the three months?
Answer: ($18.64 + $21.39 + $26.27)/3 = $22.10 per month.

13. Suppose that you averaged this amount of interest each month for one year. What would the total interest paid be for the year?
Answer: $22.10 · 12 = $265.20.

14. List alternative uses for the money that goes toward paying credit card interest.
Answer: Answers will vary.

3. A fixed payment (or installment) loan is one in which the borrower makes equal-sized payments over the life of the loan until it is finally paid off. The borrower implicitly repays both principal and interest in making the periodic installment payments. These loans, which can have a varying term to maturity, are typically made with a monthly payment. Students will probably first encounter such a loan when buying a car. Later on in life, they will discover that conventional fixed-rate mortgage loans are also fixed payment loans. A debt consolidation, student, home equity, boat, or camper loan can also be structured as an installment loan. Give each student a copy of Visual 15.2. The formula it presents is similar to the formulas found in Lesson 11. A fixed payment is calculated by setting the current value of a loan equal to its present value of future payments. Present value analysis is used by economists to mathematically express the time value of money. The general present value formula captures the notion that a dollar received one year from today is worth less than a dollar received today. This formula is converted to a form that allows students to compute a monthly fixed payment. This is the formula that students will use to complete Activity 15.2. Note that if students have not yet been introduced to the use of the summation sign, this expression of the relationship can be skipped.

4. Distribute a copy of Activity 15.2 to each student. This activity can be done in small groups with teacher support. Inform students that this simulates the calculation of the monthly payment on a 2-year auto loan. With the exception of the normal rounding errors, the payment that students calculate is exactly the same as that which can be obtained by using a calculator (or a computer program). This will help them see the mathematics that underlies these mechanical calculations. Inform students that this type of calculation is made for auto loans of varying lengths as well as home mortgage loans. Making fixed installment payments is likely to be experienced by everyone at some point during their lifetime. You may wish to note that student loans are typically repaid by making equal-sized monthly installments. Students may need some help in completing Activity 15.2. Make sure that they properly set up the problem and use the correct interest rate (expressed in decimal form as a monthly rate). If they have a calculator that uses summation notation, then feel free to let them use it to determine the sum of the present discounted value of the 24 monthly installment payments. Otherwise have them use their calculators to do this the long way. It will help them visualize the correct result. Also note that extension item number two addresses an application of the calculation of fixed payments on an installment loan.

1. $2 \cdot 12 = 24$ total payments.
2. $\$5000 = \frac{MFP}{(1.00833)^1} + \frac{MFP}{(1.00833)^2} + \frac{MFP}{(1.00833)^3} + \ldots + \frac{MFP}{(1.00833)^{24}}$

   $\$5000 = MFP \left\{ \sum_{t=1}^{24} \frac{1}{(1.00833)^t} \right\}$. Note that 1.00833 = [1 + {(10/100)/12}]. Some students may have problems with this, so provide help if they need it.
3. \$5000/21.6719 = \$230.72; \$230.72 per month.

Extension Activities

1. Have students go to the "What Will it Take to Pay Off My Balance?" financial calculator at www.kiplinger.com (the specific site is http://www.calcbuilder.com/cgi-bin/calcs/CRE4.cgi/Kiplinger). Have them insert data relevant to the exercise they completed in Activity 15.1. This includes \$1497 as the amount now owed (this corresponds to the "new balance" calculated at the end of the activity), \$0 for future monthly charges, \$45 for future monthly premiums, 21% for annual interest rate, and 0 for annual fee. Leave the "desired months until pay off" category blank and indicate "none" in future rate change. Have students guess what the answer will be. This is different than the example of always making a 3% minimum payment, because the minimum payment would decline over time. This on-line example uses a fixed \$45 payment each month. Note that the results indicate that it will take 51 months to pay off the credit card balance. Also note the total interest paid over this period.

2. Most people will purchase a home at some point during their lifetime. A typical home mortgage loan is paid off in equal monthly installments over a period of 30 years. Funds to purchase the home are commonly made available at a fixed rate of interest over the life of the loan. Suppose that after making an appropriate down payment, you borrow \$100,000 at an 8% rate of interest. You are to make fixed monthly payments over the next 30 years. Given this information, set up the calculation of the monthly mortgage payment.

[\$100,000 = MFP $\left\{\sum_{t=1}^{360} \frac{1}{(1.00667)^t}\right\}$. Note that 1.00667 = 1 + 0.08/12].

Use a financial calculator or a computer program such as that found at "How much will my payments be?" http://www.calcbuilder.com/cgi-bin/calcs/HOM2.cgi/Kiplinger to calculate the amount of the monthly payment (use \$125,000 for the appraised value and ignore taxes and insurance components of this computation). (The resulting calculation yields a MFP of \$734). Now calculate how much the monthly payment would be if the interest rate was 14% (this was a rate that was common in the early 1980s). (The new MFP is \$1185—substantially higher than the \$734 monthly payment when rates are at 8%). Now compare the monthly payment on an 8% mortgage loan when the loan term is reduced to 20 years. By how much do the monthly payments increase? (They increase to \$836 per month, but the loan is paid off 10 years earlier than a 30-year loan. This exercise illustrates how sensitive long-term payments are to changes in interest rates. Interest rate changes can have a larger effect on long-term monthly payments than changes in the term of the loan).

VISUAL 15.1 ▲ Warm-Up

Use your calculator to evaluate the following expressions.

1. (a) 35^2 (b) 56.2^2

   (c) $(-2.5)^4$ (d) $-(2.5)^4$

   (e) 3.2^{-2} (f) 2.3445^{12}

2. $(1.00256)^3$

3. $\frac{1}{(2.3154)^5}$

4. $(3.14159)^{-2}$

5. 1.25% of 786 =

6. 19.8% of 3200 =

VISUAL 15.2 ▲ The Time Value of Money—Computing Present Value

- A dollar received today is more valuable than a dollar received one year from today.
- How much would you be willing to pay today for $1 received one year from today?

$$\text{PV of future \$1} = \frac{\text{Future Value}}{(1 + \text{interest rate})^1}$$

$$\text{In symbols: PV} = \frac{\text{FV}}{(1 + \text{r})^1}$$

where FV is the future value of the payment and r is the interest rate expressed in decimal form.

A general present value calculation (for payment n years from today):

$$\text{PV} = \frac{FV}{(1 + r)^n}$$

Calculating the Fixed Payment on an Installment Loan

- Calculated by setting the current value of a loan equal to the present value of future installment payments.

Formula for calculating the *annual* Fixed Payment (FP) of an installment loan:

$$\text{Current Loan Value} = \frac{FP}{(1+r)^1} + \frac{FP}{(1+r)^2} + \frac{FP}{(1+r)^3} + \ldots + \frac{FP}{(1+r)^n}$$

Where r is the interest rate expressed in decimal form and n is the number of years over which annual payments are made. For example, if n = 20, r = 8%, and the current loan value is $1000, then 20 equal sized annual payments are made on the loan. The fixed payment on this loan is calculated as follows:

$$\$1000 = \frac{FP}{(1+.08)^1} + \frac{FP}{(1+.08)^2} + \frac{FP}{(1+.08)^3} + \ldots + \frac{FP}{(1+.08)^{20}}$$

$$= FP\left\{\frac{1}{(1+.08)^1} + \frac{1}{(1+.08)^2} + \frac{1}{(1+.08)^3} + \ldots + \frac{1}{(1+.08)^{20}}\right\}$$

$$= FP\left\{\sum_{t=1}^{20} \frac{1}{(1+.08)^t}\right.$$

The annual fixed payment is determined as the solution to this problem.

Using summation notation, the general formula for determining the fixed payment on an installment loan is:

$$\text{Current Loan Value} = \sum_{t=1}^{n} \frac{FP}{(1+r)^t}$$

Visual 15.2 (continued)

Since this expression is calculated using an *annual* rate of interest and *annual* payment, it is necessary to modify the formula to make it useful for calculating the *monthly* fixed payment on an installment loan. This is how the payment on a car, student, and home mortgage loan is calculated.

Current Loan Value

$$= \frac{MFP}{(1 + r/12)^1} + \frac{MFP}{(1 + r/12)^2} + \frac{MFP}{(1 + r/12)^3} + \ldots + \frac{MFP}{(1 + r/12)^{12n}}$$

which in summation notation is expressed as:

$$\text{Current Loan Value} = \sum_{t=1}^{12n} \frac{MFP}{(1 + r/12)^t}$$

where MFP is the monthly fixed payment, r is expressed in decimal form, and payments are made each month for n years.

ACTIVITY 15.1 ▲ The Mathematics of Credit Card Interest

Name ______________________________ Date __________ Period _____

In paying finance charges on credit cards, customers typically take as given the amount of the finance charge that is found on the monthly statement. The fine print mentions such things as the annual percentage rate (APR), the monthly rate, the average daily balance, the monthly finance charge, the minimum payment, and all sorts of other technical terms, but who knows how to meaningfully use this information?

This activity looks at some of the mathematical computations that underlie the monthly credit card statement. It also points out the hazards of perpetuating credit card debt from one month to the next. The interest rate charged on credit card balances is among the highest observed in the financial marketplace. It is very important that you understand what you are getting into before you begin charging unnecessary purchases to credit cards. You can easily dig yourself a hole from which you may find it impossible to escape. Personal bankruptcy may await those who have been unable and/or unwilling to effectively manage their personal credit. Fortunately, those who exercise wise and informed judgment in managing their credit card balances are less likely to experience bankruptcy. This lesson helps you understand how to calculate the numbers that are found in a monthly credit card statement.

A Fictitious Monthly Credit Card Statement

Suppose you have had a credit card for the past few months and have an outstanding balance of $1000 at the start of this month. Your credit card company requires that you pay a minimum of 3 percent of your outstanding balance by the 21st day of each month. Since you have only a limited income, you make only the minimum payment each month. The statement period covers thirty days of card activity. The month's card activity is as follows:

Starting Balance	$1000
Gas purchase posted on the 6th day of the month	$20
Purchase of shoes posted on the 11th day of the month	$80
Minimum payment posted on the 21st day of the month	$30
CD purchases posted on the 26th day of the month	$30

Average Daily Balance	$1065
Annual Percentage Rate	21%
Monthly Rate	1.75%
Monthly Finance Charge	$18.64
New Balance	$1118.64
Statement Period	30 days

How is the Average Daily Balance calculated? It is the average credit card balance for each day, with payments subtracted and purchases added on the date that they are posted. The balance for each day during the statement period is summed up and divided by the total number of days in the statement period. The result is the Average Daily Balance (ADB). The ADB for this statement period is calculated as follows:

Balance for the first 5 days of the month	$1000
Balance for the next 5 days of the month ($1000 + $20)	$1020
Balance for the next 10 days of the month ($1020 + $80)	$1100
Balance for the next 5 days of the month ($1100 − $30 payment)	$1070
Balance for the final 5 days of the month ($1070 + $30)	$1100

ADB = [$1000 · (5 days) + $1020 · (5 days) + $1100 · (10 days) + $1070 · (5 days) + $1100 · (5 days)]/30 days

ADB = $1065

The Average Daily Balance is used to calculate the Monthly Finance Charge. Note that had you paid off your balance in full each month, you would not have a finance charge. But since you have carried a balance, you will face a finance charge. This charge is calculated by multiplying the ADB by the Monthly Rate (expressed in decimal form). Note that the Monthly Rate is the Annual Percentage Rate (APR) divided by 12. This expresses interest on a monthly basis.

Confirm that the Monthly Finance Charge calculation stated above is correct.

The Monthly Finance Charge is added to the monthly ending balance on the credit card statement to determine the New Balance for the next month.

Confirm that the New Balance calculation is correct.

Next Month's Credit Card Bill

Now that you know the mathematics of credit card interest, fill in the missing information (where the question marks appear) on next month's credit card statement. Assume that the minimum payment of 3 percent of the starting balance is made (round this payment to the nearest whole number). You are given the following information:

Starting Balance	$1118.64
Gas purchase posted on 6th day of the month	$30
Concert ticket purchase posted on the 16th day of the month	$80
Minimum payment on 21st day of the month	?
Mall shopping spree posted on the 26th day of the month	$300

Average Daily Balance	?
Annual Percentage Rate	21%
Monthly Rate	?

Monthly Finance Charge	?
New Balance	?
Statement Period	30 days

1. How does the Monthly Finance Charge compare to the previous month?

2. Why?

3. What percentage of the Minimum Payment goes toward the Monthly Finance Charge?

4. How does this compare to the corresponding percentage calculation for the previous month?

The Monthly Finance Charge and Minimum Payment in Future Months

Suppose that after your mall-shopping spree of the previous month, you decide to put your credit card away. You still have a limited income, so you are constrained to making the 3 percent minimum monthly payment (which is posted on the 21st day of the month).

5. What is the Minimum Payment for the current month (round to the nearest whole number)?

6. What is the Average Daily Balance (assume a 30 day statement period)?

7. What is the Monthly Finance Charge?

8. What is the New Balance?

9. What percentage of the Minimum Payment is accounted for by the Monthly Finance Charge?

10. How much of the Minimum Payment is available to pay off the credit card?

11. At this rate, how long will it take to pay off the credit card?

12. What is the average total monthly interest that you paid over the three months?

13. Suppose that you averaged this amount of interest each month for one year. What would the total interest paid be for the year?

14. List alternative uses for the money that goes toward paying credit card interest.

ACTIVITY 15.2 ▲ Calculating the Fixed Payment on a Monthly Installment Loan

Name ______________________________ Date __________ Period _____

You have just decided to buy a used automobile, but will need to borrow $5000 from the bank to complete your purchase. You have already spoken with the bank loan officer about the terms of the loan. They are: it is a $5000 loan made at a 10 percent rate of interest, to be repaid in equal monthly installments over 2 years.

1. How many total payments will you have to make?

Before you go to the bank, you decide to use your mathematics and economics knowledge to determine what the fixed monthly payment should equal. This will help you make sure that there are no hidden options built into the loan. It will also help ensure that the loan officer has made the right calculations.

Since your teacher has already covered how to calculate the monthly fixed payment on an installment loan (this is one of the formulas in Visual 15.2 of this lesson), all you need to do is make a few calculations to determine what the fixed payment will be. Recall that the fixed payment computation is based on the principle of present value analysis. That is, it is calculated by setting the current value of the loan equal to its present value of future payments. This captures the essence of the time value of money—that your final payment made two years from now is worth less than a payment made today.

Given the information above, use the formula from Visual 15.2 for calculating the monthly fixed payment (MFP) on an installment loan to set up the solution for calculating your MFP.

2. Use the formula that you have developed to solve for MFP. Hint: if you have a calculator that has a summation function, use it to calculate the sum of the $\frac{1}{1.00833^t}$ terms. Otherwise, you will have to sum these terms by hand.

3. What is the value of the monthly fixed payment on your auto loan?

Congratulations, you now know how to calculate a fixed payment on an installment loan. This will serve you well throughout your life. Note that your calculation is the same amount that can be found from using a financial calculator or a computer program.

Notes

Notes